NAPOLEON'S POISONED CHALICE

NAPOLEON'S POISONED CHALICE

THE EMPEROR AND HIS DOCTORS ON ST. HELENA

DR MARTIN HOWARD

The
History
Press

First published 2009

The History Press
The Mill, Brimscombe Port
Stroud, Gloucestershire, GL5 2QG
www.thehistorypress.co.uk

British Library Cataloguing in Publication Data.
A catalogue record for this book is available from the British Library.

ISBN 978 0 7524 4857 2

Printed in Great Britain

CONTENTS

By the time I have finished, I think I shall have been
in company with *more liars* than any living author.

Sir Harris Nicols, St. Helena historian, 1848

ACKNOWLEDGEMENTS

The staffs of the British Library (London), The National Archives (Kew) and the Wellcome Library (London) have given valuable help in the location of obscure sources and illustrations. I am very grateful to David Markham for allowing me to quote from his excellent book, *Napoleon and Doctor Verling on St. Helena*. A special thanks to Ian Robertson for his continued interest and moral support.

1

THE FIRST VICTIM

Napoleon never hated England. He had a begrudging admiration for the 'nation of shopkeepers'. The Emperor respected his enemy's courage in war and its tradition of hospitality to the fallen. In his youth the great Corsican patriot Pasquale Paoli, well known to his family, had sought refuge from French oppression in England. The young Bonaparte wrote a short story in which his hero, an ex-King of Corsica, is told by the writer and politician Horace Walpole, 'You suffer and are unhappy. These are two reasons for claiming the sympathy of an Englishman.' Theodore emerges from his dungeon to receive a pension of £3,000 a year. Thirty years later, at the time of his departure to Elba, Napoleon commented to the British Commissioner Sir Neil Campbell that he was convinced that there was more generosity in the British Government than in any other. It was natural that after his decisive defeat at Waterloo he expected more understanding from the British than from the Prussians. He was not to be disappointed. When Blucher demanded that he should be hanged, Wellington remonstrated with his friend and ally. The Duke did not wish his greatest victory to be tainted by his subsequent role as an executioner. It has to be admitted that not all Englishmen were so magnanimous. Lord Liverpool, the Prime Minister, declared that he hoped that the King of France would shoot Bonaparte as the 'best termination of the business'.

After his last battle, Napoleon fled to the Élysée Palace and then to his old house at Malmaison in the suburbs of Paris, the scene of the happiest of times spent with Josephine. Here, he was still in real danger of falling into the hands of the advancing Prussian army and, on 29th June 1815, he left for Rochefort. In this Atlantic seaport the local people received him with enthusiasm; there were still a few cries of '*Vive L'Empereur!*' The French authorities were less accommodating and were intent on his arrest. He was faced with a stark choice. He could either make a determined effort to escape or he could surrender to the most munificent of his adversaries. There was discussion of flight to America. Frigates manned by sympathisers were moored off the coast but there was also a British naval blockade and there was a serious risk of capture. His brother Joseph offered to impersonate him to buy vital extra time. The Emperor was unconvinced. In truth, he had long known that he would ultimately place himself at England's mercy. In America he would be no safer than on mainland Europe; the emissaries of Louis XVIII would be sent to assassinate him. He remained calculating and pragmatic to the last.

> There is always danger in confiding oneself to enemies, but it is better to take the risk of confiding to their honour than to fall into their hands as a prisoner according to law.

He reminded his followers of the incident in Greek history when Themistocles requested refuge from the King of Persia.

On 15th July, Napoleon, dressed in his favourite uniform of the Chasseurs of the Guard, boarded the British ship the *Bellerophon*. Her Captain, Frederick Lewis Maitland, had not been instructed as to the honours to be paid to the ex-Emperor and he therefore gave none, taking advantage of the rule that no salutes should be given before 8am or after sunset. Napoleon stepped on to the deck and removed his hat, before advancing to meet Maitland, 'I am come to throw myself on the protection of your Prince and your laws.' The Captain, careful to make no commitment as to his captive's future treatment, introduced him to the other officers. A week later, the Dartmoor hills became visible and Napoleon changed his dressing gown for an overcoat to go on deck to have his first view of England. Was this to be his home?

When the *Bellerophon* was ordered to sail from Torbay to Plymouth, to the west and away from London, the French began to fear that they were not to be allowed to land. The crowds of sightseers at Plymouth were remarkable. The sailors of the *Bellerophon* displayed a blackboard on which they wrote the famous prisoner's current occupation; 'at breakfast', 'in the cabin' and so forth. Napoleon had not forgotten his earlier allusion to Greek antiquity.

He now composed a dramatic appeal to the Prince Regent, which perfectly expressed his hopes and emotions.

Royal Highness

A victim to the factions which divide my country, and to the enmity of the greatest Powers of Europe, I have terminated my political career, and I come, like Themistocles, to place myself at the heart of the British people. I place myself under the protection of their laws, which I claim of Your Royal Highness as of the most powerful, the most constant, and the most generous of my enemies.

Napoleon[1]

The British government was not willing to accommodate Napoleon's further requests that he be treated as a guest and be given an English country house in which to live out the rest of his days. The appeal for clemency had saved his life but it was clear to Ministers that their prisoner would have to be exiled to a most isolated spot. The memory of his escape from Elba, when he had slipped through the fingers of the unfortunate Campbell to create havoc in Europe, was still fresh. Rumours started to circulate that the Emperor's ultimate destination was the remote Atlantic island of St. Helena. Internment on St. Helena was not a novel idea; the conspirators of 1800 who had attempted to kidnap Premier Consul Bonaparte had planned to deport him there and the island had been suggested as an alternative to Elba at the Congress of Vienna. Liverpool wrote to Lord Castlereagh, the Foreign Secretary, to confirm the Government's choice. The confinement of Napoleon in England had been ruled out as this could lead to 'embarrassing legal questions' and make him an object of public curiosity or, worse still, compassion. This would not happen on St. Helena. 'At such a distance and in such a place, all intrigue would be impossible; and, being withdrawn so far from the European world, he would very soon be forgotten.'

Napoleon's followers were in a state of despair at the prospect of being exiled to a remote island, quite possibly for the remainder of their lives. Their leader appeared surprisingly unaffected by the news of his fate. He was a realist and whilst making some routine protestations – *'Je n'irais pas à Sainte-Hélène'* – he quizzed Maitland about the island's size and climate and began to consider who he would take with him. He knew that the continental Allies at Paris supported the British decision and that there was little hope of a change of mind.[2]

What connotations did St. Helena have for Napoleon? Curiously, there is evidence that he probably had at least a dim recollection of the island's existence. In 1788, when he was a poor student in Auxonne, he made notes on English possessions in an exercise book. One of the entries reads simply, 'St. Helena, a small island'. After these few words, there is a blank page – perhaps he was interrupted. If the young Bonaparte had continued his account, he might have recorded that St. Helena is one of the most remote islands in the world, lying in the Atlantic Ocean 1,140 miles from the nearest land in South Africa, 1,800 miles from South America and 4,400 from England. It is about the size of Jersey, being ten miles long and seven wide. Seen from the sea, it appears as a massive barren rock rising sheer from the water. In the interior, ridges of mountains alternate with pleasant wooded valleys. Parts of the island are dull and desolate whilst others have a beautiful grandeur. In the early nineteenth century, the main settlement of Jamestown consisted of only two main streets and around one hundred and sixty buildings. A few country houses were dotted about, the most notable of which was Plantation House, the British Governor's residence.

Apart from its total isolation, St. Helena had one other major advantage as a prison for the most dangerous of Britain's enemies. It was a superb natural fortress manned by a garrison and with guns in position to defend all possible landing places. In 1812, the British Governor Major General Alexander Beatson expressed the opinion that the island was 'absolutely impregnable' and that it was more secure than Gibraltar or Malta, two famous British strong points. Telegraphs were placed on all the principal heights and no vessel could approach within sixty miles without it being common knowledge to the island's defenders. The consequence of this combination of natural obstacles and military power was that a state prisoner could be allowed significant personal liberty with no opportunity for escape.

The climate of St. Helena might be supposed to be tropical – it lies one third of the way within the Tropic of Capricorn – but its distance from any large tract of land and the influence of the trade winds make it more temperate. Whether this moderate atmosphere meant a safe environment is a question that has been vigorously debated by historians of the Napoleonic period. The British Government insisted from the outset that they were sending the exile and his entourage to one of the healthiest places on earth. Certainly, British officers who resided on St. Helena in the years before

Napoleon's arrival were almost unanimous in their praise of the climate and the wellbeing of both locals and Europeans. Wellington spent two weeks on the island on his way home from India in 1805 and wrote to friends that it was beautiful and that the climate was 'apparently the most healthy that I have ever lived in'. Previous Governors contested that the weather was especially suited to the constitution of Europeans and that it was possible to reside there for many years without any malady. Walter Henry, an Army doctor on St. Helena at the time of Napoleon's internment, thought it to be 'a healthy island – if not the most healthy of its description in the world'.

Others were less convinced of the island's wholesomeness. Pro-Napoleon French historians have been keen to paint an entirely different picture, inferring that the Emperor was sent to die in a pestilential backwater. One contemporary doctor wrote:

> The most trifling cold or irregularity is frequently succeeded by a violent attack of dysentery, inflammation of the bowels or fever proving fatal in a few days, if the most active and efficacious practice is not instantly followed ... Dysentery especially, and liver affections (which are indeed frequently combined) appear with the most concentrated and fatal symptoms, baffling the prompt exhibition of the most active and powerful remedies.

The British authorities acknowledged that these diseases existed; an Admiralty secretary admitted that St. Helena was less healthy than widely believed, and a garrison report of 1817 indicated a high incidence of both fevers and dysentery. The most objective evidence we have are the mortality statistics. These are available for the decades after the exile and they suggest that nineteenth-century St. Helena, despite the prevalent bowel and liver diseases, was an unusually healthy place. For instance, in 1823, only two years after Napoleon's death, the annual death rate was remarkably low at only ten per thousand. This compares favourably with the rates among troops in Great Britain (17 per thousand) and regiments stationed in India (85). Arnold Chaplin, a noted historian of the St. Helena period, has calculated the expected and actual longevities of the main British and French characters on the island during the exile and has shown that their sojourn did not shorten their lives. The Emperor died before his predicted age but, if the British Government were intent on this, there were many Crown possessions more insalubrious than St. Helena where he could have been incarcerated.[3]

The *Bellerophon* was too old and slow to carry the captives to the distant isle and, on 7th August, they were transferred to the *Northumberland,* which carried the flag of Rear-Admiral Sir George Cockburn who had been appointed Naval Commander-in-Chief of the Cape and St. Helena stations. Napoleon said farewell to a number of his entourage who were not to sail with him; most were weeping. On the short journey between the two vessels he was accompanied by Admiral Lord Keith. Captain Maitland, acting against the advice of ministers, gave Napoleon a royal salute on his final departure from the *Bellerophon.* Once aboard the *Northumberland,* Keith introduced him to Cockburn who recollected his prisoner's first words, 'Here I am, Admiral, at your orders!' Napoleon then, as was his habit, introduced himself to all the British naval officers and asked them a few trifling questions such as their place of birth. Many were quickly won over by the disarming grace of the 'Corsican Ogre'.

Napoleon's relationship with the Royal Navy was close to being one of mutual admiration. He had always had a sure touch with the ordinary man and this was particularly so with sailors. During the Elba episode in 1814, the Emperor attended a reception to celebrate George III's birthday on board the *Undaunted* and received a rousing 'three cheers' from all the crew. Little had changed on the *Bellerophon* and the *Northumberland.* The young British officers vied with each other for the chance of a few words with the fallen hero and wrote home enthusiastic descriptions. When Maitland asked his crew what they thought of Napoleon, the general view was that he was 'a fine fellow who does not deserve his fate'. This was more than a perverse desire to kick sand in the eyes of landlubbers, who mostly despised the Emperor. It was a sure sign that Napoleon had retained his dangerous charm. 'Damn the fellow,' said Lord Keith after meeting him, 'if he obtained an interview with His Royal Highness [the Prince Regent], in half-an-hour they would have been the best friends in England.' On St. Helena, others were to fall under the spell.[4]

Napoleon was accompanied by an entourage of 27 people who were to follow him into what must have felt like oblivion. Among them were four men and two women who were the senior members of the party and who were all to become main players in the drama of the exile. Best known to the Emperor were the Bertrands. General Bertrand had been with his master at Elba and the Emperor's Aide-de-Camp since 1807. He had thrived under the Empire, receiving the Legion of Honour, governing the Illyrian Provinces and commanding a corps of the *Grande*

Armée. When Duroc died, he was chosen to perform the extravagant functions of the Grand Marshal of the Palace, a role that required a dazzling uniform. Despite these successes, Bertrand was more of an engineer than a soldier. He was still only forty-five years old but he was slight, round-shouldered and beginning to bald. By nature, he was timid and self-effacing; one colleague said that he was 'a man incapable of any greatness. He is absent minded and undecided to the last degree.' Napoleon valued his honesty and his sense of duty.

Madame Bertrand, previously Fanny Dillon, belonged to a reckless but influential Irish Catholic family. Her father fought with the Revolutionary army and was guillotined during the Terror. She was hoping to marry an Italian or German Prince but made do with the unprepossessing General. Having lived for a long time in England, she was essentially English in her tastes and thinking. From all accounts she had a singular charm and commanding appearance but her addiction to the pleasures of high society and her capriciousness made her a difficult companion in exile. She was distraught that the Emperor had not been allowed to settle with his followers in England. Napoleon was cool towards her; during one of her frequent illnesses on St. Helena he expressed the hope that the Countess would die so that he could have the Grand Marshal's exclusive attention.[5]

The second man and wife in the Emperor's inner circle were the Montholons. Charles Tristan de Montholon was thirty years old and was of an ancient family; one of his ancestors was reputed to have saved the life of Richard Coeur de Lion. His life was inextricably linked with the Bonapartes. He had been an acquaintance of Napoleon since he was a child of ten years old on Corsica when he had received lessons in mathematics from the young captain of artillery. Later, he was at school with the brothers, Lucien and Jerome, and it was his strange fate to accompany both Napoleon Bonaparte and Napoleon III into captivity. He was not a natural soldier and he left the army for 'health reasons' to be appointed as chamberlain to Josephine. He was the ultimate diplomat and courtier with perfect manners and a talent for scheming; he acquired the nickname '*le menteur*'. He was also a spendthrift and, in 1815, he was both out of favour with the King and heavily in debt. When he met Napoleon at the Élysée, he decided that he would follow him to the ends of the earth.

Madame de Montholon, originally Albine-Hélène de Vassal, had been divorced before her clandestine marriage to the Count. Napoleon initially frowned on the liaison and Montholon suffered a period of disapproval.

Despite her colourful past, Madame Montholon was one of the peacemakers in the French party. A quiet unassuming woman, she was gracious and desirous to please. A French historian describes her as 'an expert in praising', an invaluable quality in the strained atmosphere of St. Helena. The Emperor later treated her generously, leading to speculation that she was his mistress.[6]

Unlike the aristocratic Count de Montholon, Gaspard Gourgaud was a born soldier. He joined the army at eighteen and fought through the great campaigns of Austerlitz, Jena, Friedland and Russia. He was ambitious and always keen to attract attention to himself. In Moscow, he discovered a mine which had been laid in the Kremlin, a service which earned him the title of Baron of the Empire. At the battle of Brienne in 1814 he saved Napoleon's life by killing a Cossack who was intent on piercing the Emperor with his lance. As an experienced and capable officer, he might have survived the disaster of the Waterloo campaign and served under the Bourbon government, but he was entirely devoted to Napoleon. The Emperor must have been pleased to have an old soldier with him, but this brave, loyal man had none of the arts of the courtier. He had the unfortunate habit of humouring nobody and of saying exactly what he thought. He was self-assured and quick to criticise others. Napoleon was worn down by his sincerity: 'Don't worry me with your frankness' he advised Gourgaud, 'Keep it to yourself...' This was painful for the *Grande Armée* veteran who, frustrated by the boredom and celibacy imposed by the exile, wanted to be all to the Emperor. Such relentless devotion also wearied Napoleon. He once snapped, 'I am not his wife; after all I can't go to bed with him.'[7]

The Emperor commented to Gourgaud that whilst he was 'so rough', Las Cases had the 'delicacy of a woman'. Emmanuel Auguste Diéudonné, Marquis de Las Cases, was the final member of Napoleon's intimate entourage. Born in 1766 in the Languedoc, he belonged to the old nobility. He was only five feet and one inch tall and could be nervous and fidgety. Conversely, he was well travelled and cultured and the possessor of exquisite manners. He understood that the Emperor liked nothing more than subservience and he hung upon his master's every word. Las Cases was, like Montholon, a chamberlain at the Élysée at the time of Napoleon's banishment. He expected to accompany the Emperor to England or America and probably would not have volunteered if he had known the prisoner's true destination. Nevertheless, he quickly accommodated himself to his fate. Like some of his fellow travellers, Las Cases had an ulterior motive. He was a man of letters – he had already published a famous historical atlas – and he saw a chance to link his name inextricably with his time. He was determined to write the definitive history of the captivity; to be the Homer of this new Iliad.[8]

None of these men were fit companions for the greatest personality of the age. Bertrand was insignificant, Montholon and Las Cases were mere courtiers, and Gourgaud was an uncouth, self-seeking soldier. The Emperor was to lack congenial company but there was a more damaging omission from his immediate suite. Although he was healthy at the time of his departure for St. Helena, he needed a personal physician to tend to him should this change. He had always a favoured doctor in close attention during his military campaigns and his stays in Paris and yet he was now to be sent into exile with no expert medical help.

The obvious choice of doctor for Napoleon was Fourreau de Beaurégard. Fourreau had been a talented student of the famous Baron Corvisart, Napoleon's First Physician in the early years of his rule. Following Corvisart's resignation due to poor heath, he was attached to the Emperor's household and he accompanied him through the campaign of 1814, the captivity on Elba, and then the Hundred Days. Napoleon greatly valued his consultations with Fourreau and intended to retain his services. When the Emperor returned to Malmaison after Waterloo, he instructed the doctor to stay on in Paris in order that he could receive his prestigious election to the Chamber of Representatives before rejoining the Emperor at Rochefort. The loyal Fourreau tried to leave the capital but he was delayed by the Prussians and was unable to reach the *Bellerophon* in time.

Deprived of his first choice of physician, Napoleon consulted the aging Corvisart who recommended another of his pupils, Louis-Pierre Maingault. The young doctor had recently obtained his diploma and was apparently willing to follow Napoleon to America where he had family connections. Maingault accepted his new employment on the *Bellerophon* but when he learnt of the actual destination of the exiles he had an abrupt change of mind. Bertrand tried to persuade him to stay, pointing out the embarrassment that the absence of a doctor would cause the Emperor. Maingault retorted that there had only been a verbal agreement and that he thought himself to be under no obligation. He had no intent of giving up a potentially lucrative private practice in Paris to spend much of the remainder of his days on a small rock in the South Atlantic. This was for the best as the Emperor would not have tolerated an unwilling attendant. Napoleon impulsively offered the vacant post to Barry O'Meara, an obscure naval surgeon aboard the *Bellerophon*. The seasoned sailor O'Meara had sympathetically tended the Imperial followers for sea-sickness and had also engaged the Emperor in conversation in fluent Italian.[9]

Having described Napoleon's close entourage, we should consider the main British players on St. Helena. It is logical to start with Rear-Admiral Sir George Cockburn, as he commanded the squadron taking the Emperor into exile and was then entrusted with the governorship of the island and the surveillance of the prisoner for the first six months of the captivity. Cockburn entered the navy in 1786 as a captain's servant at the age of fourteen. He had fought under Nelson and played a prominent role in the war against the United States including the attack on Washington. He was a typical old sea dog, fair but strict and determined to follow the Government's instructions to the letter. When the Emperor became seasick and Bertrand asked for a larger cabin for him, Cockburn replied, 'Tell the General it is contrary to the ship's regulations to lend the Admiral's cabin to anyone, much less a prisoner of war.' He did, however, for the most part treat Napoleon with civility and respect and Las Cases summed up the ambivalent French attitude towards the Admiral when he described him as a good gaoler but a poor host. The veteran sailor no doubt believed that it was inappropriate to be overly hospitable to a state prisoner.[10]

On 14th April 1816, Cockburn was replaced as Governor by Sir Hudson Lowe. The vitriolic relationship that developed between the French exiles and Lowe is the central theme of the St. Helena story. Whilst French historians are almost universally antagonistic towards the Governor, the British literature is largely defined by its pro- or anti-Lowe stance. This was particularly so in the nineteenth century when a number of authors rallied to the defence of the pilloried British officer. The Dutch historian Peter Geyle has written a classical double-edged account of Napoleon's life entitled *For and Against* and it would be possible to produce an equally judgemental synthesis of Lowe's St. Helena service.

The object of all this vitriol and praise was born in 1769, the same year as Napoleon and Wellington. He belonged to an old Lincolnshire family and his father was a surgeon who served in Germany in the Seven Years War. Becoming an Ensign at eighteen, the young Lowe participated in all the operations against France in the Mediterranean during the Revolution and Empire. He was an ambitious and scholarly officer, who learnt French,

Spanish and Italian in his leisure time. During the British occupation of Corsica he was stationed at Ajaccio. He went on to Elba and then to Minorca where he organised a unit of Corsican refugees called the Corsican Rangers whom he led in Egypt. After service in Portugal and Capri, he obtained the rank of Colonel in 1812. Now, unusually for a British officer, he had the opportunity to view the continental Allies at first hand. Following a diplomatic mission to Scandinavia and Russia, he was present at the Battle of Bautzen in 1813 where he saw Napoleon for the first time. Attached to the Prussian army, he followed Blucher to Leipzig and then into France – it was Lowe who carried the news of Napoleon's first abdication to London, an act which brought him a knighthood and a promotion to Major-General.

After the Waterloo campaign, Lowe was awarded the governorship of St. Helena with the local rank of Lieutenant General and a salary of £12,000 per annum. He was surprised at this offer but he did appear to be very well qualified to serve as Napoleon's gaoler. Apart from his fluency in several languages, he had obtained his senior rank entirely by his own efforts, he was an experienced Governor of islands in the Mediterranean, he had knowledge of Corsica, and he was well acquainted with kings, statesmen and generals on the continent. Napoleon himself at first believed Lowe to be a sensible choice.

> I am glad of it; I am tired of the Admiral [Cockburn] and there are many points I should like to talk over with Sir Hudson Lowe. He is a soldier and has served …

The Emperor knew of his connections with his home island and that he had been a participant in the campaigns of 1813 and 1814; surely this was a man with whom he would be able to discuss his former grandeur.

Lowe had good points. A number of witnesses testify to his intense sense of duty, his honesty and humanity. He was capable of making and keeping good friends. However, he also easily made enemies. He was narrow-minded, irritable and, despite his cosmopolitan background, strikingly ignorant. Crucially, for a man placed in such a sensitive situation, he lacked tact. The humanity witnessed by some was not always demonstrated and others found him unsympathetic. His introverted nature made him awkward in company and he often seemed ill at ease; he did not have the unconscious grace of a gentleman. Napoleon commented on first seeing him that his expression was that of 'a hyena caught in a trap'.

One of Lowe's assets, his extreme conscientiousness, became a handicap on St. Helena. Strained by the responsibility of the guardianship of such a notorious figure, he became preoccupied by minutiae, endlessly exploring the smallest events and generating copious amounts of turgid correspondence. This characteristic worsened during his time on the island such that his behaviour displayed profound pedantry; one author has reasonably suggested that he had developed a psychiatric illness termed obsessive-compulsive disorder in which everyday tasks are repeated ritually and the sufferer becomes a hapless slave to his self-imposed routine. Worse still, Lowe became gradually more suspicious of all around him. The foreign Commissioners on St. Helena dealt closely with the Governor and were shocked at his demeanour. The Austrian wrote:

> I know not by what fatality Sir Hudson Lowe ends up by quarrelling with everybody. Overwhelmed with the weight of his responsibility, he harasses and worries himself unceasingly and feels a desire to worry everybody else … He makes himself odious … everyone agrees that he is half crazy.

The Russian Commissioner agreed.

> The Governor is not a tyrant but he is troublesome and unreasonable beyond endurance … Lowe can get on with nobody and sees everywhere nothing but treason and traitors.

The man most tested by the Governor's irrational tempers and bloody-mindedness was his Military Secretary, Major Gideon Gorrequer, who was in almost constant close contact with him.

> Mach's [Lowe's] endeavoured to awe, by the severity of his tone and the strangeness of his aspect and his black frown, ragged and brutal manners. He wished to be surrounded by mean slaves, like a cruel Eastern tyrant. Gloomy, unsocial and ferocious … His countenance, his gesture, his tone of voice were all subjects of aversion. Darting glances of reproach; breaking out in sharp rebukes and overwhelming you with angry, bitter, wanton taunts.

Behind this austere façade, Gorrequer sensed that a gentler person existed, or might have existed.

Mach [Lowe] is but a machine – he is what his nature and circumstances have made him. He slogs the machine which he cannot control. If he is corrupt, it is because he has been corrupted. If he is unamiable, it is because he has been marked and spitefully treated. Give him a different education, place him in other circumstances, and treat him with as much gratefulness and generosity as he has experienced of harshness, and he would be altogether a different nature. A man who would be anxious to be loved rather than feared, and instead of having the accusation of being a man who was satisfied to spread around him anguish and despair, one who has an instinct for kindness.

Gorrequer's description is the best psychoanalysis of Lowe. In simpler terms, he may be judged to be a fundamentally decent man who was promoted beyond his capacity and was then destroyed from within by his deficiencies.

Before taking up his new role, Lowe dallied long enough in London to marry. His new wife accompanied him to St. Helena. Lowe's right hand man on the island was the Deputy Adjutant-General Sir Thomas Reade; Lady Lowe liked to say that he was the real Governor. Reade performed all his duties with zeal and was an enthusiastic proponent of all the measures designed to ensure the safe custody of Napoleon. He was probably the only man on the island who thought Lowe to be too lenient. The French, who grew to detest Reade, believed his perpetual smile to be one of malevolence. The only other member of the British party who is worthy of introduction at this stage is Dr Alexander Baxter who was appointed as Deputy Inspector of Hospitals on St. Helena at the request of the Governor. The 39-year-old Baxter had previously served under Lowe in the capacity of Surgeon to the Corsican Rangers. A tall, heavily built, distinguished man, he was for a time one of the favoured few on the island and he frequently dined with the Governor and Lady Lowe.[11]

If the St. Helena episode is a 'Greek tragedy' of the early nineteenth century, then we have just met the *dramatis personae*. The extras are conveniently divided up into five groups: the remainder of Napoleon's entourage; the British military; the officers of the East India Company; the Foreign Commissioners; and the local population. At Plymouth, Napoleon had been allowed to take twelve servants with him. Most of these were to remain peripheral figures but two are worthy of mention as they were close to the Emperor and were valuable witnesses of events. Louis Marchand, the Emperor's First Valet, had accompanied his master at Elba and through the Hundred Days. He was twenty-four years old, handsome, cultivated and talented. He wrote a fluent memoir and was also an able artist. More importantly, he was entirely loyal to Napoleon and a valuable friend to the end. The Second Valet, Louis Étienne Saint-Denis (also known as Ali), was equally devoted to his employer and also left a detailed memoir of St. Helena. In addition to his duties as valet, he was an outrider when Napoleon drove in his carriage and a copyist and amanuensis. He was given charge of the books in the Emperor's library.

Prior to Napoleon's arrival on St. Helena, there were round 1,000 British soldiers on the island. This number was nearly doubled to guard the prisoner. The detailed comings and goings of troops do not need description here but, essentially, Hudson Lowe brought with him a battalion of the 66th Foot to join a battalion of the 53rd already encamped at Deadwood, a large plateau in the centre of the island. The 20th Foot arrived in spring 1819. All these regiments had served in the Peninsular War and they included all the usual officers, including the 'medical gentlemen'. By all accounts, the soldiers had an uneasy relationship with the sailors of the vessels stationed off St. Helena. Any attempt by the Army to lord it over the Navy was much resented. Among these professional military men, questions of seniority and rank were not easily resolved. For instance, Lowe was the Governor of the island but he was only a Major General with the temporary and local rank of Lieutenant General, whereas Cockburn, and his successor Lambert, had full right to their rank and, in different circumstances, would have had precedence over their army compatriot. Walter Henry, Assistant Surgeon in the 66th Foot, comments that the better pay of the soldiers in garrison 'could scarcely fail of exciting some slight soreness and envy in the minds of our friends afloat'.

The bolstering of the Army establishment also caused resentment among the staff of the East India Company. The Company had controlled the island since the seventeenth century and its officials continued to be responsible for its civil administration during the captivity. They did not easily adapt to the sudden influx of 1,500 Europeans who immediately fell upon the limited provisions and conscripted the local workforce. Although the imprisonment of Napoleon had been entrusted to Britain, three continental powers – Russia, Austria and France – decided to send a Commissioner to St. Helena to watch over the common enemy and to ensure that the Governor was not duped by him as had happened at Elba. The British disapproved of these appointments and the Commissioners proved to be an ill-disciplined group only united in their hostility to Lowe, their belief that their salaries were inadequate, and the poor state of their health. 'Far from acclimatising myself to this horrible rock,' wrote the Russian, Balmain, 'I suffer constantly from my nerves.' Sturmer, the Austrian, developed a sort of hysteria. His nervous attacks became so violent that he had to be held down by four men and to be calmed with opium. The French representative, Montchenu, was an object of ridicule; his eagerness to accept any form of hospitality was such that he was known as '*Monsieur Monter-chez-vous*'.[12]

It was to this cosmopolitan but incestuous world that Napoleon set out on board the *Northumberland* on 9th August. The Emperor was given a cabin nine feet wide and twelve feet long – quite appropriate for a 'distinguished general'. He quickly developed a routine. Cockburn describes this in his diary.

> General Bonaparte, since on board the *Northumberland*, has kept nearly the same hours: he gets up late (between ten and eleven); he then has his breakfast (of meat and wine) in his bedroom, and continues in his *déshabillé* until he dresses for dinner, generally between three and four in the afternoon; he then comes out of his bed cabin and either takes a short walk on deck or plays a game of chess with one of his Generals until the dinner hour (which is five o'clock). At dinner, he generally eats and drinks a great deal and talks but little; he prefers meats of all kinds highly dressed and never touches vegetables. After dinner, he generally walks for about an hour or an hour and-a-half, and it is during these walks that I usually have the most free and pleasant conversations with him. About eight he quits the deck, and we then make up a game at cards for him, in which he seems to engage with considerable pleasure and interest until about ten, when he retires to his bedroom, and I believe goes almost immediately to bed. Such a life of inactivity, with the quantity and description of his food, makes me fear he will not retain his health through the voyage; he however as yet does not appear to suffer any inconvenience from it.

At first the Emperor's moods matched the stormy weather and rough seas. Cockburn found him to be 'uncouth and disagreeable' and noted that he behaved in a most overbearing manner to his French friends. As the days passed, he became more placid and apparently more resigned; the Admiral's secretary thought that he appeared 'perfectly unconcerned about his fate'.[13]

Those who flew too close to the Emperor's dimming sun could still have their wings burnt. In the light of subsequent events on St. Helena, an account of the experiences of William Warden might be regarded as a cautionary tale. Warden studied medicine at St. Andrews and entered the navy as a Surgeon's Mate in 1795 at the age of seventeen. He was popular with the sailors – after the Mutiny of the Nore, it was one of the conditions of the crew of a return to obedience that their current surgeon should be replaced by the 'little doctor'. His Captain advised Warden not to accept this promotion which would have been a black mark against his name, but he soon made full Surgeon and served at the Battle of Copenhagen. When war broke out with America in 1812, Warden accompanied Rear-Admiral Cockburn and was with the joint naval and military forces which entered Washington the following year. Cockburn was well disposed towards the young doctor and when the Admiral received the command of the *Northumberland* with orders to convey Napoleon to St. Helena, he nominated Warden as the ship's surgeon.

Warden wrote regular letters home and in these he described his conversations with the French aboard the *Northumberland*. He particularly talked to the Bertrands and Las Cases. His first impressions of the captives were mixed and he was relived that it was Surgeon O'Meara and not himself who had become Napoleon's doctor. 'Deuce take me if I would reside in the island of St. Helena with this gang if they would make me bishop of St. Asaph. They have got a volunteer, and I heartily rejoice at it.' Warden took a dislike to Gourgaud who he dismissed as a 'Cossack bully'. Conversely, he grew to like the Grand Marshal and his wife. 'My friend Bertrand wins in every person's opinion. He certainly is an honest man, the kindest friend and the best of masters. Such a father and such a husband will seldom be found.'

In a letter of 17th March, written to his future wife Miss Hutt, he admits that he has become quite close to the French. 'You say I shall become an inmate [sic] among them. No, never! But, indeed, I have a fair opportunity for I know I am not a little in favour.' The surgeon's chance to befriend the exiles was limited by his lack of French. The Montholons spoke almost no English and the Emperor only a few words. Nevertheless, Warden did speak to the illustrious prisoner with Las Cases acting as an interpreter. Napoleon was interested in the health of the crew and also in the British doctor's faith in the use of bleeding as a cure-all – Warden describes the sailors as 'young, healthy and florid' and says that their complaints 'required a free use of the lancet'. The Emperor was bemused by this blood letting and, when he saw Warden on deck, he enjoyed ribbing him about it.

On meeting me, he would apply his fingers to the bend of the opposite arm, and ask, 'Well, how many have you bled today?' Nor did he fail to exclaim, when any of his own people were indisposed, 'O, bleed him, bleed him! To the powerful lancet with him; that's the infallible remedy.'

On one occasion, Napoleon summoned the surgeon to the quarter-deck and quizzed him both about bleeding and also blistering, another popular contemporary treatment. Warden's contact with the French entourage did not end on their arrival at St. Helena. He remained on the island for nine months and, after attending Gourgaud for an attack of dysentery, he was invited to dine with Napoleon and his retinue. The Navy surgeon was seated next to the Emperor who was in the habit of referring to him as 'Bertrand's friend'. Napoleon first asked after Gourgaud's health and then launched into a detailed and often critical discussion of other medical matters. Las Cases describes the evening in his *Mémorial* and he says that Warden was taken aback by the Emperor's deep knowledge of the subject. When Warden left the island, he parted company with the captives on friendly terms. After being given the honour of breakfasting with Napoleon, he was presented with a chess set and buckles from some trousers that had belonged to the Emperor. Gourgaud remembers that the young doctor was enchanted.[14]

All this was harmless enough and would usually have been no more than a trivial footnote in the story of the exile. However, after his return to England, Warden edited his earlier letters and published them as a book, the full title of which was *Letters written on board His Majesty's Ship the Northumberland and Saint Helena in which the Conduct and Conversations of Napoleon Bonaparte and his suite during the voyage and the first months of his residence in that Island are faithfully described and related*. In the introduction, the surgeon admitted that he had not originally intended to publish his writings but that he had been persuaded to do so by the entreaties of his friends and by the realisation that every word and action of Napoleon was of extraordinary interest to the British public. He was, he said, a reluctant author. As to the content of the letters, Warden acknowledged that he had procured the assistance of a 'literary gentleman' to make grammatical corrections but he vehemently insisted that they were factually correct.

In their style, the letters are a curious mix of picturesque detail, literary allusions and childlike conceit. The surgeon is continually astonished by his proximity to Napoleon and the attention he receives from the great man's entourage. A short extract from his account of his dining with the French gives a flavour of the book.

> A very short time before dinner was announced, General Montholon whispered in my ear that I was to take my seat at table between the *Emperor* and the *Grand Marshal* – Here are honours for you, and I will give you leave to figure your plain, humble, unassuming friend in his elevated station. I cannot say that my situation resembled that of Sancho Pancha [a character from *Don Quixote*] because every dish was at my service; but a piece of roast beef or a leg of mutton with apple sauce would have afforded a relief to my appetite which has never been familiarised with ragouts and fricassees – I had Napoleon on my right, and the Marshal on my left; and there was a vacant chair, that had the air of ceremonial emptiness, as a reserved seat for Maria Louisa. A bottle of claret and a decanter of water was placed by each plate…

Warden interspersed his descriptive prose with allegedly verbatim accounts of his conversations with the Emperor. Much of this dialogue was of a medical nature and was entirely inoffensive but Napoleon was allowed to give his version of a number of controversial events which had occurred during the wars, such as the poisoning of the French sick in Egypt. Far from demonising the former Emperor, the surgeon portrays him in a human light. On the *Northumberland*, he applauds the prisoner's 'placid countenance and unassuming manners'.[15]

In his original manuscript letters to his future wife, Warden is dismissive of his literary efforts; 'If any person else than the best of friends were to read this trash I have been uttering I should bite my fingers off.' His letters had now been polished and many fingers were leafing through the pages. The book was a resounding success, entering an astonishing sixteen editions in 1816 and the following year. Whereas the average British reader was desperate for any news of St. Helena and was unlikely to find fault with the surgeon's reflections, more informed opinion was divided as to the merit of the work. In March 1817, news of the book reached St. Helena and Napoleon eventually obtained a copy. 'Warden,' he said, 'is a man of good intentions and the foundation of his work is true; but many of the circumstances are incorrectly stated, in consequence of misconception and bad interpretation.' Gourgaud, who believed himself to have been libelled by Warden, tried to convince his master that the book had caused harm but Napoleon was having none of it. The book had, to the contrary, done him 'an immense good' and there only remained the need to clear up some of Warden's errors. The Emperor dictated his reply to the surgeon's letters to Bertrand. In 1817, there arrived in London a small volume entitled *Letters from the Cape of Good Hope in reply to Mr William Warden*. It was generally attributed to Las Cases.

The British press divided along political lines. The *Edinburgh Review* gave Warden a thumbs-up, saying that it was one of the few works on Napoleon that was 'neither sullied by adulation nor disgraced by scurrility'. The readers of the *Quarterly Review* were told that the work was a fake. The author was a 'blundering, presumptuous and falsifying scribbler'. The official British response was equally scathing. Hudson Lowe, who also first read the book in March 1817, believed Warden to have been a puppet in the hands of the French, a view that he communicated to Earl Bathurst, Secretary for War and the Colonies.

> General Bonaparte seems to have found in Mr Warden an instrument even out stepping his own immediate view. This person was at the time in the service of the Government, and had obtained access to Longwood [Napoleon's residence] only through the ostensible pretext of his professional duty.

Lowe was also unconvinced of the veracity of the letters, reminding the Minister that Warden and Napoleon did not share a common language and that much of the information collected by the doctor was very likely second hand and garbled.

The British authorities at home were doubly displeased. It was bad enough that a British naval officer had published an account of his experiences on St. Helena without their prior approval and even worse that he had written it in a manner that was sympathetic to Bonaparte. Most of the British public remained antagonistic to their old enemy but there were an outspoken minority who admired the ex-Emperor. In 1815, this hero-worship was widespread enough for the Tory Sir Walter Scott to complain of the 'nonsense' that people spoke – it was 'enough to make a dog sick'. Warden hardly helped himself by being a frequent visitor to Holland House, the seventeenth-century mansion in Kensington that was home to Lord Holland and the social headquarters for the Whig opposition and a clique of Bonapartists who were popularly caricatured as dupes of the French. The irritation of the Admiralty with the recalcitrant surgeon grew to the point that he was summarily erased from the Naval List. His immediate financial security was guaranteed by his book sales – Napoleon said that the doctor had made 50,000 francs – but he was disgraced and his promising naval career was apparently over.

Warden was reinstated to his surgeon's post shortly after. The precise sequence of events is unclear but it is almost certain that he was saved by his old Captain, George Cockburn. The Admiral had remained friendly with the doctor despite being very disappointed at the contents of his book. This is proved by correspondence between the two men found among Warden's papers. In January 1817 the Admiral wrote to Warden grieving the loss of his child from illness and regretting that Warden himself had not been there to tend him. Several years later, Cockburn was to congratulate the surgeon on the birth of his own son, the product of his marriage to Miss Hutt. Warden was forever grateful to the Admiral – the boy was given the Christian names 'George Cockburn'. The doctor was later a senior surgeon in the Navy for many years, holding appointments at Sheerness and Chatham dockyards up until his death in 1849. He was a recipient of the war medal with ribbon and three clasps. If it had not been for a fortunate connection in the Admiralty, his dalliance with Napoleon and his circle would have cost him all this.[16]

The voyage from England to St. Helena lasted for seventy-one days. On 1st October 1815 the *Northumberland* anchored in Jamestown roads and Napoleon came on deck to view the third island, together with Corsica and Elba, which was to be associated with his name. The British authorities, notably the retiring Governor Colonel Mark Wilks and Cockburn, inspected several houses on the island and decided that the most suitable for the Emperor and his entourage was Longwood, the home of the Lieutenant-Governor Colonel Skelton. This required some repairs and enlargement and, in the meantime, Napoleon was first lodged in the town and then at the summer house of 'The Briars' the residence of a local merchant, William Balcombe. Here, he was at first distracted by the charming setting and his friendship with the Balcombe family, particularly the children who he enjoyed teasing. By early December he had grown weary of his cramped surroundings and the incessant rain and he was relieved when Cockburn informed him that his definitive accommodation was ready.[17]

Longwood House had been built in 1753 as a cow-house and barn. In 1787 the Governor converted the cow-house into a four-room dwelling. Cockburn made numerous additions to try and make it a suitable abode for an ex-Emperor but it remained a hotchpotch of small rooms grouped around a court. Eventually there were thirty-six rooms on the ground floor and a number of garrets. Napoleon, who had slept in so many palaces, was confined to two rooms of equal size – about fourteen feet by twelve. Each was lit by two small windows from which he could see the regimental camp. In one corner was the small camp bed with green silk curtains that he had used at Marengo and Austerlitz.

There was no cellar or any air space between most of the rooms. Originally a farm, the wood flooring covered a soil still impregnated with the manure of the stables. The build quality may have been adequate for cattle, but Longwood was a damp and unhealthy human habitation. A Captain of the French Engineers who lived in the house a few decades later, complained that 'Silk stuffs and gloves, even when placed in closed boxes, become quickly covered with ineffaceable reddish spots; leather articles are, in the space of a few days, thickly covered with mildew'. The Longwood residents fought a constant battle against rats that lived under the floors and in the wooden partitions. Bertrand was seriously bitten whilst asleep and special precautions had to be taken to protect the children at night.

Cockburn's planned extensions had not been completed when Napoleon first moved into Longwood. Gourgaud originally had to make do with a tent but ultimately he, Las Cases, and the Montholons were all housed in hastily constructed additions and conversions. Madame Bertrand refused to live at such close quarters with so many people and the Grand Marshal asked the Emperor's permission to use a small cottage at Hutt's Gate a mile and a half away. The Bertrands eventually moved to a new house much closer to Longwood. Lowe was fully aware of the shortcomings of the prisoners' accommodation and a second new house was built for Napoleon but this was never occupied. Outside Longwood there was park consisting of two or three rows of pine and about a hundred scattered gum trees. The latter were twisted and distorted by the relentless trade wind. Around this copse stood a low wall about four miles in circumference which was known as the 'four mile limit'. Sentries were posted at intervals of fifty paces; they only came inside this perimeter at night. The enclosure covered around a third of the plateau on which the house was built. An imaginary line, called the 'twelve mile limit', encompassed it almost entirely. Within this second boundary, Napoleon was allowed to walk freely but outside it he had to be accompanied by a British officer.[18]

Despite the gloomy surroundings, Napoleon was determined that his entourage should retain the habits of his old Imperial Court. Thus Bertrand kept his appellation of Grand Marshal of the Palace and he remained the intermediary for presentations and was the representative of the Emperor on formal occasions. Montholon was styled 'Lord Chamberlain' and given responsibility for the service, provisioning and domestic details. Las Cases was 'Secretary of State' and Gourgaud was both '*Aide de Camp General*' and 'Master of the Horse'. The Pole, Piontkowski was 'Equerry' and Mesdames Bertrand and Montholon were '*Dames d'honneur*'.

A daily routine was soon established at Longwood. Napoleon rose early, had his cup of coffee and shaved himself. He then washed and dressed with the assistance of Marchand or Saint-Denis. In the early days, the Emperor went out as early as 6am for his morning ride dressed in his green hunting coat. After having completed the prescribed circuit, he took a hot soak in the zinc bath provided for him by Cockburn. He was inclined to take his breakfast either in the bath or immediately afterwards in his sitting room. Then there was the dictation of his memoirs. All the followers had to take a share in this daunting task; the unwilling Bertrand was given the Egyptian Expedition, Gourgaud had the Battle of Waterloo, Las Cases the first Italian Campaign and Montholon worked on more general subjects. Napoleon interspersed his dictation with extensive reading. He had brought with him a library of about six hundred volumes and he was always keen to acquire British and French newspapers. Batches of new books sporadically arrived and he would sometimes read through the night.

In the early afternoon, the Emperor went for a drive in his carriage drawn by six horses. The route was about six miles and high speeds were attained. Madame Montholon, who often accompanied him, declared that they went so fast that it was difficult to breathe. If in a more sedate mood, he might alternatively have a walk in the wood or the garden. It was during the afternoon that an outsider had the best chance of being presented to the famous captive. In the first two years Napoleon met more than a hundred British visitors, but in later times this was a rare event. Before dinner he went to the drawing room for a game of chess or cards. The meal itself was a formal affair attended by the whole suite; the men were in uniform and the ladies in evening dress. It was not necessarily an enjoyable experience. George Bingham, the Commander of British troops on the island, wrote that it was 'stupid enough'. He added that the 'people who lived with him scarcely spoke out of a whisper; and he was so much engaged in eating that he hardly said a word to any one'. When there was no foreign guest, the Emperor wolfed down his food even more quickly – twenty minutes usually sufficed. The meal was followed by coffee and reading aloud in the salon. Napoleon was not talented at oration and he took revenge on those who dozed off by waking them abruptly and handing them the book to continue. He retired to bed after the desultory conversation fizzled out.[19]

This humdrum routine must have been almost intolerable to a man such as Napoleon. His life had been one of excess but now, as he commented himself, he had only a superfluity of time. At his peak he had been egotistical and brutal. He says to Gourgaud, 'After all, I only care for people who are useful to me, and so long as they are useful.' He was happy to make courtiers but reluctant to make friends. He was, however, not all bad. Those closest to him witnessed a gentler side. On St. Helena, he still believed himself to be the Messiah and expected abject self-sacrifice from his disciples but he also showed them sympathy and consideration. Saint-Denis confirms this.

> The Emperor had a really kind heart and was capable of a strong attachment. In his household at St. Helena he was an excellent father of a family in the midst of his children. His bad humour never lasted long; it disappeared a short time after it had shown itself. If he was in the wrong, he would soon come and pull the ear of the one on whom his anger had fallen, or give him a slap on the back.

If Napoleon treated his inner circle as children, it was perhaps because they behaved so. They were, as Las Cases freely admitted, a disparate group of people thrown together quite by chance. The Emperor should have been the unifying force but, despite his efforts, he was the opposite. His imitation court strove for his attention and preference and endless jealousies arose. The Montholons schemed against the Bertrands who joined with Gourgaud in their hatred of Napoleon's pet, Las Cases. Gourgaud, in turn, disliked Montholon, who, he believed, had jumped ahead of him in the pecking order. These divisions were out in the open; Gourgaud wrote in his journal that if Las Cases again tried to go before him into the dining room, he would kick him.[20]

Among the papers pertaining to the exile held in the British Library is a 'Nominal list of persons composing the establishment at Longwood' dated March 1816 (see Appendix II). This serves as a reminder that there were two separate groups of people in residence. Of the 52-person total, 28 belonged to 'General Bonaparte and his suite' and 24 were British officers and their attendants. The household was divided unambiguously into prisoners and guards. There was, however, one Longwood resident who did not quite belong in either of these camps and whose true loyalties were unclear.

Notes

1. Aubry, O, *St. Helena*, pp. 63–89; Young, N, *Napoleon in Exile*, Vol. I, pp.23–57; Masson, F, *Napoleon at St. Helena*, pp. 7–34; Korngold, R, *The Last Years of Napoleon*, pp. 12–44.

2. Aubry, pp. 85–94; Young, Vol. I, pp. 55–62, 346–7; Roseberry, Lord, *Napoleon The Last Phase*, pp. 57–8; Masson, pp. 28–34.

3. O'Meara, B, *Napoleon in Exile*, Vol. II, pp. 421–3; Aubry, p. 85; Young, Vol. I, pp. 60–106, 153, 178; Korngold, pp. 64–7; Roseberry, pp. 98–9; Frémeaux, P, *Napoléon Prisonnier*, pp. 24–6; Henry, W, *Surgeon Henry's Trifles*, pp. 165–6; Martineau, G, *Napoleon's St. Helena*, pp. 138–43; Antommarchi, F, *Les Derniers Moments*, Vol. I, p. 343; Chaplin, A, *A St. Helena Who's Who*, pp. 187–94.

4. Cockburn, Sir George, *Napoleon's Last Voyage*, pp. 5–7; Aubry, pp. 95–108; Young, Vol. I, pp. 62–7; Gonnard, P, *The Exile of St. Helena*, p. 11; Roseberry, pp. 60–1; Giles, F, *Napoleon Bonaparte: England's Prisoner*, pp. 14–17; Forsyth, W, *History of the Captivity of Napoleon*, Vol. I, p.30.

5. Masson p. 49; Aubry, pp. 82–3; Martineau, pp. 24–5; Roseberry, p. 124; Young, Vol. I, pp.67–8, 85.

6. Gonnard, pp. 91–3; Young, Vol. I, 69–71; Aubry, pp. 78–81; Roseberry, pp. 126–7; Masson, pp. 57–71; Martineau, pp. 25–6.

7. Gonnard, pp. 181–93; Martineau, pp. 27–8; Roseberry, pp. 56–7; Aubry, pp. 81–2; Young, Vol. I, pp. 71–4; Masson, pp. 71–9.

8. Young, Vol. I, pp. 74–5; Gonnard, pp. 45–7; Aubry, pp. 77–8; Martineau, pp.28–31; Masson, pp.79–87; Roseberry, pp. 128–30.

9. Masson, F, *Autour de Sainte-Hélèna*, Vol. III, pp. 165–70; St. Denis, LE, *Napoleon from the Tuileries to St. Helena*, pp. 159–60; Tulard, J, *Dictionnaire Napoléon*, Vol. II, p. 247; Young, Vol. I, pp. 76–7.

10. Masson, *Napoleon at St. Helena*, pp. 110–11; Young, Vol. I, p. 79; Aubry, p. 99; Chaplin, pp. 66–7; Roseberry, pp. 62–5.

11. Aubry, pp. 175–6; Young, Vol. I, pp. 203–15, 316–7; Jackson, B, *Notes and Reminiscences*, pp. 137–8; Roseberry, pp. 66–9; Korngold, p. vii; Gregory, D, *Napoleon's Jailer*, pp. 188–9; Balmain, Count, *Napoleon in Captivity*, p. 85; Gorrequer, Major G, *St. Helena during Napoleon's exile*, pp. 261–7; Chaplin, pp.55–7; Forsyth, Vol. I, p. 123; Masson, *Autour de Sainte-Hélèna*, Vol. III, p. 180; Martineau, pp. 76–86.

12. Aubry, pp. 149–50; Young, Vol. I, pp.155, 108–10, 222–5, 260–73; Chaplin, pp. 22–40; Martineau, pp. 120–2, 134; Henry, pp. 158–9; Roseberry, p. 148.

13. Young, Vol. I, pp. 80–6; Aubry, pp. 103–9; Cockburn, pp. 10–11, 25, 41–2.

14. Shorter, C, *Napoleon and his Fellow Travellers*, pp.144–50, 119–22, 193–7, 217–9; Roseberry, p. 28; Warden, W, *Letters written on board the Northumberland and St. Helena*, pp. 75–80, 111–17; Las Cases, le Comte de, *Le Mémorial de Sainte-Hélène*, Vol. II, p. 261, Vol. III, p. 243; Gourgaud, Général Baron, *Journal de Sainte-Hélène*, Vol. I, p. 151.

15. Shorter, pp. 122–36; Gonnard, p. 115; Roseberry, p. 28; Warden, pp. 101, 113–4.

16. Lowe Papers 20146 f.23; Shorter, pp. 111–7, 124–5, 136, 263; Aubry, pp. 264–5; O'Meara, Vol. I, pp. 409–19; Marchand, *Mémoires de Marchand*, Vol. II, p. 156; Gourgaud, Vol. II, p. 152; Forsyth, Vol. I, pp. 443–4; Bertrand, Général, *Cahiers de Sainte-Hélène*, p. 52; Giles, pp. 49, 53.

17. Aubry, pp. 119–29; Young, Vol. I, pp. 111–3.

18. Korngold, pp. 84–5; Young, Vol. I, pp. 127–42; Aubry, p. 145–8; Frémeaux, P, *The Drama of St. Helena*, p. 34; Roseberry, pp. 134–5, 149–50.

19. Aubry, pp. 153–63; Young, Vol. I, pp. 154–77; Roseberry, p. 151; St. Denis, pp. 173–82; Marchand, Vol. II, p. 70.
20. Roseberry, pp. 46–52; St. Denis, p. 183; Malcolm, Lady, *A Diary of St. Helena*, p. 156; Young, Vol. I, pp. 195–8; Korngold, pp. 97–8.

2

DOUBLE AGENT?

Although he played a pivotal role in the events of St. Helena, Barry O'Meara remains an elusive figure. His life prior to his fraught appointment as Napoleon's surgeon was apparently unremarkable but there are inconsistencies and unanswered questions from his earliest years.

We know that he was born in Ireland in 1786 into a respectable Protestant family. His father, Jeremiah, served in the British army and was rewarded for his bravery by George III for quelling a rebel uprising in the North. The French historian Frédéric Masson implies that O'Meara exaggerated his father's achievements and rank. In later conversation with Napoleon, O'Meara claimed to have studied medicine in Dublin and London but the rolls of Trinity College and other universities do not contain his name and it is not possible to confirm that he practised in the English capital. In 1804, at eighteen years of age, he joined the 62nd Regiment as Assistant Surgeon and served in Sicily, Calabria and Egypt. His Army service was short-lived as, in 1807, he was obliged to resign his commission for having acted as a second for a fellow medical officer in a duel at Messina. Although neither party was injured, O'Meara's action was in direct contravention of the orders of Sir John Stuart who was determined to stamp out the practice. Undeterred, the young doctor made his way to Malta where he was appointed as a naval surgeon. He served in three different vessels in the Mediterranean and the West Indies before transferring, fatefully, to the *Bellerophon*.[1]

When Napoleon boarded this ship in July 1815, Surgeon O'Meara was among the officers formally presented to him. The Emperor could not have suspected that the affable Irishman would become so associated with his fortunes. Marchand witnessed the subsequent unlikely coming together of the two men.

> Since the Emperor had been on board the *Bellerophon*, he had talked several times to Dr O'Meara, surgeon on this vessel, who spoke Italian very well and whose appearance was frank and open. This surgeon had been in Egypt and he spoke with the Emperor about the glory of his conquest and the administration left by him in this country. This circumstance joined to the ease with which he expressed himself in a common language made him very interesting to the Emperor who, when he saw him on deck, would call him over and question him regarding the health of the crew and other medical subjects. During the voyage we had just made, Dr O'Meara had tended to several people in the Emperor's suite who had become seasick (M. Maingault was ill himself). Everybody applauded his kind, affectionate manners. All efforts, even those of the admiral, having failed to convince M. Maingault to follow the Emperor, he thought of having Dr O'Meara join him and he charged the Duke of Rovigo [Savary] to ask him if he would accompany him to St. Helena as his private surgeon. The doctor replied that he would willingly accept this honour if his government did not oppose it and if he was able to keep his rights as an Englishman. Admiral Keith, advised by the Grand Marshal of the Emperor's wishes, quickly gave O'Meara an unlimited leave of absence with full pay and permission to accompany General Bonaparte to St. Helena to act as his doctor.

Marchand's account concurs exactly with O'Meara's. The surgeon confirms that because of his medical duties and fluent Italian he had more contact with Napoleon than any other officer on the ship with the exception of Maitland. On receiving the offer to become the Emperor's surgeon, he was flattered and quickly seized the opportunity. In his own words, he was 'highly gratified' to take up the prestigious post. Admiral Keith advised O'Meara to accept the appointment, reassuring him that he would receive the Government's approval as ministers were anxious that Napoleon should have a surgeon of his own choice.

O'Meara must have been both surprised and excited at his sudden elevation but he was also cautious, perhaps sensing that his life was now to be much more complicated. In his letter to Keith of 7th August, 1815, accepting the post, he makes a number of stipulations.

...I beg to inform your Lordship that I am willing to accept the situation (provided that it meets with your Lordship's approbation) and also on the following conditions, viz. that it should be permitted to me to resign the situation, should I not find it consistent to my wishes, on giving due notice of my intentions thereof. That such time as I shall serve in that situation shall be allowed to count as so much time served on full pay in his majesty's navy or that I shall be indemnified in some way for such loss of time as surgeon on full pay, as it may occasion to me. That I am not to be considered in any wise depending upon, or to be subservient to, or paid by the aforesaid Napoleon Bonaparte: but as a British officer employed by the British Government; and lastly, that I may be informed, as soon as circumstances will admit, of which salary I am to have, and in what manner and from whom I am to receive it.

This is a surprisingly assertive and legalistic letter from a junior medical officer to the Admiral of the Fleet. O'Meara gives the impression that he thinks he is getting the British Government off the hook by accepting the appointment and that he is keen to provide himself both with financial security and a watertight escape route should things not work out.

As a naval doctor, O'Meara's duty had plainly been to his naval superiors, ultimately the Admiralty. While on the *Bellerophon*, he was already indulging in a 'private' correspondence with a friend who was a clerk in the Admiralty offices in London, John Finlaison. As the following short letter from Finlaison attests, this correspondence had a clandestine air from the start.

My Dear Barry

Thank you for your kind letter which was so extremely interesting that I showed it to Lord Melville who made some corrections in it and then expressly permitted and was well pleased that I should insert it in the *Sun* of tomorrow. This will do you no harm. You will on no account mention a hint of this to a soul, except your Captain if you find that necessary for your justification in having written. I cannot tell you now my reasons for printing it. When we meet, you will find them good as they are partly political. It is the highest authority that did it.

Yours truly
John Finlaison

This letter is typical of the whole O'Meara episode; secretive, political, and ambiguous. Lord Melville, the First Lord, was happy to obtain first hand information on Napoleon via the surgeon's correspondence. O'Meara's indirect contact with the heads of the Navy may have been harmless to him on the *Bellerophon* but his continued writings to Finlaison were to prove a major factor in the poisoning of his relationship with Hudson Lowe.[2]

Before following O'Meara on the *Northumberland* to St. Helena, we will pause to consider the character and motivation of this man plucked from medical anonymity to be Personal Physician to Napoleon. The Emperor seems to have picked O'Meara largely because he liked him and there is evidence that he was a popular and respected doctor among his naval chiefs and peers. Frederick Maitland was well acquainted with him as the two men had served together in three different ships. The Captain had no qualms in giving the doctor a testimonial.

> The attention and meritorious conduct of Mr Barry O'Meara while serving with me in the *Goliath* calls upon me as an act of justice to him and of benefit to the service, to state, that during the fifteen years I have commanded some of his majesty's ships, I have never had the pleasure of sailing with an officer in his situation who so fully answered my expectations. Not being a judge of his professional abilities, though I have every reason to believe them of the first class, and know that to be the opinion of some of the oldest and most respectable surgeons in the navy, I shall only state that during a period of very bad weather, which occasioned the *Goliath* to be very sickly, his attention and tenderness to the men were such as to call forth my warmest approbation, and the grateful affection of both officers and men. Were it probable that I should soon obtain another appointment, I know of no man in the service I should wish to have as surgeon so much as O'Meara.

Maitland, a well respected officer, could hardly have given a more effusive reference. Furthermore, he continued his support for O'Meara in later years when the surgeon was under fire for his alleged connections with the Bonapartists. O'Meara often gave a good first impression. When Walter Henry first met him on St. Helena he noted that 'his address and manner were agreeable'. Henry was later a staunch supporter of Lowe and he decried O'Meara's appointment as Napoleon's surgeon but he had to acknowledge that O'Meara's deportment in the regimental mess was 'that of a gentleman', even if his conversation was a little animated and favourable to Napoleon.

Others witnessed a less savoury side to the surgeon. O'Meara's writings are used against him to demonstrate a coarse, even vulgar tendency. He exploited his unique situation on St. Helena to parody those around him, particularly the French contingent, in his letters to the Admiralty. Some of his comments are at best mildly amusing, and at worst sneering. For instance, his description of Count Montholon; '…were he not a liar and base, he would be a gentleman: and except for these two defects, he is a good kind of man enough'. He was close to Madame Montholon as he attended her professionally and he used his pen to deride her. The historian Norwood Young claimed to have found letters in the British Museum relating to another female patient which 'place him very low among the members of his profession'.

The Russian Commissioner Balmain judged O'Meara to be an honest man but many eminent St. Helena authors have disagreed with him. William Forsyth, in his monotonous defence of Sir Hudson Lowe, claims numerous examples of the doctor's inveracity.

Lord Roseberry accuses O'Meara of 'bad faith' and Arnold Chaplin acknowledges that the surgeon's evidence 'is not trustworthy in the absence of some form of collateral testimony'. In his contemporary journal, Gourgaud speaks of O'Meara's 'lies'. Was a degree of dishonesty an integral part of O'Meara's character or was carelessness with the truth essential for his survival on St. Helena? He made the following admission to Lowe when pressed as to why he had given the Governor information against Napoleon's wishes.

> Because you had asked me and I thought it might be interesting to the government. But though I told you some parts, I did not tell you all; besides I thought I might in some things depart from the promise [to Napoleon] without impropriety.

One problem in dissecting O'Meara's character is that most of the St. Helena writers have an axe to grind, determined either to extol or belittle him. Lord Dudley, who met O'Meara at dinner in later times, was probably impartial and he remembered his guest as being 'cheerful, good humoured and communicative, and, in spite of an air of confident vulgarity, which is diffused over all his behaviour, the impression he made was rather favourable'. Dudley's ambivalent assessment may be the best description we have of Napoleon's Irish surgeon.[3]

O'Meara's motivation to take on what would prove to be an onerous duty appears straightforward. Apart from the obvious excitement and curiosity engendered by becoming physician to a man who had dominated world affairs for fifteen years, he could surely expect rapid advancement for rendering such a conspicuous service. The alternative was to pass up the opportunity and to take his chances as just another Navy surgeon. In an attempt to keep his independence, he refused Napoleon's offer of a salary of £480 stating simply that the British Government remained his master and would remunerate him. The Emperor presumably believed the young doctor to be competent in his medical duties and a man he could easily communicate with and, to some degree, trust. He might be able to manipulate him toward his own ends. Shortly after their arrival on St. Helena, Napoleon tackled O'Meara regarding his new status.

> You know that it was in consequence of my application that you were appointed to attend upon me. Now I want to know from you precisely and truly, as a man of honour, in what situation you conceive yourself to be, whether as my surgeon, as M. Maingault was, or the surgeon of a prison-ship or prisoners? Whether you have orders to report every trifling occurrence or illness, or what I say to you, to the governor? Answer me candidly; what situation do you conceive yourself to be in?

O'Meara replied that he had orders only to report any illness to Sir Hudson – referred to by Napoleon as the 'head of the spies' (*un capio di spioni*) – and the Emperor seemed to be mollified. The surgeon added that in his professional capacity he did not consider himself to belong to any particular country.[4]

O'Meara's dismissal of his nationality, even in the context of his medical role, was wishful thinking. Irish by birth, 'English' in the eyes of Napoleon and the French, his military superiors expected him to behave as a loyal British citizen and officer and to fulfil his duties on St. Helena accordingly. He was not helped by the fact that he had no written contract of employment to be the Emperor's doctor, only the verbal encouragement of the Admiralty and his immediate naval chiefs. His exact relationship to Napoleon, and indeed to the British Navy, Army and Government, was open to interpretation. The surgeon later claimed that Lord Keith and others had granted him the special title 'Surgeon to Napoleon Bonaparte' and that 'this nomination did not confer on the officers of His Majesty's Land

Forces any right or power over me … I consequently was not subject to ordinary military discipline'. Unsurprisingly, St. Helena's military Governor was subsequently to disagree with O'Meara. For Napoleon's British surgeon to have been a completely free agent, entirely detached from normal military protocol, would have been unprecedented. The British authorities approved of having a British officer in Napoleon's entourage as this was an excellent opportunity to watch over the captive, but he had to be under control. Despite his posturing, O'Meara must have had considerable concerns. He later recalled that he was only a short period on St. Helena before he fully understood the 'embarrassments' of his situation whereby he had to choose between becoming an accessory to 'vexations for which there was no necessity' or 'incurring suspicions of no very comfortable nature'. He was to be trapped between two warring factions. The two chief protagonists acknowledged as much, Lowe accepting that the doctor's position was 'delicate' and Napoleon frankly informing him of his 'dangerous situation'. As O'Meara later admitted to Marchand, he was 'between the anvil and the hammer'. He created unnecessary complications by continuing his subversive contact with the Admiralty in London. When he had stepped aboard the *Bellerophon* he had been an ordinary navy surgeon. When he disembarked on St. Helena he was attempting to be three things; Napoleon's medical attendant, a British officer, and an Admiralty informer.[5]

In his early days on the island O'Meara had time to cement his relationship with the Emperor. A good doctor has to be a good listener and this was one of O'Meara's talents much appreciated by the great man. Napoleon enjoyed dominating a good conversation and he was tired of the constant bickering of Bertrand, Montholon, and Gourgaud. Marchand says that the doctor was particularly allotted the time that the Emperor spent dressing. It is clear that Napoleon enjoyed O'Meara's company and that he treated him affectionately, not hesitating to give him the familiar friendly 'slap in the face' or a gentle tug of the ear. When O'Meara suffered a faint, Napoleon showed great concern, loosening his collar and reviving him with smelling salts. 'I feared' said the Emperor 'that it was a stroke; your face became that of a dead man; I thought your soul had left you.' Were we to have only O'Meara's account of this episode, we might think it embroidered or even fabricated, but it is fully confirmed by Marchand.

Napoleon chatted to his surgeon about a wide range of subjects, not least medicine. He quizzed O'Meara regarding anatomy and physiology and observed that he had studied anatomy himself for a few days but had been sickened by the putrefied corpses. The Emperor knew that his doctor was avidly documenting his conversations for later publication and it is little coincidence that many of the military and political subjects that he addressed involved much self-justification. As with Warden, he spoke of controversial aspects of his rule such as the murder of the Duc D'Enghien, the alleged poisoning of the French sick at Jaffa, and his abortive invasion of Russia. As his exile lengthened, he increasingly attacked Lowe and the British authorities. O'Meara, who at the outset had no particular reason to be his admirer or ally, gradually fell under his spell. Las Cases witnessed the relationship and was touched by the genuine concern that the British navy doctor had for his eminent patient.[6]

Prior to Lowe's arrival, things went quite smoothly for O'Meara, as the interim Governor, Cockburn, was not only from the surgeon's own arm of the service but also more understanding than his Army successor. This was not much appreciated by Napoleon and his retinue, who were quick to find fault with the sailor. Relations between Napoleon and the Admiral became strained; the Emperor referred to the Englishman as a 'veritable shark', refused his dinner invitations and expressed relief that he would soon be replaced. O'Meara was present during one of the Emperor's grumbles regarding Cockburn and as he left the room he commented to Marchand, 'I wish the shark could stay with us; we will regret his departure, I am sure of it'. In view of subsequent events, this shows perspicacity on O'Meara's part. His warmth towards Cockburn was reciprocated. The Admiral later discussed events on St. Helena with Lord Dudley, who wrote in his letters;

> He [Cockburn] defends Sir Hudson Lowe only just as far as prudence and
> decorum obliges an official man to do so. Indeed; he acknowledged that,
> with respect to what passed on St. Helena, he was disposed to take O'Meara's
> part.[7]

Whilst fulfilling his dual role as physician and British officer, O'Meara was continuing to busily wield his pen as an unofficial Admiralty spy. Before Lowe's appearance in April 1816, he had already sent three letters to his friend Finlaison. These are long and detailed and their writing must have taken up much of O'Meara's spare time. They are also opinionated and amusing, containing much St. Helena gossip, and they were enthusiastically received. Finlaison encouraged O'Meara to continue the correspondence. On 3rd July, he replied to the doctor.

Your letters of the 16th March and 22nd April came duly to hand and furnished a real feast to some very great folks here ... I hope sincerely that
your letters to me, which have done you so much credit with the Admiralty,
and made you well known, will hereafter be the means of favouring your
advancement, which will give me great pleasure.

The 'great folks' were a number of cabinet ministers and the Prince Regent.
The letters were circulated by Crokin, Secretary to the Admiralty, although
Finlaison confidently asserted that they were not seen by anyone outside
this elite group. Earl Bathurst can hardly have been ignorant of the nature of
the letters, but he was apparently in no hurry to share this information with
the new Governor of the island.

O'Meara trusted Finlaison to edit his correspondence. After a self-seeking passage in a letter of March 1816 in which O'Meara tries to justify
his claim for extra pay – 'I have had to perform every duty of physician,
surgeon, apothecary, and indeed orderly man, if I must be a prisoner it is
only the hopes of emolument which will induce me to continue in this
case' – he stresses that much of his letter is unsuitable for the public eye and
notes that it might not be 'altogether agreeable' to the Government. He
adds, 'However, of this you are, of course, the best judge.' O'Meara appeared
sympathetic to Napoleon.

He frequently breaks into invectives against the British Government for
sending him to this island which he pronounces (with some reason) to be the
most detestable spot in the Universe. Behold the English generosity, said he,
gazing around at the frightful and stupendous rocks which encompassed him
... Your Ministers laugh at your Laws!

The need for circumspection became even more acute, when, later in
the year, O'Meara began to criticise Lowe directly. In a letter penned in
December, he refers to the 'unnecessary rigor' practised towards Napoleon,
the first of a series of adverse comments regarding his military superior.
He reminds Finlaison of the need to conceal his letters from the Governor,
'though it remains a little strange and unaccountable to me that Sir Hudson
should be so dreadfully alarmed at the idea of His Majesty's Ministers being
made acquainted with the truth'.[8]

If the arrival of Hudson Lowe was the touchpaper, it was a slow burn-
ing fuse. Indeed, he initially made efforts to befriend O'Meara who was

in a unique position to inform him of the activities of his prisoner. Later, O'Meara was to claim that the Governor had 'loaded him with civilities', invited him constantly to dinner and conversed with him for hours. Lowe denied these assertions, saying that he had treated him as any other officer and, certainly, these claims are not entirely consistent with O'Meara's contemporary comment to Finlaison that the Governor was polite but a man of few words. O'Meara also states that Lowe sought his advice on the most appropriate way to approach Napoleon, for instance, whether it was good etiquette to invite him to a ball at Plantation House as 'General Bonaparte'. The doctor says that he defended the Governor in conversation with Napoleon, accepting that he was 'hasty' but also pointing out that he was 'not devoid of talent' and emphasising his great responsibility and rigid orders. In subsequent correspondence to Bathurst, Lowe comments that he originally believed O'Meara to be close to Napoleon but ultimately loyal to the British Government, '...he considered his duties as a British officer paramount to every other consideration'. He then adds cryptically, 'Certain views, however, which I had taken of his character, would have still induced me to have removed him upon my arrival on the island had not the decided repulse of Napoleon Bonaparte to receive the advice of Mr Baxter and the suspicion insinuated that I was sent out here to poison him, proved the difficulty I should have to encounter in placing any other person than Mr O'Meara near him.' This was written in 1818, long after the first rift between the two men and Lowe's judgement of O'Meara's character may have benefited from hindsight. That their relationship was, at the outset, relatively harmonious is suggested by the Governor's acceptance of O'Meara's petition for an increase in his salary from £365 to £520.[9]

As O'Meara was the only individual close to both Lowe and Napoleon it was inevitable that he would become a 'go-between', carrying messages and general information between the British and French camps. In justifying this role, he claimed that Lowe had actually appointed him as 'an organ of communication' with Longwood. This arrangement was approved by the French and it quickly evolved such that O'Meara became a mediator between the Governor and the prisoners. He transmitted complaints relating to cooking utensils, poor provisions and washing facilities. Much of this was trifling – he informs Gorrequer that Madame Bertrand would prefer to be supplied with 'ale' rather than 'brown stout'. In addition, he wrote a number of more complex diplomatic letters addressing various unresolved issues including Napoleon's proper title, the possible modification of the restrictions pertaining to Longwood, medical bulletins, and the fate of Las Cases after his abrupt removal from the island. French historian Philippe Gonnard sympathises with the surgeon. 'On reading these letters it is very evident that the negotiator was to be pitied. His position was a trying one between two parties equally difficult to please.'[10]

When first arriving on St. Helena, O'Meara had to be content to live under canvas but he was subsequently accommodated in a fair size room at Longwood. Beyond his futile attempts to keep the peace between the Emperor and the Governor, his greater freedom of movement meant that he was ideally placed to keep the French entourage in touch with events on the island, to liaise on their behalf with visiting ships and to bring them news-papers. He could also deal with local tradesmen and purveyors. The French had originally been allowed to access all parts of St. Helena if accompanied by O'Meara, but this arrangement was quickly changed by Cockburn such that it had to be another British officer of his choice, a sure sign that the Admiral viewed O'Meara as a less reliable safeguard than a strictly military escort. Isolated and frustrated, the Longwood occupants much appreciated O'Meara's sudden arrivals from Jamestown with news gleaned from a new vessel in the harbour. Gourgaud's journal is peppered with such incidents. In the early days of the exile, Napoleon's health was of no great concern to the doctor but he was occupied as Longwood's General Practitioner tend-ing to the minor ailments of the Bertrand children and others.[11]

Living in such close proximity to the French on a daily basis it was natu-ral for the young surgeon to form a close bond with them. What did they think of O'Meara? We have the accounts of Gourgaud, Las Cases, Bertrand and Montholon to refer to but we have to read between the lines. Gourgaud had an uneven relationship with O'Meara but the two men parted on good terms when the doctor left St. Helena. The old soldier comments in his journal that O'Meara had fallen out with the Montholons, but that Count Montholon was quick to defend O'Meara when Balmain accused the surgeon of impropriety. Bertrand often acted as a messenger between the Emperor and the doctor, at one point giving O'Meara explicit instruction as to his course of action after leaving the island. O'Meara's opinions of the French are probably better gauged from his contemporary letters to the Admiralty than from his writings published a decade later where he tended to idealise Napoleon's entourage. Whereas he later plays up the lack of pro-visions on St. Helena, in letters to Finlaison he claimed that the Longwood occupants were the greatest gluttons and epicures he ever saw, consuming three or four times as much as a normal English person. He delighted in making fun of the Montholons, gave a satirical account of the Longwood ante-chamber and kitchen, and added occasional coarse jokes.[12]

Lowe's initial qualified approval of O'Meara was very likely fuelled by the latter's willingness to relate Napoleon's actions and words to him. In a letter to the *Morning Chronicle* in 1823, O'Meara explained the letters that he had written to Lowe, Gorrequer and Reade in early 1816. Some of the letters were written for good reason and could not be held against O'Meara, but in others he relates Napoleon's conversations in explicit detail, leading to a possible charge of indelicacy or even of being a British spy. Balmain speaks of the doctor as 'Sir Hudson Lowe's secret agent at Longwood'. It is difficult to prove that Lowe insisted that O'Meara report on Napoleon, but the fact that the Governor says that these reports were 'generally unsolicited' implies that he sometimes asked for them. According to O'Meara, he was simply complying with the Emperor's wishes. He asserted that, as he had no written appointment, Lowe had threatened to send him back to England and replace him with his own favourite, Dr Baxter, who also spoke Italian and would be able to converse with Napoleon. At this point in his newspaper letter, O'Meara makes an outrageous reference to a conversation between the King and Buckingham in Shakespeare's Richard III.

> Cousin, thou wast not want to be so dull –
> Shall I be plain? I wish the bastards dead;
> And I would have it suddenly performed.

Lowe had little incentive to assassinate Napoleon, a man entrusted to his care, but it was equally unlikely that the Emperor would readily agree to a doctor provided by a man he regarded as his enemy. O'Meara consulted Napoleon, stating that Lowe insisted that he tell all regarding events at Longwood.

> 'Never,' said Napoleon, 'Never shall the body-physician of that governor attend me. I have seen his face and the proposal needs no other commentary. You may do any thing, only keep me out of the hands of that man's body-physician … Speak as you will of us all; gratifying his nature by abusing or decrying us.'

This dramatic account was undoubtedly written for public effect but the more sober version of events in his later book suggests that the Emperor gave the doctor at least partial permission to repeat his conversations, particularly his favourite themes. Furthermore, many St. Helena writings confirm Napoleon's reluctance to be Baxter's patient. However, O'Meara is not entirely frank and the content of his letters subtly changed over time. His later statement that he discontinued his reporting of Napoleon's words after the odious regulations established by Lowe in October 1816 is untrue, as more than half of the letters were written after this date. Initially he focussed on subjects which a loyal Englishman might feel bound to report to his superiors, quite in accordance with his comment to Lowe in October 1817.

> If Napoleon said something of political importance, if he were to tell some anecdote likely to throw light on any part of his history or might be useful, I would tell you of it.

In later letters, O'Meara's ink flows more freely and he begins to make allusions to subjects, for instance, the Emperor's criticisms of Warden's letters, that he had little need to share with the Governor. He seems to have exceeded the admittedly loose permission given by Napoleon to only report, on the one hand, his idle chatter on selected themes or, on the other, topics of key political importance. Was he really complying with Napoleon's dictate to act as a gentleman or was he becoming perilously close to being a spy? Perhaps the doctor was unsure where this thin line lay.

O'Meara can thus be accused of double disloyalty to Napoleon, both in his communications to Lowe and in his continued letters to the Admiralty. The latter correspondence only became favourable to Napoleon after O'Meara started to quarrel with the Governor. The Emperor can hardly be accused of naivety and he cannot have entirely trusted O'Meara. The Longwood retinue were also becoming suspicious of their foreign physician, Gourgaud commenting in February 1817, 'Is not the doctor the Governor's spy?' Napoleon was displeased when he learnt of O'Meara's reports to the Admiralty.[13]

It is ironic that O'Meara, a man who was to be remembered as Lowe's worst enemy, should initially have been identified as the Governor's stooge. The relationship between O'Meara and Lowe soon deteriorated such that the doctor was pushed irretrievably into the French camp. The reasons for this disastrous falling out between the two are not clear-cut. It is possible to document specific disagreements but the depth of antagonism was disproportionate and suggests a more fundamental clash of personalities and motives. O'Meara's account of his conflict with the Governor is emotive – at times, such as in his *Morning Chronicle* letter quoted earlier, melodramatic and self-seeking – whereas Lowe's version, contained in his correspondence with Bathurst, is more circumspect and contains less self-justification.

In the summer of 1816, Lowe began to believe that O'Meara was too close to Longwood; in Marchand's words, '…he reproached the doctor for being overly eager to carry out the petty errands of the French in town'. The surgeon's loyalties were under intense scrutiny from Plantation House. When Lowe heard that Napoleon had referred to him as 'The Little Tyrant of Italy', he accusingly asked O'Meara if he had said anything to 'draw forth such remarks'. The doctor denied it. The first hint of the scale of the trouble to come was a communication from Bathurst to Lowe of 12th July regarding a letter which had been published in a Portsmouth newspaper. This was clearly written by someone on St. Helena and was critical of Napoleon's treatment by the British. O'Meara was an obvious candidate and although Bathurst acknowledged that he was not necessarily the author, he was sufficiently confident of his involvement to warn the Governor. 'It appears therefore that it will not be prudent to place any confidence in Dr O'Meara; and unless his explanations are more satisfactory than I expect they will be, it will, I am afraid, be impossible not in prudence to remove him from the island, although I fully enter into the difficulty you may have in supplying his place near General Bonaparte's person.'

The Governor already had serious doubts regarding O'Meara's actions but, as the Secretary of War pointed out, his replacement would be no easy matter and the British Government would surely be censured for leaving Napoleon without medical attendance. Lowe tackled O'Meara over the matter of the newspaper letter but he denied any part in it, suggesting that the offending article may have been written by Warden. In the ensuing conversation, it transpired that O'Meara had held on to an important letter from Montholon detailing Napoleon's grievances rather than delivering it immediately to Lowe. This disclosure understandably irritated the Governor and O'Meara's justification of his action, that he wished to make the contents known to the Admiralty, brought his hitherto secret correspondence into the open. It is not easy to feel sorry for Lowe but he deserves some sympathy at this point. He can hardly have expected these revelations and he must have felt undermined by the Cabinet blithely receiving information behind his back. O'Meara comments that he 'appeared surprised and annoyed' and that he demanded that any further correspondence should go via him alone. The doctor countered that he had acted with the full approval of the Admiralty and that, under the circumstances, he believed he should resign his position. The Governor now backed off, saying that he 'was far from desiring' such a step.[14]

The tension between the two men increased at the end of 1816 when Lowe became more suspicious that O'Meara was acting as a Longwood agent. Las Cases was under arrest for his involvement in covert correspondence and was awaiting deportation. O'Meara contended that Las Cases's son was very ill and that both should therefore be sent directly to England rather than via the Cape as in the standing instructions. Lowe doubted the validity of the medical advice, believing that O'Meara was now a tool in Napoleon's hands. The physician must have been encouraged to stand up to his protagonist by a letter from Finlaison of 25th February 1817 in which the Admiralty clerk informed him, 'We did hear that the Governor had determined to send you home. Lord Melville, however, immediately applied to Lord Liverpool to interfere and prevent it.' He had support at the highest possible level.[15]

The disputes continued. Rear-Admiral Sir Pulteney Malcolm, Cockburn's successor, had employed O'Meara to give Napoleon newspapers without the Governor's knowledge and against his orders. O'Meara continued to deliver these papers on his own initiative, receiving them from Joseph Cole, the island's postmaster. In late May 1817, Lowe learnt of this infringement of the regulations and ordered him to stop. When the Governor challenged O'Meara regarding some pamphlets in his possession, the surgeon retorted that he 'did not consider himself amenable to any tribunal for receiving books from England'. Lowe also believed O'Meara to have misrepresented his motives in the 'affair of the bust'. In July, a marble bust of Napoleon's son, the King of Rome, arrived on the island in a rather mysterious manner. The Governor was accused by the French of delaying its delivery to Napoleon and even of considering its destruction, a charge which was likely to cause further damage to his reputation. Whatever the truth of this episode, Lowe perceived that O'Meara did not adequately support him. When O'Meara again offered a verbal resignation, the Governor stated that if it was placed in writing he would consider it – the doctor did not respond.[16]

O'Meara perhaps derived vicarious pleasure from the depth of ill feeling between his two employers. He was quick to inform Lowe, in front of Gorrequer, that Napoleon desired the Governor's recall: 'He did not think [any] man could have more dislike for another than he [Napoleon] had for the Governor.' By November 1817, Lowe was writing to Bathurst expressing his dissatisfaction with the surgeon and making it clear that he only hesitated to remove him because of the political capital Napoleon would reap from this. O'Meara now refused to report Napoleon's conversations and the situation deteriorated, witnessed by Balmain.

> There is a serious misunderstanding between Sir Hudson Lowe and Dr O'Meara. The latter, disgusted with the Governor's undue sensitiveness and instability, has ceased to see him and informs him no longer of what is happening at Longwood. The Governor asked him the reason and, as is often the case, used threats. The other answered shortly that he was a doctor, not a spy.

The meetings between the two were now violent clashes. On 28th October, Lowe accused the physician of being 'a jackal running about in search of news for General Bonaparte'. He again forbade O'Meara to converse with the Emperor on non-medical subjects and when the doctor asked for this order in writing, he flew into a rage and ordered him to leave Plantation House. On 25th November, O'Meara defended himself staunchly, claiming that he had discussed nothing of importance with Napoleon, only for the Governor to cry out, 'You are no judge, Sir, of the importance of the conversations you may have with General Bonaparte. I might consider several subjects of great importance which you consider as trifling or of no consequence.' The physician responded that he was not a *mouton* (stool pigeon) and was brusquely shown the door.[17]

In a meeting on 18th December, O'Meara admitted to the Governor that he had pledged to Napoleon in May 1816 only to reveal his private conversations when they might involve a plan of escape – an admission which, we have already noted, did not reflect well on O'Meara and which was seized upon by the Governor as proof of his duplicity. He was betraying Napoleon to Lowe, Lowe to Napoleon, and both to Finlaison. In O'Meara's account of this confrontation, he claims to have feared for his safety. 'The Governor followed me out of the room, vociferating after me in a frantic manner, and carried his gestures so far as to menace me with personal violence.'[18]

A few days later, O'Meara wrote to Lowe;

> He who, clothed with the specious garb of the physician, insinuates himself into the confidence of his patient and avails himself of the frequent opportunities and frailties ... to wring disclosures of his patient's sentiments and opinions for the purpose of afterwards betraying him, deserves most justly to be branded with the appellation of *mouton*.

A statement tinged with hypocrisy in the light of O'Meara's original willingness to tell all to the Governor. The doctor concluded his letter with a stinging and unprecedented rebuke to his senior for 'making use of language and treatment [to and of me] unworthy of and degrading to an officer'. In two dispatches of late January 1818, Lowe reiterated to Bathurst his chief complaints against O'Meara and added that there was little hope of restricting Napoleon's communications and correspondence whilst he remained near him.[19]

From late 1817, the rupture with the Governor meant the O'Meara was unequivocally 'Napoleon's man'. He now understood that he could not please both parties and he decided to serve the Emperor rather than the irritating Governor. This state of affairs can only have pleased Napoleon; Marchand notes that the Emperor was amused at the verbal clashes between the two 'Englishmen' and that he wished that Lowe 'might one day die of anger'.

O'Meara's loyalty to the French was probably cemented by a bribe paid to him in early October 1817. Napoleon discussed the payment with Gourgaud.

> The English have no exalted sentiments, they may all be bought. I should have done well to buy Poppleton [British Orderly Officer]; he would have let me take rides alone on horseback. Do you think that O'Meara is on our side? He looks for a substantial reward. He values his place at £3,000 sterling.

After money had allegedly changed hands, Gourgaud says that the Emperor was convinced of O'Meara's devotion to him. 'The Doctor was not so much on our side until I gave him money. Ah! I am quite sure of that one.' Marchand confirms that the surgeon was a 'faithful reporter' to Longwood and that Napoleon now trusted him. He was, according to the valet, 'too precious a resource for the Emperor to voluntarily get rid of him'. In his journal, Bertrand details how Napoleon asked him to brief O'Meara regarding his relationship with the Governor. He was to reject Lowe's attempts to embroil him in 'politics and government' and to try to supplant these with considerations of 'medicine and morality'.[20]

There is also British testimony that O'Meara was, by this stage, very much a Longwood agent. Walter Henry recalls that after the death of Cipriani, Napoleon's *maitre d'hôtel*, in February 1818 he was approached by a smiling O'Meara who informed him that, as the English doctor who had attended Cipriani, he was to receive a present from the Emperor. Henry was suddenly the potential beneficiary of a breakfast service of silver plate which had already been ordered from London and he was understandably flattered. A few days later, O'Meara returned in more serious mood stating that it had been forbidden by statute to accept any gift from Napoleon or his suite. If Henry was to receive his reward it would have to be done secretly without the knowledge of the Governor. Henry sensed danger and rejected the offer.

> The thing was plain enough – a palpable attempt at a bribe to enlist even so humble an individual as myself, *l'homme d'Empereur*, and to bind him down to future obedience by making him first commit himself in a wrong action.

The regimental surgeon had no doubt that O'Meara had allowed himself to be 'cajoled and fascinated' by Napoleon with the result that he was his 'admirer, adherent, agent and tool'. This was almost certainly not an isolated incident as O'Meara tried to enlist a group of British sympathisers on St. Helena. It is difficult to be precise as to their identity but some, such as Lieutenant Reardon of the 66th and Major Poppleton of the 53rd, were later to support him in his legal defence against Lowe.[21]

O'Meara derived his confidence to act autonomously beyond the Governor's authority from his support from the Admiralty at home and also from Napoleon's approval on St. Helena. His role as the Emperor's doctor gave him a certain power over Lowe who was terrified of possible accusations that he had deprived Napoleon of proper medical care. O'Meara's medical bulletins were the only portrayal of the Emperor's health available to Lowe and the outside world. These reports could be manipulated for political purposes; for instance, Napoleon's ill health might be exaggerated and his symptoms attributed to the negligent care provided by the British authorities. There are no anecdotes of medical incompetence relating to

O'Meara and it is likely that he was of an average professional standard for a Navy doctor of the time. In early October 1817, Napoleon complained for the first time of a pain in his right side with an odd sensation in his right shoulder. O'Meara believed that he could feel an enlarged liver and that his patient had hepatitis. This was a diagnosis with political implications that was unlikely to please Lowe. Hepatitis was prevalent on the island and if Napoleon had contracted the disease it left the British Government and its agents open to the accusation that the Emperor had been consigned to an early grave by his banishment to an unhealthy location.[22]

We will return to Napoleon's illness and death in later pages but the consensus of informed modern medical opinion is that O'Meara's diagnosis, whilst perhaps not correct, was quite reasonable. On the other hand, O'Meara's detractors accuse him of playing up Napoleon's symptoms for personal gain, pointing out that his new diagnosis of hepatitis followed shortly after his receipt of a bribe. Was this all invention? After October 1817, O'Meara reports a gradual deterioration in the Emperor's health, information bound to cause concern to the British authorities. Shortly before his departure from the island, the doctor wrote to the Admiralty stressing that the symptoms of hepatitis had much increased and that Napoleon would likely die of this unless he was treated more equitably and removed from St. Helena. He pointed out that many men of the 66th Regiment and around one sixth of the crew of the *Conqueror* had died of hepatitis within the previous six months. This explosive information was also passed to the Foreign Commissioners. In December, Balmain wrote that O'Meara had informed him that Napoleon's health was 'seriously affected', that his condition 'excited pity' and that he was unlikely to live another two years.[23]

Napoleon's illness had become another point of contention between O'Meara and Lowe. The Governor was understandably dubious of his adversary's motives; in Marchand's words, 'He [Lowe] came to Longwood, announced himself to the Grand Marshal, and said to him that Dr O'Meara reported in his bulletins that General Bonaparte was sick when this was not the case and that this rumour had spread throughout the town. Everyone was trying to deceive him.' Despite his doubts, it was awkward for Lowe to entirely ignore the increasingly alarming medical reports emanating from Longwood and they served to heighten his already considerable anxiety. He was convinced enough of O'Meara's account to later write to Bathurst; 'Napoleon's illness seems to have taken a serious turn and his surgeon not to be a little alarmed on his account.'[24]

The medical bulletins issued by O'Meara were ammunition in the struggle between Longwood and Plantation House – hardly a dignified way to manage a sick man. Marchand tells us that disagreements over the bulletins 'renewed the bitterness' in relations. Napoleon complained to O'Meara that his reports, which were being sent to the courts of Europe, described him as 'General Bonaparte' and that unless he was titled 'The Emperor Napoleon' he would decline to receive him. He subsequently stated that he would also refuse to see O'Meara unless he was allowed to approve the bulletins prior to these being sent to the Governor. Lowe therefore instructed the surgeon to discontinue the issue of written reports and to restrict himself to verbal communications to Baxter who would be the Governor's messenger. Napoleon declined to see O'Meara for a few days in mid October and when he consented to be consulted by him again his symptoms were relayed by O'Meara to Baxter, who passed the news on to Lowe.[25]

Baxter was placed in an invidious situation. The senior surgeon had no opportunity to see Napoleon as a doctor but had to translate O'Meara's words into a medical report which would satisfy the Governor. He did express some tentative views regarding the Emperor's illness – he suggested 'dropsy' (heart failure) and questioned the diagnosis of hepatitis – but without proper access to Napoleon he was no more than a medical clerk. The key question is whether Baxter was forced to amend O'Meara's reports to downplay the seriousness of the symptoms and protect the British from charges of mistreatment of the Emperor. In his subsequent writings, O'Meara implies that this was the case, talking of 'fictitious bulletins' which were sent to the Commissioners from Plantation House, '…it appeared that the surreptitious bulletins were made by a person who never saw Napoleon and who consequently could never be a judge of his complaint'. When these accusations became public in later years, Baxter had to defend himself, stating that he had 'scrupulously' attended to O'Meara's words prior to reporting to Lowe. It is normal to portray Baxter as Lowe's poodle but there is evidence that the doctor became increasingly indignant at his demeaning role in the reporting of the Emperor's health.[26]

In the spring of 1818, Lowe was in a quandary regarding Napoleon's troublesome physician. Up to a point, he needed him to provide medical attention to his captive and to maintain a British presence in Longwood, but the degree of estrangement between O'Meara and himself was such that it was inconceivable that the doctor could continue in the post indefinitely. The Governor hesitated to dismiss O'Meara but remained vigilant, seeking any opportunity to embarrass him and undermine his position. This brings us to the 'snuff box affair' of April 1818. It is tricky to discover the truth of this incident but the basic facts are as follows. Napoleon wished to give the two clergymen, the Reverends Boys and Vernon, a token of his appreciation to acknowledge their role in the burial of Cipriani. On the 20th of the month, O'Meara handed a silver snuff box to Boys as a present from the Emperor. This date was selected as Boys was about to leave the island and it was hoped that the secret present – against the Governor's regulations – would not be discovered. Vernon alerted Boys of the severe penalties attached to the acceptance of such a gift and the clergyman nervously returned the snuff box to O'Meara. There is little doubt that the doctor was Napoleon's gift bearer although he later denied this, insisting that Boys actually received the snuff box from Montholon and that he simply returned it to him. James Vernon claimed that O'Meara had tried to conceal the matter from the Governor, demanding that Boys' letter to the surgeon rejecting the gift be destroyed. O'Meara is supposed to have said to Vernon, 'Boys could not have taken a more effective method to ruin me … You have no idea what serious consequences may result from this: I am not a man likely to be frightened at a trifle neither.'[27]

On learning of O'Meara's most recent misdemeanour, Lowe was predictably outraged. Balmain recorded his reaction.

'Dr O'Meara', says the Governor 'has committed unpardonable faults. He informed the people there [at Longwood] of what was going on in the town, in the country, onboard the ships; he went in search of news for them and paid base court to them. Then he gave an Englishman, on behalf of Napoleon, and secretly, a snuff box! What infamy! And is it not disgraceful of this grandisseme Emperor to break the regulations.

Lord Roseberry commented, 'This is not burlesque; it is serious.' Lowe's exaggerated response to a minor infringement of regulations was designed to ensnare O'Meara and he sent the doctor an order via Thomas Reade that he must not quit Longwood unless something extraordinary occurred there or he was directed to do so by the naval Commander-in-Chief Admiral Plampin. O'Meara disobeyed this directive by going immediately to The Briars in an unsuccessful attempt to converse with his naval superior. Oddly, the letter from Reade contains no allusion to the snuff box. Forsyth struggles to explain this; 'Probably Sir Hudson Lowe thought that O'Meara must be sufficiently conscious of his own improper act and he did not require to be told why he was thus openly mistrusted.' The obsessive Lowe rarely made careless omissions in his orders and correspondence; more likely he was a little ashamed at the petty reason he had found to persecute O'Meara and did not wish it to be more widely known.

Bertrand states in his journal that O'Meara now decided, with some regret, to tender his resignation to the Governor as he believed the new restrictions both to have been unfairly imposed and incompatible with his role as the Emperor's physician. Lowe formally accepted this resignation but O'Meara was to remain at Longwood until instructions had been received from the British Government and some arrangement had been made to find a new doctor acceptable to the French. From mid April, Napoleon had refused to see O'Meara in protest at what he perceived to be the Governor's unwarranted interference. This allowed the doctor to raise the stakes, demanding his reinstatement. On 5th May, he wrote to Lowe.

> As Napoleon Bonaparte has declined seeing me since the 14th of April last and I feel that some dangerous effects may follow, I beg leave to propose putting matters on the footing they formerly were until the arrival of an answer from England ... The actual state of matters is now appalling, and will probably produce very unpleasant sensations both in England and Europe. *His Excellency may perhaps reflect upon the terrible responsibility which weighs upon him* if (as is possible and very probable) Napoleon Bonaparte, deprived of assistance, was to die before the expiration of the five or six months required to obtain an answer from England.[28]

We can imagine the neurotic Lowe repeatedly reading this letter with sweat forming on his brow. O'Meara well understood his antagonist's profound sense of duty and was quite prepared to exploit this to achieve his own objectives. A few days latter, the Governor decided to discuss the matter openly with Russian Commissioner Balmain, who recorded the conversation in some detail. Balmain noted that the 'O'Meara affair' was now the subject of gossip all over the island.

> 'There is a vessel leaving today for England. Write a report for your [Russian] Government. But I cannot give you any more bulletins, O'Meara is out, and Baxter is in disgrace with the French. I cannot give you a word about his

health. He sees nobody and I hardly know whether he is even living. What do you think of his illness?'

'They tell me that he is suffering in his head, liver and stomach, that Montholon spends the entire night at the bedside putting warm clothes on his stomach.'

[Lowe now criticised O'Meara for his role in the snuff box affair.]

'Has Dr O'Meara', I asked him, 'violated the regulations?'

'No, not exactly.'

'Have you asked him about that, and has he acknowledged it?'

'No, I have not yet asked him directly. I have my reasons.'

'May I speak to you frankly? Tell you my candid opinion, not as Russian Commissioner – for I haven't the right – but as a friend?'

'I shall be greatly obliged to you.'

'If Dr O'Meara is guilty, accuse him and try him publicly, so that in St. Helena, Longwood and Europe they may know what he has done and why you have punished him. But if he is innocent and should be reproached only for peccadilloes, forget about the affair and set him at liberty. Remember that if Bonaparte dies without having seen a doctor, as he seems determined on doing, the English will be accused of having poisoned him and it will be easy for the Bonapartists in France and other places to produce false witnesses against you. And millions of men will henceforth look upon you as his assassin.'

This observation impressed the Governor. He fell into a reverie, then thanked me cordially for my frankness and left.'

Two days after this interview, Lowe rescinded his previous order limiting O'Meara's movements and permitted the surgeon to continue as normal at Longwood. O'Meara later claimed that the Governor was also forced to acknowledge him as Napoleon's 'private surgeon', an entitlement he had previously contested.[29]

Although Lowe had backed down, he remained determined to ostracise O'Meara. Accordingly, he instructed Colonel Edmund Lascelles, who had recently arrived in command of the 66th Regiment, that the doctor was no longer a fit person to be admitted as an honorary member of the regimental mess. Lascelles, in turn, informed O'Meara's friend, Lieutenant Rodolphus Reardon who suggested to the surgeon that it would be better for him not to make any more appearances. This was a red rag to O'Meara and he immediately wrote to Lascelles asking to present his case to the officers of the 66th. In his own words, he had no intention of 'slinking away secretly'. At first, events favoured the doctor. O'Meara was a respected figure in the regiment and Lascelles told him that, although he could no longer be an honorary member, he and the officers would be happy to dine with him as a 'stranger'. Encouraged by this, O'Meara had the gall to visit the mess but, realising he could not indefinitely ignore the interdict of the Colonel, he then wrote to the officers thanking them for their friendship and regretting that he would no longer be able to enjoy their society. On the following day he received a reply.

> Deadwood, 26th June, 1818
>
> Dear Sir – As president last night I had the honour of communicating to the mess the contents of your letter of the 25th instant and am directed by the commanding officer and officers composing it to say it is with much regret they hear of your departure as an honorary member of the mess and to assure you they always conceived your conduct while with them to be perfectly consistent in every respect with that of a gentleman. I am directed to say, the mess felt much indebted for the very flattering expressions of esteem contained in your letter, and have the honour, & c.
>
> Chas. M'Carthy
> Lieut. 66th Regiment

Forsyth, O'Meara's harshest critic, has to concede that 'he possessed many agreeable and social qualities' and that he was 'very probably a popular member of the mess'. We have no reason to doubt the sincerity of this letter or its authorship.[30]

O'Meara later alleged that Lowe had employed Thomas Reade to turn Lascelles against him and to convince the Colonel that his expulsion from the mess would greatly please the Governor. If this was a premeditated scheme of Lowe's then it was unlikely that O'Meara would remain unscathed. He was not the only target. The Governor regarded the conduct of both Lascelles and Reardon to be unsatisfactory and, following a summary investigation by Sir George Bingham, both officers were removed from the island. Major Henry Dodgin succeeded to the command of the 66th and by November there was a change of heart among the officers of the regiment with regard to O'Meara. A letter addressed to Bingham by twenty seven officers assured him that they had no knowledge of the supportive letter written to the surgeon and that they wished the Governor to be informed of this. A further seven officers who were acquainted with the letter to O'Meara wrote to Dodgin stating that they had had no knowledge of any impropriety attached to the doctor and were acting out of 'the common rules of politeness'. When the officers of the 66th became aware of O'Meara's defence of his conduct in a letter to the Admiralty of October 1818 (a letter to which we will return) they again felt obliged to distance themselves from him, writing to Bingham that the letter signed by McCarthy was merely 'a mark of common civility'.

Walter Henry was a close observer of these events. He was not a supporter of his fellow medic.

> It is, I think, much to be regretted that the officers of the 66th mess should have given Mr O'Meara any written certification of good character while a member of the mess. However correct his behaviour might have been before, the gross insult to our commanding officer, and indirectly to ourselves, of sitting down to dinner after the prohibitory note he had received, ought to have prevented any verbal or written testimony being given to a man who could act with such effrontery.

Henry thought O'Meara to be culpable with respect to the snuff box affair and he raised the possibility that O'Meara had repeated confidential mess conversations at Longwood. On the other hand, he did not believe that Lowe should have expelled the surgeon from the mess thereby dragging his regiment into the quarrel.[31]

Whether the regimental officers' backlash against O'Meara was spontaneous or orchestrated by the Governor and Reade is difficult to decipher. Certainly, it was dangerous to be O'Meara's friend. The fate of poor Lieutenant Reardon, who was perceived by Lowe to be too close to the doctor, is adequate proof of this. The charges against Reardon in the military enquiry held by Bingham were firstly that he had held a conversation with the Bertrands in which the Governor's conduct towards O'Meara was censured and, secondly, that he had disseminated the content of a letter from O'Meara to Lascelles in which the surgeon had referred to the Governor in insulting terms. The transcription of the enquiry survives and it is obvious from his replies to Bingham that Reardon understood himself to be guilty by association with Napoleon's doctor. He refers to O'Meara as a 'villain' but this was probably a vain attempt to conceal his true loyalties. Referring to John Stokoe, the surgeon of the *Conqueror*, Reardon 'lamented that two innocent persons were brought into trouble by being his [O'Meara's] friend. Dr Stokoe regretted having anything to do with O'Meara … he considered it very hard after so many years service that he might be ruined by his intimacy with him.' Stokoe's fate is described in later pages. Reardon never recovered from his association with O'Meara. His later apologetic letters to Lowe failed to win the Governor's forgiveness and his military career was destroyed.[32]

Notes

1. Forsyth, W, *History of the Captivity of Napoleon*, Vol. I, p. 75; Young, N, *Napoleon in Exile*, Vol. I, pp. 76–9; Gonnard, P, *The Exile of St. Helena*, pp. 69–70; Masson, F, *Autour de Sainte-Hélène*, Vol. III, pp. 172–3; Chaplin, A, *The Illness and Death of Napoleon Bonaparte*, pp. 96–7.

2. Marchand, *Mémoires de Marchand*, Vol. II, pp. 17–18; O'Meara, B, *Napoleon in Exile*, Vol. I, pp. 6–8, II, 444–5; Young, Vol. I, pp. 77–8.

3. O'Meara, Vol. I, pp. 7–8; Henry, W, *Surgeon Henry's Trifles*, p. 148; Forsyth, Vol. I, p. 163; Young, Vol. I, p. 79; Balmain, Count, *Napoleon in Captivity*, p. 170; Roseberry, Lord, *Napoleon The Last Phase*, p. 76; Chaplin, p. 16; Gourgaud, Général, *Journal de Sainte-Hélène*, Vol. II, p. 360; Korngold, R, *The Last Years of Napoleon*, p. 297; Seaton, RC, *Napoleon's Captivity in Relation to Sir Hudson Lowe*, pp. 117–8.

4. Gonnard, p. 70; O'Meara, Vol. I, pp. 42–4.

5. Forsyth, Vol. II, pp. 582–6; O'Meara, Vol. I, pp. vii–viii, Vol. II, pp. 385–6; Marchand, Vol. II, p. 115; Young, Vol. I, p. 78.

6. Richardson, F, *Napoleon's Death: An Inquest*, p. 118; Marchand, Vol. II, p. 69; O'Meara, Vol. I, pp. 118–9, 190–6, 233, 300, 442; Young, Vol. II, pp. 249–50; Las Cases, le Comte de, *Le Mémorial de Sainte-Hélène*, Vol. VII, p.84.

7. Gonnard, p. 71; Masson, Vol. III, p. 176; Marchand, Vol. II, p76; Korngold, pp. 79–81; Seaton, p. 118.

8. Lowe Papers 20146 f. 49; Young, Vol. II, pp. 47, 57; Masson, Vol. III, pp. 177–80; Gregory, D, *Napoleon's Jailer*, p. 142; Gonnard, pp. 71–2; Forsyth, Vol. I, pp. 259–60, 72–3, 398–9; Giles, F, *Napoleon Bonaparte: England's Prisoner*, p. 87.

9. Forsyth, Vol. I, pp. 583–4, Vol. II, p. 533; Giles, p. 72; O'Meara, Vol. I, p. 86, 446; Young, Vol. I, p. 249.

10. Lowe Papers 20145 ff. 9, 33, 54, 58; Forsyth, Vol. II, p. 586; O'Meara, Vol. I, pp. 97–100, 117–8, 124–5; Gonnard, p. 73; Malcolm, Lady, *A Diary of St. Helena*, p. 79.

11. Young, Vol. I, pp. 133–4; Forsyth, Vol. I, p. 57; Gourgaud, Vol. I, pp. 152, 194, 259, Vol. II, p. 333; Bertrand, Général, *Cahiers de Sainte-Hélène*, p. 24.

12. Gourgaud, Vol. II, pp. 99, 313, 359; Balmain, pp. 195–6; Montholon, Comte de, *Lettres du Comte et de la Comtesse de Montholon*, p. 41; Bertrand, pp. 120–1; Young, Vol. I, pp. 193, 343; Forsyth, Vol. I, pp. 282–3; Gonnard, p. 72.

13. Gonnard, pp. 72–6; Forsyth, Vol. I, pp. 76–8; O'Meara, Vol. I, pp. 46–7; Masson, Vol. III, p. 178; Gourgaud, Vol. II, p. 290.

14. Lowe Papers 20146 f. 7, 20145 ff. 41–4; Forsyth, Vol. I, pp. 260–2; Gonnard, p. 77.

15. Lowe Papers 20146 f. 15; Gregory, p. 143; Forsyth, Vol. II, p. 534.

16. Young, Vol. II, p. 96; Forsyth, Vol. II, p. 538; Lowe Papers 20146 ff. 7, 23.

17. Balmain, p. 147; Korngold, pp. 296–7.
18. Young, Vol. II, pp. 96–7; O'Meara, Vol. II, pp. 346–7; Gourgaud, Vol. II, p. 326.
19. Balmain, pp. 171–5; Young, Vol. II, p. 97.
20. Gonnard, pp. 78–9; Young, Vol. II, p. 54; Gourgaud, Vol. II, pp. 270–4; Marchand, Vol. II, pp, 175–6; Bertrand, p. 33.
21. Henry, pp.162–4; Gonnard, p. 79.
22. Richardson, pp. 123–4; Chaplin, pp. 11, 79–80.
23. Young, Vol. II, pp. 64–5; O'Meara, Vol. II, pp. 517–8; Lowe Papers 20145 f. 248; Balmain, p. 146.
24. Marchand, Vol. II, p. 159; Masson , Vol. III , p. 186; Young, Vol. II, p. 102.
25. Marchand, Vol. II, pp. 179–89; Masson, F, *Napoleon at St. Helena*, p. 207; Young, Vol. II, p. 69; O'Meara, Vol. II, pp. 402–3.
26. Young, Vol. II, pp. 65, 70; O'Meara, Vol. II, p. 398; Forsyth, Vol. I, pp. 549–50; Richardson, pp. 172–3.
27. Gonnard, p. 80; Young, Vol. II, p. 97; Forsyth, Vol. II, pp. 592–4, Vol. I, pp. 562–5.
28. Roseberry, p. 72; Young, Vol. II, pp. 98–9; Forsyth, Vol. I, pp. 558, 565–6; Bertrand, pp. 105–6.
29. Balmain, pp. 177–9; O'Meara, Vol. II, p. 402.
30. Young, Vol. II, pp. 99–101; Forsyth, Vol. I, p. 572.
31. Forsyth, Vol. II, pp. 594–7, Vol. I, pp. 572–6; O'Meara, Vol. II, pp. 407–14; Young, Vol. II, pp. 99–101; Henry, pp.163–4.
32. Chaplin, A, *A St. Helena Who's Who*, pp. 195–204.

3

HIS MASTER'S VOICE

O'Meara's dismissal from St. Helena was prompted by events off the island. For reasons that remain obscure, Gourgaud departed for England in March 1818. Montholon later claimed that Gourgaud was entrusted with a secret mission in Europe but it may be that the long-suffering officer had simply tired of Longwood and his petty arguments with the Emperor. On arrival in England in early May he gave interviews to the British Undersecretary Henry Goulburn and the French and Russian Ambassadors in London. Among other revelations, he dropped the bombshell that General Bonaparte was in fact very well and that O'Meara had been duped. Indeed, Bonaparte was no more ill than when he had first arrived on St. Helena.[1]

Bathurst had written to Lowe at the end of April expressing his opinion that O'Meara should not be removed from his post as he did not believe that the doctor's disagreements with the Governor and his refusal to reveal Napoleon's conversations were sufficient reasons to satisfy public opinion. Now, having learnt of Gourgaud's utterances, he viewed the matter in a new light and he wrote to Lowe on 16th May instructing him to dismiss the surgeon and return him to England. Bathurst was unsure whether O'Meara had given false health reports because of 'professional ignorance' or out of a 'blind devotion' to Napoleon, but the end result was the same.

> We must expect that the removal of Mr O'Meara will occasion a great sensation and an attempt will be made to give a bad impression on the subject. You had better let the substance of my instruction be generally

known as soon as you have executed it that it may not be represented that Mr O'Meara has been removed in consequence of any quarrel with you, but in consequence of the information furnished by General Gourgaud in England respecting his conduct.

O'Meara still had allies within the Admiralty offices. A letter from Finlaison sent only a month or so earlier contained confirmation of Lord Melville's approval of his ongoing correspondence. The doctor was asked to 'continue to be equally full, candid and explicit in future'. Finlaison continues, 'Admiral Pulteney Malcolm , who is now beside me, begs I should express to you his particular wish that in every future discussion or report, you will as much as possible avoid bringing up his name as he is of opinion it can do no good. He sends his compliments and wishes you well through your arduous employment which he thinks no one could ever be found to fill so well.'[2]

Malcolm's wish for anonymity is more revealing than his fulsome praise. O'Meara's supporters in London were now unable or unwilling to save him. Lowe set about removing him from Longwood. The following letter was placed in O'Meara's hands by the Assistant Military Secretary.

> Plantation House, July 25th, 1818
>
> Sir, – I am directed by Lieutenant General Sir Hudson Lowe to inform you that by an instruction received from Earl Bathurst, dated the 26th of May, he has been directed to withdraw you from your attendance upon General Bonaparte and to interdict you all further interviews with the inhabitants at Longwood. Rear-Admiral Plampin has received instructions from the Lords Commissioners of the Admiralty as to your destination when you quit this island. You are in consequence to leave Longwood immediately after receiving this letter without holding any further communication whatsoever with the persons residing there.
> I have the honour, & c.
> Edward Wynyard

O'Meara ignored the central instruction to depart forthwith – 'I determined to disobey it whatever might be the consequences.' He justified his actions by citing his duty to his sick patient. If Napoleon was now to be left without a doctor acceptable to him, as appeared very likely, it was necessary to make provision for this, to prepare his drugs and to leave

a medical plan of action. After ordering his servant to pack his belongings, O'Meara spent his last two hours in the company of the Emperor.
Marchand witnessed the scene and noted that Napoleon was unsurprised
by the course of events. He urged his doctor to seek out Joseph, his brother,
and the rest of his family on his return to Europe.

> Dr O'Meara took away with him testimony of munificence equal to the
> Emperor's trust, which his conduct merited. A small bronze statue of the
> Emperor, made during the Hundred Days, which I had brought, was on the
> mantelpiece. The Emperor noticed that he was looking at it with interest; he
> took it down and gave it to him as well as a note written in his own hand: 'If
> he sees my good Louise, I beseech her to let him kiss her hand.' The Emperor
> gripped his hand, embraced him, said goodbye to him and added: 'Be happy.'
> As he was leaving, he called him back and said to him, 'Tell Lady Holland how
> much I value her good wishes.' I accompanied the doctor for a few steps after
> he had left the Emperor and I told him how disastrous I thought his departure
> was. The Emperor's health was visibly worsening and there were not even any
> instructions to follow in the future. I thanked him for his conscientious care
> for all of us and wished him a safe voyage. The shameful act was played out;
> Dr O'Meara was taken away from the Emperor at the moment when he
> needed him the most.

French commentators and Lowe's detractors have claimed that the
Governor was aware of Napoleon's poor health and that his removal of
O'Meara was a wilfully malicious act. This is unfair. He was following
explicit instructions from the Secretary of War. Also, he was understandably dubious of Napoleon's supposed symptoms when Gourgaud, his close
companion for several years, had just informed the British Government
that his illness was a sham. A protest from Longwood was inevitable and
Montholon wrote to the Governor re-emphasising Napoleon's determination to select his own doctor and adding that if he died deprived of
that man then he would be a victim of murder. O'Meara was challenged
by Wynyard for having flagrantly disobeyed the instructions of the letter
and he replied that he did not acknowledge its authority. He was directed
to collect his belongings and to go to Jamestown where he was to await
the departure of the sloop *Griffon* for the passage to England.[3]

The doctor's imminent departure did not break the cycle of accusation and retaliation. O'Meara claimed that his baggage had been 'secretly

rummaged' and his papers examined. He also alleged that he was deprived of a change of clothes and that his writing desk, in the custody of the Governor's agents, had been opened and a gold watch and precious jewellery removed. Sir George Bingham, the sitting magistrate, undertook an enquiry, but this proved inconclusive. The doctor applied to Admiral Plampin for redress but the senior naval officer, for reasons which will become clearer, was unwilling to support an opponent of the Governor.

O'Meara did not forget his patient and he sent a detailed report on the Emperor's illness to Bertrand. He was reluctant to share this information with the British authorities. Baxter was *persona non grata* at Longwood and so it is unsurprising that when, acting on Lowe's instructions, he asked O'Meara for his medical journal, he was refused. O'Meara argued that he required his patient's consent before delivering his medical details into the hands of a 'strange surgeon'. According to O'Meara, Baxter hesitated and then replied that he would be prepared to give up such a journal without consulting the sick person or caring about his feelings. Their meeting caricatured the awkward dual role of British medical officers on St. Helena; O'Meara adopted the guise of the ethical physician and Baxter, albeit reluctantly, that of the loyal military officer.[4]

O'Meara left the island on the *Griffon* on 8th August, 1818. Filled with hatred against Lowe, he was unable to resist the temptation to slander the Governor. Both Midshipman Blackwood of the *Favourite* and Mr Hall, Surgeon of the same ship, confirmed that whilst on Ascension O'Meara had stated that if he had complied with Lowe's wishes it was unlikely that Napoleon would still be alive. Mr Hall drew the inference that Lowe had wished to poison the Emperor or that he had at least planned to shorten his life by withholding proper medical assistance.[5]

On 17th September, O'Meara reported to the Admiralty that he had arrived back in England; on the following day, Barrow, the Secretary, wrote to him communicating Their Lordships' approval of his recall. O'Meara, who had been confident of support from this quarter, viewed the response as a slap in the face and he resolved to write a long letter in reply justifying his own conduct and criticising the role of Hudson Lowe. This letter of 28th October 1818 is the most explicit expression of O'Meara's defence and a valuable source for the whole episode. The young surgeon had become convinced of his eventual triumph over his senior adversary and he spectacularly overplayed his hand. He wrote:

> [Sir Hudson Lowe] made to me observations upon the benefit which would result to Europe upon the death of Napoleon Bonaparte, of which he spoke in a manner which, considering his situation and mine, was publicly distressing to me.

O'Meara added that, because of his liver disease, Napoleon's life would be endangered by a longer residence on St. Helena, particularly if he continued to be subjected to 'disturbances and irritations'. He signed off this explosive piece of writing with a request to the senior officers of the Admiralty to communicate to him their judgement of his actions. His optimism was based on his known support within the department. Lord Melville, no friend of Lowe, was still rooting for him. However, he had clearly gone too far – intending murder, he had committed suicide. A junior surgeon could not be allowed to publicly accuse the Governor of St. Helena of attempted assassination and to openly criticise the British Government's choice of Napoleon's exile. Melville was over-ruled by the Prime Minister Lord Liverpool, a reflection of the importance which was now attached to the 'O'Meara affair', and Sir George Cockburn agreed that the doctor should be dismissed from the service.[6]

Mr Croker, Secretary to the Admiralty, replied to O'Meara on 2nd November. It was, as Forsyth gleefully points out, a *réponse sans répliquer*.

> Their Lordships have lost no time in considering your statement and they command me to inform you that (even without reference to the complaints made against you by Lieut.-General Sir Hudson Lowe) they find in your own admissions ample ground for marking your proceedings with severest displeasure.

Having quoted the paragraph in which O'Meara implied that Lowe wished Napoleon dead, he continues:

> It is impossible to doubt the meaning which this passage was intended to convey, and my Lords can as little doubt that the insinuation is a calumnious falsehood; but if it were true, and if so horrible a suggestion were made to you directly or indirectly, it was your bounden duty not to have lost a moment in communicating it to the Admiral on the spot, or to the Secretary of State, or to their Lordships … Either the charge is in the last degree false and calumnious or you can have no possible excuse for having hitherto not expressed it.

O'Meara's position was indefensible even if his allegations were true. Croker finished his letter by informing O'Meara that his name was to be erased from the list of naval surgeons. Up to this point, the doctor was probably ambivalent as to his wider allegiances but from this time on he was undoubtedly as hostile to the British Government as he was to the Governor of St. Helena.[7]

O'Meara now acted as Napoleon's agent in London. His true motivation to undertake this role was only known to him but it was almost certainly catalysed by a complex mix of considerations: he perceived that he had been mistreated by Lowe and the British authorities; he was flattered that such a celebrated figure as Napoleon trusted and liked him; he had a genuine sympathy for Napoleon as a man and as his patient; he was likely to become rich by strengthening his links with the Bonapartists.

The Emperor had begun to brief O'Meara on his new role while the doctor was still on St. Helena. At their final meeting, O'Meara recalled Napoleon giving him instructions.

> When you are in Europe, you will either go yourself or send to my brother Joseph. You will inform him that I desire he shall give you the parcel containing the private and confidential letters of the Emperors Alexander and Francis, the King of Prussia, and other sovereigns of Europe with me, which I delivered to his care at Rochefort. You will publish them, *couvrir de honte* [to shame] those sovereigns, and manifest to the world the abject homage which those vassals paid to me, when asking favours or supplicating for their thrones.

The doctor was also told to actively oppose any public criticism of the Emperor and his entourage on St. Helena. O'Meara failed to find the letters referred to but he was able to wield his pen to his patron's advantage. As early as 1818, the *Morning Chronicle* published details of his rupture with Lowe. When, in 1819, Theodore Hook, a colonial officer returning to England from St. Helena, wrote an account favourable to the Governor, O'Meara made a detailed reply (*An Exposition of some of the transactions that have taken place at St. Helena since the appointment of Sir Hudson Lowe as Governor of that Island*). This publication became known to Napoleon's supporters in Europe and Joseph Bonaparte wrote to congratulate him. O'Meara then proceeded to publish other works relating to Napoleon. He had received some of the Emperor's notes on the *Manuscrit de Sainte-Hélène* and he published them in

1820. He also released a revised version of Gourgaud's *The Campaign of 1815* in London, Paris and Philadelphia and, in 1821, he sent a further letter to the *Morning Chronicle* containing details of the disease of which Napoleon had died. His contribution to Napoleonic propaganda peaked with the first appearance of his notorious *Napoleon in Exile or a Voice from St. Helena.*[8]

This frenetic activity was financed from the Emperor's coffers. O'Meara was well rewarded. In addition to his earnings from his literary efforts, the bribe of October 1817 and the gifts presented to him on his departure from St. Helena, a letter of Napoleon of April 1818 directed Joseph or Eugene to pay him £4,000, he was the recipient of further presents from Joseph, and he acquired a pension of £320 per annum from Napoleon's mother, Madame Mère.[9]

The Emperor's supporters in London operated in the shadows. It is clear that O'Meara was not working alone. He had a very active colleague in William Holmes, a man whose name crops up repeatedly in accounts of Napoleon's affairs. Holmes was both O'Meara's close friend and business partner. He was an Army and Navy agent, acting for officers on service abroad, drawing their pay, meeting their bills and keeping their accounts. Hudson Lowe, admittedly not an impartial source, claims that he was not much respected and not connected with any *bona fide* business. The formal connection between O'Meara and Holmes started at the beginning of 1818 when the doctor, presumably authorised by Napoleon, asked the agent to be the financial representative of the Longwood exiles in London. The Emperor was coming to the end of his funds and Holmes was asked to raise money in Europe. This involved much clandestine correspondence between England and St. Helena. After O'Meara's return to the capital, Holmes continued to manage the Emperor's finances, making a number of substantial payments including those to the doctor. In September 1819, O'Meara reassured Madame Montholon, now residing in Brussels and one of the recipients of the money, that she could entirely trust the agent; 'Consider him in everything as if it were I who had the honour of applying to you and believe all that he tells you with reference to the affairs that interest us.'

O'Meara's connections in England remain cloaked in secrecy. He was increasingly regarded as an authority on and exponent of the extreme political opposition with regard to the treatment of Napoleon by Lord Liverpool's government. Was he actually plotting Napoleon's escape from St. Helena? This has been suggested but the sources are shaky and we are probably in the realms of conspiracy theory rather than historical fact.

One of the best known 'plots' to free the Emperor was reputedly instigated by Colonel Latapie, an exiled French cavalry officer, with help from General Brayer, a Count of the Empire, and Lord Cochrane, a once distinguished British admiral who had become a renegade. All three had taken refuge in South America and, according to the French Embassy in London, they were about to seize the island of Fernando de Noronha and collect enough mercenaries to capture St. Helena. As if this were not remarkable enough, they were to be assisted by an Englishman called Johnstone, 'a smuggler of an uncommonly resolute character', who was said to be a close friend of O'Meara. The smuggler was constructing a 'submarine vessel' but this was supposedly confiscated by the British Government and the bizarre scheme collapsed.

Colonel Maceroni, an officer who had served in the French army under Murat and who had been implicated in the writing of St. Helena propaganda and connected with the political opposition in London, makes his own claims. If he is to be believed, which is doubtful, O'Meara, on his return from St. Helena, made large-scale preparations for the rescue of the Emperor which relied upon the 'mighty powers of steam'. Sympathetic British officers volunteered to leave their regiments and exchange to posts on St. Helena. Maceroni declines to enter into 'particulars', which is a shame. This great enterprise failed due to lack of funding. Napoleon's mother was not willing to hand over her entire fortune until the act was done whereas O'Meara insisted that he could not proceed without her financial support. If this is all true, we must presume that the Bonaparte family was wary of such complicated escape plots, especially if they were attached to a demand for money.[10]

Lowe's apologists, authors such as Forsyth and Seaton, express their frustration that their man did not make a more robust defence of his actions with regard to O'Meara. In his letter to Bathurst of January 1818, Lowe ponderously details O'Meara's 'line of proceeding from the first period of my acquaintance with him', giving his version of the rift between the two men. He accuses the doctor of a 'system of provocation', suggesting that O'Meara was deliberately manipulating his own dismissal. In a private letter to Bathurst in early October, no doubt anticipating the furore that would attend the return of O'Meara to England, Lowe rehearses the criticisms that might be made of him. He supposes that O'Meara might accuse him of forcing the physician to be a spy, of failing to give him a fair hearing on St. Helena, and of general victimisation. When O'Meara delivered the first serious cut of the knife with his self-destructive letter to the Admiralty later in the month, Lowe made notes in response to O'Meara's specific allegations. Forsyth regrets that this vindication was not made public but, in truth, Lowe's annotations are not informative. He appears to have consulted a thesaurus; O'Meara's words are variously dismissed as being 'false', 'a false innuendo', 'a pure falsehood', 'a calumnious falsehood', 'an infamous falsehood', 'a deliberate falsehood', 'a wilful falsehood', 'an utter falsehood', and 'a fabrication'.

Lowe's indignation was not limited to O'Meara's conduct. Perhaps his initial reluctance to tackle him publicly was, in part, because he believed the junior medical officer to be unworthy of the effort. He had more important adversaries. Senior officers in the Admiralty had encouraged O'Meara to indulge in his clandestine correspondence. They allowed the physician to believe that he could accuse the Governor with impunity. This was iniquitous and Lowe's outrage was justified. He wrote to Bathurst that O'Meara's 'hopes of support from the superiors of his own service' had been 'a primary cause of much of the trouble he has given'. Later, he added a pencil note in the margin of this dispatch, 'sole cause it may now be said'.[11]

In contrast to Lowe, O'Meara employed his pen in gratuitous self-justification, commencing with his letters to the Admiralty and continuing with his newspaper correspondence and later published works. Historians of the St. Helena period generally show their hands with respect to the Lowe versus O'Meara argument, portraying one of the two as the vilified innocent. A final judgement is elusive as Lowe's account of affairs is often unrevealing and O'Meara's not entirely trustworthy. It may be simply a matter of whom we choose to believe – traditionalists have tended to trust Lowe whilst the more liberal opposition elements have favoured O'Meara. This distinction is based as much on temperament or politics as on the evidence, as it is hard to unearth the truth from the two men's accusations and counter allegations. We need a third opinion from an impartial witness; a man on the scene when the Governor and doctor clashed behind the walls of Plantation House.

With the exception of the Governor himself, Major Gideon Gorrequer occupied arguably the most important position in the British garrison. He was fluent in French, a diligent secretary, and the possessor of a remarkably retentive memory. For five years he worked at Lowe's side, ever present during official business, whether this was an interview with the French or a conversation at the Governor's residence. He documented the contents of these discussions in note books and these records were used to facilitate Lowe's subsequent lengthy letters to Bathurst. From this official correspondence it would appear that Gorrequer was a staunch supporter of Lowe, but the Austrian Commissioner, Sturmer, perceptively described him as *'un finaud'* ('a wily bird').

In the late nineteenth century it became known that this man with an unrivalled knowledge of events on St. Helena had written a private diary. The documents were stored in the Court of Chancery and were jealously guarded; the judge making the order for the deposition specified that the papers were of such a 'high political importance' that it would be better if their contents were not disclosed. In 1958, by an Act of Parliament, the diary was transferred to the Public Record Office (now The National Archives) and a surgeon with a keen Napoleonic interest, James Kemble, retrieved it and published the contents. This was a labour of love as Gorrequer, in an attempt to obscure the identity of the persons to whom he referred, employed a bewildering array of pseudonyms. Before making use of the diary, Kemble had to crack the code. O'Meara, for example, is variously referred to as 'Magnesia' or 'Magnesia Primo' whilst Baxter is 'Medico in Capito', 'Scottyese', 'Primo Fisico', or 'Medico Primo'. Lowe is most commonly just 'Mac', 'Mack' or 'Mach'. Even with the main characters identified, the diary has a peculiar shorthand style and the references are often cryptic. It is obvious that Gorrequer disliked Lowe (see also Chapter 1). We must take this into account when reading the diary but there is little reason to doubt the truth of the secretary's words. He probably wrote the journal to let off steam and his elaborate efforts to disguise the individuals to whom he refers suggest that he did not wish to share his private thoughts with others.[12]

Gorrequer's testimony is a mine of information on the St. Helena episode. He is unstinting in the description of the fallibility of his colleagues. When Lady Lowe complains that Lieutenant Colonel Lyster has blown his nose on the bed curtains in Plantation House, Gorrequer records the conversation. More importantly, the diary casts an entirely new light on the Governor's dealings with the doctors on the island. Gorrequer is no apologist for O'Meara but his account is a damning indictment of Lowe's treatment of the physician, supporting many of O'Meara's allegations. It is transparent that the Governor took an immediate dislike to the young Irishman. In the summer of 1817, Gorrequer records a conversation with Lowe.

He [Lowe] remarked to me on the 1st August that people judge sometimes from little things of the feelings of others. Dr O'Meara asked for champagne. 'What, himself?' 'Yes. Dr O'Meara is taking the liberty of calling for champagne at my house!' He was raising his head again, and it was time to pull it down again.

We know that O'Meara could be brash, and the Governor's irritation may be forgiven, but the last sentence suggests that he was determined to harass O'Meara. This is amply confirmed by subsequent entries in the diary. On 22nd December, 1817;

He [Lowe] told me after dinner he did not mean to send O'Meara from here in a hurry. He would keep him long enough yet. He would worry him with questions whenever he came to him. He did not care whether he answered them or not. He would rather he did not, for then the conclusion would be the equivalent to an acknowledgment on his side. He would consider it in that light whenever he refused to answer any question he put to him.

Later, the Governor refers to O'Meara as a fool and rants against him, '…he would not get so easily out of his [Lowe's] hands. He was not aware of all the forms he [O'Meara] would have to go through before he could get away from him.'

Lowe's scheming included attempts to isolate O'Meara from other British personnel on the island. On 1st May 1818:

After his [Lowe] dictating a letter to O'Meara, he began saying what a rascal and scoundrel he was, and, working himself up into a fit of extreme passion, he declared he never would notice or again invite any person to his house who associated, visited, or had any intercourse with him. Such a rascal and villain that fellow is. After a little consideration, at last he added 'anyone who does it after knowing the circumstance of his conduct.' Proceeding with a repetition of this, turning around upon me in a gesture of rage, he said 'I prohibit you, as an officer of my staff, from ever speaking or taking notice of him, whatsoever.'

Gorrequer, who grew used to these irrational attacks, was forced to point out that he was not in the habit of seeing O'Meara. Indeed, he had hardly met him out of the Governor's presence. In October, Lowe takes satisfaction in the subtle tactics that he believes he has employed in undermining the doctor. 'By not using his name [he] had completely defeated all his plans … to ruin his character on the island, he had succeeded in producing the same effect as if his name had really appeared.'

Lowe pressed on with his campaign of vilification against O'Meara but he also worried endlessly about how his actions might be interpreted by others, both on St. Helena and in England, and also about the possible consequences if he were actually to dismiss Napoleon's physician. He repeatedly attempts to justify his behaviour to Gorrequer by slandering O'Meara. In July 1818, he agonises over whether to send the doctor from the island. 'For a long time he cursed over the orders received from home to pack him off. He sometimes determined to do it, at others seemed undecided. No decision took place for one and a half to two hours.' After more prevarication, Lowe appears to take the decision to remove O'Meara but he feels the need to seek Gorrequer's approval for his actions. His paroxysms of anxiety were intensified by the Navy's sympathy for the Emperor and his doctor. In the spring of 1818 he moans to his secretary,

> When Captain Wallis [a naval commander who dined with O'Meara in September 1817] came here he would take the part of O'Meara. The whole Navy do it. Look at the Admiral [Sir Pulteney Malcolm] the other day; he attempted to condemn the conduct of O'Meara but did he pass any remark on these matters after reading the correspondence? It was all owing to this scoundrel and damned Polyphemes [Malcolm] visiting and bowing at Bonaparte … Mr O'Meara has been too much considered.

Lowe assures Gorrequer that it is his nature to seek appeasement but then he immediately condemns Baxter for dining with O'Meara. In reality, the Governor created acrimony all around him and he was only restrained in his actions when he paused to consider their potentially disastrous outcome. In July 1818, he snaps at Wynyard, his other Military Secretary.

> I have this day signed a death warrant [man of the 66th Regiment to be hanged] and my signing this letter [acquainting Longwood of the removal of O'Meara] may be the signing of another. I know nothing more likely to happen in consequence of my signing it, and it therefore required to be well considered, and it is not a thing to be done in a hurry.

Lowe was constantly haunted by the prospect of being blamed for the Emperor's death.[13]

Gorrequer also illuminates many of the specific battles in the war between Governor and doctor. For instance, there was the notorious meeting between the two men on 18th December 1817 at Plantation House where O'Meara alleges that Lowe abused and insulted him. In reply to O'Meara's accusation in his letter of October 1818 to the Admiralty that the Governor made him 'suffer every indignity short of blows', Lowe dismissively replied 'False'. Gorrequer describes

> ... his [Lowe's] furious gusts of passion. He scarcely had breath to articulate at times. How often he repeated: 'dishonourable, shameful, uncandid conduct'. He afterwards told me that when he ran after Mr O'Meara in the passage, on his repeating of the above expression to him, he retorted that if he had behaved in that manner, he would have been better received.
>
> As Dr O'Meara retired from the library, speaking indistinctly, he ran after him in a most extraordinary and furious manner calling out loud enough to be heard in all the house: 'What's that you say, Sir,' and followed him into the passage desiring him in a most injurious manner to quit the house. 'Leave the house, Sir, leave the house, Sir,' and repeated the words 'dishonourable', etc. as above stated. Then having once returned as far as the door of the library from following Dr O'Meara, as the latter's voice was still heard retiring, he made another sally of the same kind after him. I remained in the library not going beyond the door, shocked at all this.

Gorrequer had joined the army at sixteen years of age and had seen much active service. His reaction to this argument was unlikely to have been exaggerated.

Forsyth painstakingly finds fault with O'Meara's version of the snuff box incident but Gorrequer's brief account of Lowe's reaction is more telling: 'What a damn fool O'Meara was in giving the snuff box; he [Lowe] had never had hold of him before.' A further allusion suggests that the Governor became aware of the present because Vernon informed Baxter and the doctor 'ran to Reade' with the news. Gorrequer also supports O'Meara's claim that Lowe and Reade plotted to turn the officers of the 66th Regiment against him. On 3rd August 1818, Reade is 'furnished with everything which could be got up against O'Meara' and, a few days later, 'He [Lowe] was resolved to damn him, at all events in the eyes of the officers of the 66th.'

Whilst there is nothing in the diary to support the creation of entirely false medical bulletins by Lowe and Baxter, there is evidence that O'Meara's medical reports were tampered with. It may be significant that when O'Meara makes the allegations of falsification of reports in his October 1818 letter, there is no denial from Hudson Lowe recorded by Forsyth and the Governor's defender has to resort to appending a letter from Baxter to refute the claim. In December 1817, Gorrequer describes Lowe re-reading one of O'Meara's bulletins several times and having additions made 'at his own desire'. It is not specified whether this material was added by Lowe himself or by Baxter or Gorrequer but it is obvious that there was at least some editing of O'Meara's words. Finally, O'Meara's claim that he was shabbily treated on his departure from the island gains credence. At the time, he received no support from Admiral Plampin and Bingham's enquiry whitewashed the doctor's complaints, but Lowe acknowledges to Gorrequer on 30th July 1818 (a week prior to O'Meara's actual departure) that there had been wrongdoing.

> Lamenting the unfortunate circumstances of Magnesia's robbery and reverting to the manner of removing him, his [Lowe] saying how much better Nincumpoop [Reade] would have done it than Vignoble [Wynyard] … It was altogether very badly managed.

Not only did Lowe persecute O'Meara, but he took calculated steps to cover his tracks. In the early days of 1818, he reveals his strategy to his secretary.

> 'I'll tell you what, Gorrequer, Lord Bathurst remarks very properly to me in one of his letters that I am a person too generous and open in method towards them by allowing everything to pass through, which they think proper to say, and by this means giving it effect to a certain degree, and assisting their views. I don't see why I should do it to Mr O'Meara. I am not bound to notice all that I said to him or he to me.'

After an altercation with O'Meara a few weeks later, the Governor forbids Gorrequer to make any note of it. The Secretary does not explicitly support O'Meara's case but he is disgusted by Lowe's conduct. When Lowe later makes a pathetic attempt to justify his harassment of the doctor, Gorrequer is entirely dismissive in his usual cryptic style.

Mach speaking of his treatment of Magnesia, said as an excuse that he did not think after all he had done anything so very much out of the way, and that when Lord Stair was ambassador in France in a discussion with one of the French ministers he threatened to throw him out of the window. What a comparison. What a similitude of personages and how improbable that they affected it.[14]

The depth of hatred between the two adversaries made it inevitable that the feud would continue beyond the shores of St. Helena. This was not a one-sided affair. There is much to support the view that both parties were intent on hounding the other and their supporters by any means possible. As early as August 1818, Lowe, apprehensive of O'Meara's actions on his return to England, promised Gorrequer that he would surely take vigorous retribution.

If Magnesia published or made any noise at home on the subject of his ways here, it would not be him he would attack, but those who supported him. Anyone who took his part or spoke in his favour, those would be the people he would pursue. He would ferret them out, he would find some means of ascertaining who they were; it would be them that would suffer. All this spoken in a sort of threatening manner.

Three years latter, Bertrand notes in his journal, 'The Governor will never forgive him [O'Meara] and will pay him back some day.'

Lowe may have believed that a humble Navy surgeon without influential patrons could do him little harm. If so, he underestimated the power of O'Meara's pen. As alluded to, he wrote a copious St. Helena diary filled with Napoleon's derogatory opinions of the Governor, as well as the subversive correspondence with the Admiralty. His *Exposition* of 1819 achieved some success and a few copies of the pamphlet were smuggled back to St. Helena. He was much encouraged by a favourable reception in the *Edinburgh Review* and, in 1822, he published his more substantial *Voice from St. Helena*. The physician was not motivated to write this work solely from a desire to get even with Lowe. The amazing success of Warden's modest book had high-lighted the commercial possibilities. O'Meara, much closer to Napoleon than Warden, could expect substantial profit and fame.[15]

He was not to be disappointed. The public was already aware of the doctor who had purportedly been hounded out of the Navy for his simple acts of humanity to Napoleon. Outside the publisher's offices, the crowds were so large as to obstruct the traffic. Fresh editions of *The Voice* appeared at short intervals and there were several translations including a French reprint. The surgeon had the good sense to devote most of the pages to his conversations with Napoleon and to curtail the story of his disagreements with the Governor. Walter Henry astutely comments that the *Exposition* was more remarkable for 'the *suppressio veri* than the *assertio falsi*' and this can equally be applied to *The Voice*. There was still quite enough to portray Lowe as the arch villain and to make his name 'a synonym for heartless brutality towards the fallen'. O'Meara left little doubt that Napoleon was not the Governor's only victim. Of the violent meeting of 18th December 1817, he says,

> Summoned to attend at Plantation House by letter from Major Gorrequer. As the reader must already be disgusted with the details of the manner in which the governor took advantage of his situation to insult and suppress an officer inferior in rank, because the latter refused to be his spy; I shall not fatigue him with any further account of the conduct practised towards me on this day …

Despite lapses into pomposity, *The Voice* is a convincing and emotive piece of writing. Lowe was devastated by the impact of O'Meara's words. He reflected on the damage caused to him in a note to Lord Liverpool.

> Public curiosity flew with eagerness to the repast: nothing was wanting to satisfy the cravings of the more credulous, the most inquisitive, or the most malignant mind. The highest authorities were not spared; but I was destined to be the real victim, upon whom the public indignation was to fall.

From the outset, informed opinion was divided as to the book's credibility. The admired historian, Thomas Carlyle, believed it to be a genuine work which increased his respect for Napoleon. Sir Walter Scott was more critical, regarding it as the product of a 'disappointed man'. Forsyth was predictably antagonistic whilst those nineteenth-century British writers less attached to Lowe were reluctant to view it as a reliable source; Norwood Young thought it tainted by 'falsehood and malice' and Lord Roseberry dismissed it as 'worthless'. A degree of scepticism was understandable as O'Meara was on a crusade, but they might have been less jaundiced had they had access to Gorrequer's diary.[16]

The French historical perspective is more sympathetic to O'Meara. Gilbert Martineau describes *The Voice* as a 'proud and aggressive testimony' and Philippe Gonnard, whose analytical approach to the St. Helena period is unusually free of national prejudice, agreed with Walter Henry that O'Meara's sins were mostly those of omission. The doctor had carefully excluded the spicy anecdotes and the insinuations about Napoleon and his companions that are to be found in the earlier letters. On the other hand, if the content of *The Voice* is directly compared with the correspondence to Finlaison and other writings, there is little difference. O'Meara had sent his contemporary notes back to Holmes for safe keeping and he was able to consult these to refresh his memory.

It was common knowledge at Longwood that O'Meara was writing more than a simple private diary. Montholon noted that the physician began to write as soon as he entered his room. As early as March 1817, Napoleon commented to Gourgaud that he presumed that his doctor, like Warden, would eventually publish his own book. The Emperor was not concerned at the prospect; he knew that O'Meara liked him and that he had little to fear from the doctor's portrayal of events. He predicted that the work would be 'interesting'. After O'Meara's departure, Napoleon had the opportunity to read his diary in manuscript form and he apparently found few faults in it. He did not collaborate in the writing of *The Voice* any more than he did in Las Cases' *Mémorial* but he favoured O'Meara's work over the other mass circulation Napoleonic gospel.[17]

The response of the other Longwood inhabitants to O'Meara's revelations of their private world is more contentious. Montholon, writing to his wife in November 1819, rubbished the *Exposition*, referring to it as a 'collection of stupidities and trivialities' and saying that it left a 'bad odour'. However, interpretation of St. Helena sources is rarely straightforward and as Montholon knew that his letters from the island to his wife in Europe would be scrutinised by Lowe it is quite possible that these opinions were expressed purely for the Englishman's consumption and were not real. This view is supported by the fact that Montholon was in the habit of feeding the British Governor snippets of false information. Also, he and his wife remained on good terms with O'Meara, regularly corresponding with him.[18]

Lowe had vowed that he would not demean himself by attacking O'Meara directly, but the public humiliation he had suffered at the doctor's hands left him no option but to seek legal redress and a stage where he could clear his name. He consulted the Solicitor General, Sir John Copley, and the Chief Justice of the Common Pleas (an accomplished lawyer), Mr Tindal. Although he laid his case before them in August 1822, because of the long vacation he only received their joint opinion in November. They advised him to make a selection of what he regarded to be the most obnoxious and injurious passages in O'Meara's volumes with the object of applying to the courts for a 'criminal information' – the most serious form of libel action.

This process took Lowe a considerable period of time as he found the task to be much more difficult than he had anticipated. He moaned that the work had been composed with a 'peculiar art' and that 'truth and falsehood were artfully blended together'. It is clear that his lawyers were not confident. They emphasised to their client that he would have to prove that the passages selected from the book were not only 'abusive' but also 'false'. Moreover, many of these statements had been put into the mouth of Napoleon and it was unlikely that a jury would find the defendant guilty of libel unless they could be convinced that speeches attributed to the Emperor were actually a fabrication, a cover for O'Meara's 'malignity'.

Despite the lukewarm support of his legal team, Lowe decided to forge on and he managed to obtain twenty-three affidavits from officers who had served under him on St. Helena and were willing to testify that the accusations made against him in the book were untrue. He had powerful allies such as Sir George Bingham, but it is likely that many signed affidavits in his support out of duty or expediency. Those who made affidavits in favour of O'Meara, willing to testify that his book was truthful, were as follows: John Fernandez, Captain of the 53rd; R.H.Reardon, Lieutenant of the 44th, late of the 66th; A.W. Birmingham, late Lieutenant of the 66th; Thomas Poppleton, Captain of the 53rd; Thomas Cook, late Commander of the *Tortoise* store ship; Robert Yonghusband, Captain of the 53rd; John Cumming, late purser of the *Princess Charlotte of Wales* H.E.I.C.; and of the French residents at Longwood: – Montholon, Las Cases, Antommarchi, Marchand, Coursot, Chandelier, Saint-Denis and Pierron.

Bertrand was apparently under obligation to Lowe and Gourgaud's non-appearance in the ranks of O'Meara's supporters was almost certainly because he did not wish to repeat statements he had first made on his return from St. Helena. Norwood Young dismisses the seven British officers in this list as a 'little band of failures' but this is unfair as their lack of career progression was guaranteed by their history of conflict with Lowe.[19]

When the case finally opened in June 1823, O'Meara's counsel objected that the application should have been entered at a time nearer the date of publication of the alleged libel. The court upheld the objection and the case was dismissed. O'Meara had to pay his own costs as he had taken a stand on the time element – if he had wished to proceed with the case, he could have waived this technical flaw. He was presumably relieved to escape unscathed and was not willing to take the risk of charging Lowe with having committed perjury against him. Lowe immediately protested that he had not been informed of the time limit by his solicitor. His apologists struggle to account for the failed legal action. Forsyth glosses over the affair as an unfortunate accident, Seaton refers to it as 'very strange', and Young attributes his downfall to 'the carelessness of his eminent counsel and the incompetence of his solicitor'.

It is inconceivable that Lowe's legal advisors, the foremost lawyers in the land, were unaware of the time restriction or that they simply forgot to warn their client of it. More likely, they were so doubtful of a successful outcome that, unable to persuade Lowe not to proceed, they deliberately employed delaying tactics to save both him and the Government needless embarrassment. This was certainly the contemporary opinion of some of Lowe's friends. The Governor now considered other forms of legal redress such as indictment or a civil action for damages but Tindal advised him against this. Even if he were to succeed, the damages were unlikely to be great. There is an interesting aside in Gorrequer's diary suggesting that Lowe also had concerns regarding the vagaries of the jury system: 'That one dissenting voice and one bad character, among such men as London juries are composed of, might perhaps clear him [O'Meara].' His supporters exhorted him to instead take a stand outside the courts. Bathurst wrote to him,

> I have always thought that whatever might have been the result of your late proceedings, you owed it to yourself, after all that had been said against you, to draw up a full and complete vindication of your government at St. Helena coupled with all the documents in your statement. It will be for consideration when it will be prudent to publish it.

Bathurst's final sentence is revealing. Even if Lowe were to assemble the evidence in his favour, the Government would not necessarily encourage its immediate disclosure. O'Meara's connections within the Admiralty and particularly the support of his anti-Lowe correspondence by senior figures such as Lord Melville could cause embarrassment. Ministers might be attacked for both their cruelty to Napoleon and their treachery to the Governor.[20]

In the event, Sir Hudson Lowe was never to produce any written work defending his actions on St. Helena. William Forsyth tried to vindicate him in his *History of the Captivity of Napoleon at St. Helena* published nine years after Lowe's death. The book is valuable as it contains many original documents but, in the words of Lord Roseberry, 'as a defence of Lowe it is futile because it is unreadable.' Few who have attempted the stodgy volumes would disagree. Forsyth also weakens his own case by selectively including and excluding material to show his hero's opponents in a poor light.

In the absence of any coherent defence, either in the courts or by his own hand, Lowe was left to bear the brunt of O'Meara's broadside. He became a pariah. Men moved away from him at his club and refused to sit next to him in public. He was subjected to an unsuccessful attempt at assault by the young Emanuel Las Cases in London. The Government kept him at arm's length by appointing him Commander of the Forces in Ceylon, a subordinate position for a man of his experience. He continued to be castigated in the press and in popular literature, for instance by Walter Scott in his *Life of Napoleon*, and his name gradually became a byword for inadequacy. In the House of Lords in 1833, when Lord Teynham was speaking critically of a proposal to entrust additional powers to Ireland's Lord Lieutenant, the Marquis of Normanby, he commented, 'Now suppose the noble marquis were to be succeeded in the government of Ireland by a Sir Hudson Lowe.' This was presumably a common usage but it could not be left unchallenged in such a public arena and the Duke of Wellington rose to protest, describing Lowe in glowing terms. This testimony from Wellington would be much in Lowe's favour was it not for the fact that the Duke later revealed his true opinion in conversation with Lord Stanhope. When asked if he knew the ex-Governor personally, he replied;

> Yes, I did; I knew him very well. I conceive that he had a bad irritable temper; and in that point was ill-qualified for his post. He was a stupid man … he was not an ill-natured man, but he knew nothing at all of the world, and like all men who know nothing he was suspicious and jealous.[21]

Why did Lowe not defend himself more vigorously? His actions suggest that he was not fully convinced of the validity of his own case. It is possible that he was entirely misled by his lawyers but we know him to have been a fastidious, even an obsessive individual. It would be remarkable if he was unaware of any time constraint in a process that would define his reputation. More likely, he feared that he would lose the case and that his unsavoury behaviour on St. Helena would be more widely publicised. A dread of ultimately losing the argument with his detractors may have also served to deter him from publishing his memoirs or any form of justification of his record as Governor.

In contrast to Lowe's public decline, O'Meara had become what we would now term a 'celebrity'. Byron expressed general opinion when he eulogised the naval surgeon in his poem, *The Age of Bronze*, published in April 1823. There was little prospect of him returning to simple military service. His popularity did not alter the fact that he had been dismissed from his post. O'Meara claimed that his allies in the Admiralty had offered him the lucrative situation of surgeon to the Greenwich Hospital but John Finlaison wrote to the *Morning Chronicle* denying this. O'Meara ensured his financial security in 1823 by entering into a marriage which complemented his increasingly eccentric life. His rich wife had first married years before O'Meara's birth and had been widowed twice. Her first husband had been executed for poisoning a relative.

O'Meara now became a proponent of controversial and anti-authoritarian causes. He first involved himself in the 'Queen Caroline Affair'. This explains the odd reference in Bertrand's journal; 'O'Meara is now physician to the Queen'. Caroline had married the Prince of Wales, the future George IV, in 1795. They disliked each other from the start and their estrangement was such that popular legend states that when, upon the death of Napoleon, Wellington announced to the King, 'Sire, your greatest enemy has died', the startled monarch replied, 'What! When did the Queen die?'

In fact, she was alive, and when she returned to England from an exile in Europe in 1820 riots broke out in her support. The King appealed to his ministers to get rid of her and a bill was introduced to strip her of the title of Queen Consort and to dissolve the marriage, in part because of her alleged adultery. O'Meara decided to help her and busied himself collecting papers, evidence and witnesses on her behalf. The doctor was now addicted to opposition. Although not a Catholic, he played a prominent role in the campaign for Catholic emancipation and he became an ardent supporter of Daniel O'Connell and the First Reform Bill.[22]

O'Meara maintained close links with the Bonaparte family. The following letter was written to the physician by Louis Napoleon, the future Napoleon III, in 1836.

My Dear Doctor

I am sending you my work upon artillery, which appeared a few months ago and which will, I hope, interest you. I beg you to accept it as proof of my friendship which has too noble an origin for it ever to change.

My work was received with much indulgence in France, which gave me great pleasure, and rewarded me for my long and arduous labours.

You would be doing me a great pleasure by obtaining for me an accurate drawing of the cannons newly invented for the English Navy, which are loaded at the breach. I should be much interested to learn how they are made because I am now occupied with a new invention which is connected with that process. You will understand no doubt that whatever has reference to artillery must be of interest to me. I am happy to take this opportunity of renewing the assurance of my friendship.

Napoleon Louis Bonaparte

We do not know if O'Meara acted as a French spy and replied to this brazen request to disclose the secrets of the British Navy. That the letter was written at all suggests that the French authorities regarded him as a potential enemy of his former employer.

The doctor died shortly afterwards at his home in London on June 10th 1836 at the age of fifty-four. He had caught a chill whilst attending one of O'Connell's meetings. He was still held in high public esteem. A leader in *The Courier* which appeared three days after his death described him as a man of 'rigid integrity, capable of any sacrifice in the support of principle … A warmer-hearted or a more sincere friend than O'Meara never lived'.

He had won the war of words but he was not leaving anything to chance. He was buried in St. Mary's Church at Paddington Green and, in his will, he directed that the following should be inscribed upon his tomb.

I take this opportunity of declaring that with the exception of some unintentional and trifling errors in the *Voice from St. Helena*, the book is a faithful narrative of the treatment inflicted upon the great man Napoleon by Sir Hudson Lowe and his subordinates, and that I have even suppressed some facts which although true might have been considered to be exaggerated and not credited.[23]

Notes

1. Young, N, *Napoleon in Exile*, Vol. II, pp. 90–3; Gonnard, P, *The Exile of St. Helena*, pp. 182–4.
2. Forsyth, W, *History of the Captivity of Napoleon*, Vol. I, pp. 584–5, Vol. II, pp. 553–4; Young, Vol. II, pp. 101–3.
3. Gonnard, p. 81; Forsyth, Vol. I, pp. 589–90; O'Meara, B, *Napoleon in Exile*, Vol. I, pp. 414–6; Marchand, *Mémoires de Marchand*, Vol. II, p. 192; Masson, F, *Autour de Sainte-Hélène*, Vol. III, pp. 190–2.
4. Forsyth, Vol. II, pp. 602–4; Korngold, R, *The Last Years of Napoleon*, pp. 301–4.
5. Forsyth, Vol. I, p. 629; Young, Vol. II, p. 106.
6. Young, Vol. II, pp. 106–8; Forsyth, Vol. II, pp. 583–4, 615, 21; Korngold, pp. 304–5; Masson, Vol. III, p. 193; Seaton, RC, *Napoleon's Captivity in Relation to Sir Hudson Lowe*, p. 109; Jackson, B, *Notes and Recollections*, pp. 170–1.
7. Forsyth, Vol. II, pp. 19–21; Young, Vol. II, pp. 107–8; Gonnard, p. 81.
8. Masson, Vol. III, pp. 195–6; O'Meara, Vol. II, pp. 416–7; Gonnard, pp. 83–4.
9. Masson, Vol. III, pp. 191–3; Young, Vol. II, p. 98; Korngold, p. 303.
10. Gonnard, pp. 82–5; Roseberry, Lord, *Napoleon The Last Phase*, pp. 102–3; Martineau, G, *Napoleon's St. Helena*, pp. 204–5.
11. Forsyth, Vol. II, pp. 532–9, 581, Vol. I, pp. 625–7; Young, Vol. II, p. 138; Seaton, p. 149.
12. Chaplin, *A St. Helena Who's Who*, pp. 78–9; The National Archives J 76/8/1; Gorrequer, Major G, *St. Helena during Napoleon's exile*, pp. 2, 5.
13. Gorrequer, pp. 18, 30, 55–6, 60, 97, 38, 70–1, 61, 71–2, 62.
14. Gorrequer, pp. 29, 56, 99, 81–3, 31, 75–6, 33, 43, 111–2; Forsyth, Vol. II, pp. 587–94.
15. Gorrequer, p. 79; Bertrand, General, Napoleon at St. Helena, p. 265; Markham, JD, *Napoleon and Dr Verling on St. Helena*, p. 104; Richardson, F, *Napoleon's Death: An Inquest*, pp. 126–8; Young, Vol. I, pp. 249–50.
16. Young, Vol. II, pp. 359–60, Vol. I, p. 574; Giles, F, *Napoleon Bonaparte: England's Prisoner*, p. 164; Roseberry, p. 31.
17. Martineau, p. 39; Gonnard, pp. 87–90; Gourgaud, Général, *Journal de Sainte-Hélène*, Vol. II, p. 290.
18. Montholon, Comte de, *Lettres du Comte et de la Comtesse de Montholon*, p. 41; Gonnard, pp. 84–6.
19. Forsyth, Vol. II, pp. 186–9; Korngold, pp. 409–10; Young, Vol. II, pp. 261–5.
20. Forsyth, Vol. II, pp. 189–92; Young, Vol. II, pp. 265–7; Seaton, pp. 231–2; Gregory, D, *Napoleon's Jailer*, p. 175; Gorrequer, p. 153.
21. Forsyth, Vol. II, p. 192; Gonnard, p. 112; Roseberry, p. 76; Young, Vol. II, p. 268; Giles, p. 166; Gregory, pp. 185–6; Stanhope, Earl, *Notes of Conversations with the Duke of Wellington*, p. 244.

22. Young, Vol. II, pp. 260, 267; Seaton, p. 119; Forsyth, Vol. II, p. 647; Masson, Vol. III, pp. 194–5; Richardson, p. 129; Chaplin, A, *The Illness and Death of Napoleon Bonaparte*, p. 97; Bertrand, p. 265.
23. Young, Vol. II, pp. 267–8; Chaplin, *The Illness and Death of Napoleon Bonaparte*, p. 97; Chaplin, *A St. Helena Who's Who*, pp. 109–110.

4

TRAFALGAR VETERAN

After the departure of O'Meara, the medical care of Napoleon was largely left to chance. The Governor appointed James Verling of the Royal Artillery to the post of British physician at Longwood but Napoleon stubbornly refused to see any doctor offered by Lowe. Verling (to whom we will return) only caught a few glimpses of his 'patient' despite residing in the same house for over two years. Because of the lack of a reliable medical witness, little is known of the health of the Emperor at this time. Montholon infers that he was far from well. Verling notes in his journal of September 1818 that one of the servants described their master as 'looking old, pale, and sallow', and he later adds, 'I thought from the slight views I had occasionally that he looked very ill'. Lowe remained sceptical of Napoleon's illness but, if real, it was surely only a matter of time before his prisoner agreed to consult one of the Governor's favoured doctors. However, when the call for medical help came, it was not to Verling or Baxter, but to John Stokoe, the surgeon of the *Conqueror*.[1]

Stokoe was born in 1775 at Ferryhill in Durham. In 1794 he entered the British Navy as Surgeon's Mate and was attached to a sloop of war, getting his first taste of action at the bombardment of Copenhagen. He was transferred to the *Monarch*, a ship of the line, and then to a frigate, the *Acosta*, and he spent two years in the Channel and the North Sea. He served at the Battle of Trafalgar on the *Thunderer*, which was last but one in Admiral Collingwood's line. Relatively late into the action, she engaged a number of enemy ships and was fortunate to suffer only light damage, with sixteen casualties, four killed and twelve wounded. From September 1805 to November 1808 he was on the same vessel and saw the terrible siege of Gaeta, took part in an expedition to the Dardanelles and visited Sicily and Egypt. The vagaries of war next took him to a blockade of the Île de France and, on his return, he was appointed doctor to a prison ship anchored on the Medway. At the fall of Napoleon in 1814, he was selected by the Admiralty to accompany a Russian battalion which was being repatriated at Cronstadt. He was stationed at Sheerness and Leith in 1815 and 1816. We have no testimonies as to Stokoe's character during these earlier years. His portrait suggests a country gentleman rather than a hardened naval veteran. Whatever his appearance, we may assume that he was no shrinking violet. By the end of 1816, he had been in the Navy for twenty-two years of which sixteen and a half had been at sea on active service. He had cured himself of typhus by quickly downing two bottles of wine. He was a survivor of hard times.[2]

At Portsmouth, in December 1816, Sir Robert Plampin hoisted his flag on the *Conqueror*. This ship of the line was to take the Admiral to St. Helena in the spring and was not due to return until 1820. Stokoe was offered the post of Surgeon of the vessel and was faced with a life-changing decision. He would very soon be entitled to a retirement pension and there was no doubt that his previous service allowed him to refuse the posting and to remain at home, perhaps serving in a naval hospital. If he still had the urge to travel, he could have reasonably requested a pleasanter station than the isolation of the South Atlantic. He chose St. Helena. 'I thought', he says in his memoirs, 'that I should see the great man and probably have the honour of conversing with him – little did I think at the time that the honour would be so dearly purchased!'

Having made his decision, the surgeon tried to research his new post-ing. He scoured the papers in vain. The press had been mostly silenced by the Government. William Warden's letters were a little more help but they focussed largely on Napoleon's conversations and gave only a vague picture of life on the island. Other pamphlets purporting to emanate from St. Helena were clearly bogus – most notoriously the *Manuscrit venu de Sainte-Hélène d'une manière inconnue*. When the *Conqueror* set sail on 15th March, 1817, St. Helena was an uncertain and mysterious destination. Jamestown harbour was reached on 29th June, well into Napoleon's second year of captivity.

Plampin was to replace Pulteney Malcolm, and was to prove much more compliant with Lowe's wishes than his predecessor. Malcolm had not been deliberately obstructive to the Military Governor but he had harboured rather more sympathy for Napoleon and had operated independently of Lowe to a greater degree than was proper for the Commander-in-Chief of a naval station. In contrast, Plampin was to be putty in Lowe's hands, moulded to fulfil his every whim. The reason for this change was not simply Plampin's personality, although this was a factor. Napoleon was unimpressed by the new Admiral, '… that little man of some 60 years with a very unpleasant appearance. He resembles one of those vulgar Dutch sailors who are always drunk and whom I have seen in their country, seated at a table, pipe in mouth, with a piece of cheese, and a bottle of gin in front of them.' Balmain was less unkind but equally dismissive of Plampin; 'a good man, timid, who wishes to live peacefully and to mix into nothing which does not concern him.' The Russian Commissioner then adds that, despite this inherent dullness, the Admiral had caused a scandal on the island by bringing with him 'a lady from London, who, though she uses his name, is only his mistress'. Plampin had severely compromised himself and, if he wanted his life on the island to be tolerable, he was going to need Lowe's help.

Stokoe confirms this state of affairs in his memoirs, commenting that all on board were surprised that 'Mrs Plampin' joined the ship surreptitiously from the Isle of Wight rather than at Portsmouth as would have been customary for the wife of a senior officer.

> Our suspicions gained strength and were verified on our arrival at St. Helena. There being great lack of feminine society at St. Helena, any new arrival aroused intense interest. No sooner were the officers of the *Conqueror* seen on the quay at Jamestown that they were plied with questions, one of the first being, 'Is Admiral Plampin a married man?' 'Has he brought his wife out with him?' Laughing in their sleeves, the officers answered in the affirmative.

Plampin landed alone and visited the Governor and Lady Lowe but he made no mention of his female companion. The inevitable storm soon burst.

> Its fury was most severe at Plantation House. The ladies who formed the court of the queen of the island were unanimous in the opinion that the Admiral's conduct was the grossest insult that could possibly be offered them, considering that he was second in rank in the island. They regarded it as the Governor's duty to punish him severely. The report soon spread from

Plantation House that the lady would immediately be sent off the island, that the Admiral would be reported and in all probability recalled. These rumours, no doubt, reached his ears, together with the curious fact that he had been preached at from the pulpit.

The Reverend Richard Boys, the senior chaplain on St. Helena, had attacked the Admiral in his sermon. It was obvious to Plampin that only Lowe could save him and it seems that a deal was done between the two senior officers. Lowe would protect Plampin from the public disapproval of his social arrangements if Plampin was prepared to give him unconditional support for his own actions. The Admiral, no longer a free agent, brought his mistress ashore and installed her at The Briars. The existence of such a pact between Admiral and Governor is suggested by all Plampin's subsequent behaviour. Lowe knew that he had him in his pocket. Gorrequer's diary entry for 20th July, 1818:

> When the order was sent for the removal of Magnesia [O'Meara] and the row about Il Grazzioso [Colonel Lyster] took place, he [Lowe] exclaimed how very fortunate it was that he had little Polyphemes [Plampin] here at the juncture – what trouble he might have had if such a fellow as his predecessor XXX [Malcolm] had been here now.

The subjugation of Plampin to Lowe meant that O'Meara could expect no help from his naval commander; Plampin referred to the surgeon as a 'dirty vagabond' and vowed that he would have nothing to do with him. We can suppose that if Malcolm had remained in post he would have taken a more sympathetic view of the plight of his doctors. Stokoe was not only to lack support from Plampin, but the Admiral was to combine forces with the Governor to bring about his downfall. It may be that Plampin bore a grudge against the doctor before the *Conqueror* arrived at Jamestown. A footnote in his memoirs reveals that Stokoe refused to sit at the same table as the Admiral's mistress on the voyage to St. Helena.[3]

The Governor's treaty with the Admiral meant that he could immediately impose harsher restrictions pertaining to the captivity without the danger of interference. Among other edicts, it was directed that naval officers were forbidden to visit Longwood without explicit approval from Plampin. This was a grave disappointment to Stokoe and his comrades as it was unlikely that the Admiral would see any advantage in them visiting

Napoleon. Previously it had been customary for a newly arrived military or naval attachment to be presented to the Emperor, but petitions to Plampin brought the predictable response that they were not to be introduced as 'it was not the wish of Sir Hudson Lowe'.

Stokoe soon met and befriended O'Meara. This was a dangerous liaison, although it is unlikely that Stokoe initially understood this. Later, as is clear from the transcription of the Lieutenant Reardon inquest alluded to in the previous chapter, he would regret his intimacy with the Irishman, realising that the association had contributed to his troubles. O'Meara partly owed his undoubted popularity to his privileged relationship with Napoleon; he was overwhelmed with questions regarding the Emperor whose allure had only grown with his isolation. Napoleon's physician dined several times on board the *Conqueror* and he invited his hosts back to Longwood – Gourgaud makes an allusion to Stokoe sleeping in O'Meara's quarters. This provided a good excuse to seek the Admiral's permission to enter the otherwise prohibited zone around Longwood and there was always the possibility of spotting its most important occupant. Stokoe admits that he hoped for a sighting but this was a remote chance as the Emperor had shut himself in his rooms, refusing to exercise in the open.[4]

On 10th October, 1817, Stokoe had a stroke of remarkable good luck – at least he thought so at the time.

> O'Meara and I had been walking for some time about the grounds at a considerable distance from the house, when we saw Napoleon come out of the billiard-room, accompanied by Count and Madame de Montholon. After taking a few turns before the house, he seated himself on the steps with Madame de Montholon beside him, and with his back towards us. We approached to the distance of fifty yards and stopped for a minute or two then turned to walk away. The Count came to O'Meara and asked who I was; he returned to Napoleon and came back immediately saying the Emperor would be glad to see me. I was delighted, and yet I felt a dread in approaching the man whose fame as a warrior had reached the remotest corner of the earth.

Although Stokoe does not concede the fact, it seems that the meeting was engineered by the two doctors. They could easily have avoided approaching the Emperor and they had no other reason to loiter only fifty yards away. As previously noted, a regulation dated 4th July 1817 had been issued to every ship's commander with instruction to disseminate the contents to all on board; this stipulated that not only should no naval officer visit Longwood but also that there was to be no conversation of any sort, upon any subject whatsoever, with any of the prisoners without the Admiral's permission. Stokoe had a permit allowing his presence at Longwood but this did not nullify the remainder of the restriction. He had now placed himself in a situation where he had either to snub the Emperor or ignore the regulation.

After some initial awkwardness – Stokoe was unsure whether or not to remove his hat – he spoke with Napoleon in Italian. The relaxed conversation focussed on his previous naval service and his origins in the north of England. The Emperor asked him if he was married, a question that appeared to amuse the French contingent. It later transpired, from O'Meara's explanation, that there was a widespread rumour on the island that the English doctor was paying a lot of attention to Jane Balcombe, the daughter of the purveyor who supplied Longwood. In truth, he had attended her professionally for a serious illness shortly after his arrival. This exchange led to the bizarre aftermath of Napoleon accosting William Balcombe a few days later, 'Why have you refused your daughter to the surgeon of the flagship? *C'est un brave homme'*. The bemused purveyor denied any approach for his daughter's hand. Napoleon had obviously warmed to Stokoe and he was not alone among his entourage. Gourgaud approvingly refers to him as 'a very honest man'.

This feeling was reciprocated. Like most of his countrymen, Stokoe had been conditioned to despise Napoleon but the Emperor's charisma had completely won him round.

> During the short time I was in the presence of Napoleon, my opinion of his character underwent a complete change. I had formed in my imagination the man I expected to see, but I found him so totally the reverse that I had not been two minutes in conversation before I felt myself as much at my ease as if talking to an equal. I am not ashamed to confess this sudden change with such a friendly feeling towards him that I could have been at that moment his ambassador to Sir Hudson, to plead for a rescinding of those orders that caused him to convert his miserable retreat into a voluntary prison.

Napoleon had lost little of the personal magnetism that he had used to seduce far more worldly men than the naval surgeon. The two doctors left the Longwood lawn to retire to O'Meara's apartment where they lamented Britain's lack of generosity to its fallen enemy. Incidents such as this were bound to fuel Lowe's suspicions.

Stokoe called at The Briars the next morning to give an account of the meeting to Plampin. He had no concern that he would be censured; he was permitted to be at Longwood and he had been summoned to speak to the Emperor quite by chance. Plampin took a different view, immediately reminding him of the order forbidding all contact with the Longwood inhabitants. 'You could quite easily,' he said, 'have refused to speak to Bonaparte and you ought to have done so. It is not at all necessary to be polite to the General.' Having warned Stokoe regarding his 'improper' conduct, the Admiral decided to write to the Captain of the *Conqueror* reminding him and his officers that an invitation to visit O'Meara did not imply permission to be presented to Napoleon and other members of his retinue.

Stokoe did not help himself with a disarming display of frankness. He had not been on St. Helena long enough to appreciate the Machiavellian nature of the local politics and the real dangers that lurked in the simplest exchanges. Plampin's mistress was present during the interview and she asked the doctor what he thought of Napoleon. He replied that his opinion had completely changed since his brief meeting. This revelation, much better left unsaid, cannot have improved the Admiral's temper. Plampin only ever spoke of Britain's greatest foe in disparaging terms. In almost all other circumstances, this meeting and admonition would have been judged sufficient and the matter left to rest. The exigencies of St. Helena would not permit such a simple denouement and Plampin sent Stokoe on to Lowe to make a further report of the incident. The Governor expressed surprise that he had not seen the surgeon earlier and interrogated him regarding his conversation with Napoleon, particularly asking him which language had been used. When Stokoe replied that he had spoken in Italian, which he had learnt during his service in Sicily, Lowe's mood worsened. The doctor's reaction to the Governor could hardly have contrasted more with his first impression of Napoleon.

This interview fully confirmed in my mind the justice of the opinion entertained of him at Palermo, and I quitted him with mingled feelings of contempt and disgust, as well as sorrow that such a man had been chosen for so important a command. Every transaction connected with his illustrious charge would be judged by the conduct of one man, and he unworthy of the name of an Englishman.[5]

The surgeon had committed the unpardonable sin of ruffling the Governor's feathers but, provided that he complied with regulations, there was no reason for future confrontation. He managed to keep a low profile until July 1818. At this time, Napoleon's health was starting to give O'Meara serious cause for concern. He believed the Emperor's 'hepatitis' to be progressing. Accordingly, he tried to persuade Napoleon to see another doctor in addition to himself and suggested either Baxter or Stokoe. The former remained repugnant to the Emperor but, after some prevarication, he authorised O'Meara to send for the surgeon of the *Conqueror*. O'Meara relates his attempts to gain his colleague's help in a note to Gorrequer dated 10th July.

> I wrote him [Stokoe] a letter on the spot, and awoke Captain Blakeney [the Orderly Officer at Longwood] in order to have it sent and to procure him a pass. Since that time, I have seen him [Napoleon] three times and have found considerable debility to prevail. Mr Stokoe, came up about three o'clock, not with a view of entering into a consultation, or seeing Napoleon Bonaparte, but to excuse himself upon the plea of the responsibility being too great, and not wishing to run the risk of getting himself into any scrapes.

Stokoe was no longer under any illusion as to the risk attached to social or professional contact with Napoleon. Prior to discussing the matter with O'Meara, he had already begged Plampin to allow him to refuse the request. The Admiral was non-committal, indeed unhelpful, neither commanding Stokoe's attendance nor forbidding it. Stokoe was, however, informed that any 'blame' that resulted from his not consulting at Longwood would be his responsibility alone. In conversation with O'Meara, he explained his diffidence.

> I told him that he must be well aware of the delicate position in which the request had placed me. I was known to be his friend. His quarrel with the Governor and the latter's disbelief in his report of the patient's declining health were also known ... This state of things prevented me from visiting the General with him alone, for, if I did so, and coincided in his opinion, the Governor would immediately say: 'Oh, so Stokoe is a friend of O'Meara's and is biased by his opinion'.

O'Meara, unable to persuade Stokoe, informed Napoleon. Bertrand then appeared, clearly irritated by Stokoe's refusal. When the doctor tried to explain his reluctance, the Grand Marshal interrupted him, saying, 'No, no, sir, it is only an additional proof of the tyranny to which we are exposed.' The Longwood retinue were not in doubt as to why the English doctor was so reticent to attend their master. In his journal, Bertrand notes that Stokoe had said to him that he was already suspected by the Governor who was 'behind him'. The doctor could feel the knife in his back.

Lowe was meanwhile writing to Montholon (12th July) restating his case that the Emperor could employ 'the assistance of Mr Baxter or any other medical person on this island'. He made it quite clear that Baxter was his preferred choice. With regard to Stokoe, he declared himself mystified by the surgeon's reluctance to answer the call. On the following day, Stokoe was required to present himself at the office of Sir Thomas Reade. Lowe entered the room. 'Mr Stokoe, I cannot convince those people at Longwood that I did not influence you in your refusal to see General Bonaparte the other day, and I wish you to state to me particularly your reasons for having done so.' The doctor could hardly share his real concerns with the Governor and he confined himself to saying that he was very unwilling to go to Longwood without the assistance of other medical men as the case was a complex one. Lowe asked him to restate this in a letter to the Admiral but he added that he would like to see it before it was sent. The doctor penned a short note confirming that he did not want to take on such responsibility alone and closed it with the following statement, 'I should be happy to share it with any other medical man who might be permitted to see him.'

Stokoe returned to Lowe, who he found alone. The Governor read the letter but seemed not to approve of it. He took his pen and wrote himself that he had questioned Stokoe regarding his actions and that the surgeon objected to going to Longwood but, if obliged to do so, he would prefer to visit the General with other medical men, 'excluding his private attendant'. At this point, Stokoe, who was looking over Lowe's shoulder, inferred that this was a premeditated attempt to slur O'Meara by implying that Stokoe was unwilling to consult with him. He therefore requested that Lowe omit the words alluding to the 'private attendant', which the Governor did with ill grace, not bothering to finish the letter. He then, according to Stokoe, threw his pen down and left the room in a rage, exclaiming, 'You can send your letter, sir.' This behaviour is in keeping with Gorrequer's descriptions of the Governor's evil temper but it is not certain that Lowe was trying to manipulate the situation. He may have been conspiring to use Stokoe against his colleague but, equally, it may have been an innocent attempt to clarify an ambiguity in Stokoe's letter to Plampin in which he asked for another doctor to attend with him but made no specific allusion to the role of O'Meara. Nevertheless, Stokoe strongly suspected that Lowe was plotting against O'Meara and the recall of his friend to England shortly afterwards was only likely to convince him of this.[6]

John Stokoe's reluctance to treat the Emperor was known beyond the precincts of Longwood and Plantation House. Balmain wrote home on 15th July: '[Stokoe] has refused to see Napoleon and to consult with O'Meara … he is afraid of offending Mr Baxter, the Governor's protégé.' Lowe had revealed his reservations regarding Stokoe to the Commissioners; he had offered Napoleon any medical man *on* the island but, as a naval surgeon, Stokoe was really *off* it! In the wake of O'Meara's departure, his friends on St. Helena were nervous. They perceived themselves to be under the ever closer scrutiny of Lowe and his accomplices. Stokoe believed that he was being spied upon. He cites an episode in which he vigorously defended O'Meara at the mess-table on the *Conqueror* only to have his words later repeated back to him by the Admiral. This was not paranoia – Lady Malcolm comments in her diary that her husband, Plampin's predecessor, discovered a 'system of spies' on the island with 'every trifle' reported to the Governor. On the other hand, Lowe's behaviour was now that of a paranoid man. Encouraged by his henchman Reade, he was starting to question his own supporters. Of all the doctors on St. Helena, Walter Henry appears most sympathetic to the Governor's cause but, in the autumn of 1818, no person was beyond suspicion. We find the following in Gorrequer's diary.

> Nincompoop [Reade] at his country house observed how extraordinary it was Fisico Henrico [Henry] should have been called by Shrug's [Bertrand's] wife and immediately after told Fisico Primo [Baxter] that he did not wish to go to the Cape, though the night previous he had shown himself so desirous to go there, and settled it all with Fisico Primo. 'It looks very odd; there must be something in it, depend upon it; it's damn strange'. 'I'll be damned,' said Mach [Lowe], pacing the room with animation and filled of anger, red in the face, 'if there is not an intrigue. You are right Nincompoop; that fellow [Henry] is intriguing to be appointed medico to our Neighbour [Napoleon] …'[7]

In September, Stokoe, through no fault of his own, became more closely associated with the activities of O'Meara in the eyes of the Governor and the Admiral. William Balcombe, father of the young woman to whom Stokoe had been almost betrothed, had by now returned to London. Lowe had suspected him of being too close to Longwood and of aiding the French in clandestine correspondence, and the purveyor's actions in the capital showed him to be sympathetic to O'Meara and Napoleon. William Holmes, O'Meara's friend and business contact, had been having problems in communicating with his client, letters either going astray or remaining unopened. Balcombe suggested to him that he address them to Stokoe instead – the surgeon could easily pass them on to his medical colleague. Unfortunately, from the autumn of 1818 onwards, Stokoe was required to open any correspondence in front of the Admiral. This was a result of his friendship with O'Meara and the discovery by Lowe and Plampin that Napoleon's doctor, now off the island, had been involved in secret communications with Europe. Although the Admiral accused him of being implicated in this, Stokoe was quite relaxed as he knew that his genuine letters from friends could contain nothing to incriminate him. Indeed, he directed the St. Helena postmaster to send any letters or parcels addressed to him from home or the Cape to the Admiral for his perusal. Stokoe relates the denouement of the scheme of Holmes and Balcombe.

Very soon another parcel of books and pamphlets arrived, addressed to me and from the same sender as the box, Mr O'Meara's agent, a gentleman to whom I was a total stranger. Puzzled to account for this unwarrantable proceeding, I followed the box to the Admiral's house. When it was opened, two letters fell out addressed to me, one from Mr Holmes, the agent, containing a note for Count Bertrand, which he begged I would deliver to him, as, though it contained nothing of importance, he did not wish the Governor to see it. In this note, the Emperor was entreated to take exercise, in order to preserve his health, and not to give up hope that affairs would take a favourable turn for him. It also spoke of the interest which his purveyor, Mr Balcombe, took in his case, besides touching on money matters, books, and on visits which Holmes intended to pay in Paris to Las Cases and Laffitte, the banker.

When the Admiral opened the second letter he found that it also contained an enclosure; holding it up, he exclaimed: 'For Napoleon Bonaparte,' regarding me at the same time with a significant side-glance. Disappointed, perhaps, in his experiment, he corrected himself with: 'Oh, no, for Barry O'Meara, Esq.' Mr Balcombe was the writer; his style was laconic and expressive. Here is a specimen: 'Dear Stokoe, – Be so good as to hand the enclosed to our friend O'Meara. I find that he has many partisans here, and I hope the B–g—ers will soon be turned out.'

Balcombe also indulged himself in some ribald comments on Plampin and his mistress at his old home, The Briars, and the Admiral decided not to share the contents with the Governor. However, Lowe was informed of the substance of the matter and Stokoe, although entirely innocent, was bound to be tainted by it. In fairness to Holmes, once he realised that O'Meara was no longer on St. Helena and that his plot had backfired, he made efforts to disentangle the hapless Stokoe. In letters to Bathurst and to Plampin, he explained why he had used the surgeon's name (and that of a Mr Fowler) and emphasised that not only had he not been authorised to do this by Stokoe, but also that he had never heard from him or seen him. This confession satisfied Bathurst who wrote to Lowe in November advocating a measured response.

> I am willing to believe that neither Dr Stokoe nor Mr Fowler are parties in this transaction and that those who have taken a part on the side of Mr O'Meara have been duped by him, and are sincere in the regret which they express. At any rate, I am sure you will do right to show no ill-humour and (if you still entertain) to conceal any suspicion regarding them.

Lowe had 'entertained suspicions' with regard to Stokoe before Holmes's clumsy intervention. The Governor was less inclined than the Minister to give the doctor the benefit of any doubt and 'evidence' of an illicit connection would ultimately be used against him.[8]

By the end of 1818, Lowe had despaired of his attempts to install Baxter as Napoleon's physician and he was instead making the case for James Verling who was still installed at Longwood. Napoleon remained equally determined not to consult with any doctor appointed or championed by the Governor. Stokoe was a marked man. Whilst he kept his distance from the French he had realistic hopes of self-preservation, but the whirlpool of Longwood was about to suck him in and swallow him up. Towards midnight on 16th January 1819, Napoleon suddenly became much more ill, complaining of sharp pain in the groin and shoulders, a violent fever and giddiness. He was actually unconscious for several minutes.

For an account of what happened next and in the following few days, we have four witnesses; Stokoe, Verling, Bertrand and Captain George Nicholls. Montholon's account was written years after the events and is unreliable. Nicholls was Orderly Officer at Longwood and was required by Lowe, in the absence of O'Meara, to confirm the presence of Napoleon on a daily basis, preferably by actually sighting him. The Emperor cooperated little and poor Nicholls found himself in a ludicrous situation, having to adopt a variety of ruses to get a view of the prisoner. His journal is a useful record of comings and goings at Longwood.

Although allegedly very unwell, Napoleon declined to see Verling – who was only a few yards away – and instead asked for Stokoe who was aboard the *Conqueror*. This refusal of immediate medical help renewed British scepticism as to the nature of his symptoms. Reade wrote to Verling, 'How Stokoe will act, I am at a loss to know, but is Napoleon really so ill? I do not entertain a very serious idea of the urgency of the illness from the circuitous mode of seeking relief.' Bertrand scribbled a short letter to Stokoe and handed it to Nicholls at around 3am on 17th January.

> Sir, The Emperor has just had a sudden and violent attack. You are the only medical man at present in this country in whom he has shown any confidence. I beg you not to lose a moment in hastening to Longwood. On your arrival, ask for me. I hope that you will come in the course of the night. I am much troubled.

The Orderly Officer woke Verling to inform him of the French request and two dragoons were dispatched, one to take the Bertrand letter directly to Plantation House and the second to take a note written by Nicholls to the Admiral, briefing him of the situation. At 3.45am, Lowe penned a further note to Plampin and forwarded the original letter – the dragoon rushed to The Briars and found that his comrade had by now raised Plampin and his secretary, John Elliot, and had galloped on with a communication from the secretary to the Captain of the *Conqueror*. This was sent out to the ship by the duty officer in Jamestown. Stokoe was woken and read the following:

> The Admiral has desired me to say that you are to order Dr Stokoe (surgeon of the *Conqueror*) to go directly to Longwood and call on Dr Verling as Bonaparte is very ill.

Briars, 17th January, 1819, 20 minutes past four o'clock in the morning. To be delivered immediately. John Elliot.

It is not clear whether Stokoe also had the Bertrand letter in his hands at this time but it was obvious that he had no alternative but to answer the call. 'No discretionary power was allowed me as on the former occasion, therefore I obeyed the order with all possible speed, but in the greatest distress of mind.' He was rowed to the shore where a horse was readied and he arrived at Longwood, five miles away, at 6.45am. Allowing for the labyrinthine communications, the distances travelled and the hilly nature of the country, this was as early as could be expected, less than four hours after the alarm had been raised.[9]

On his arrival, the doctor was informed that the greatest danger had passed and that, relieved by a hot bath, Napoleon was sleeping. Stokoe was asked to delay the consultation. This sequence of events was to prove important as the fact that the surgeon did not see the Emperor immediately served to heighten the suspicion of Lowe and his cronies that the symptoms were exaggerated. The doctor complied with the request to wait to see his patient and ate with the Bertrands.

> After breakfast, Count Montholon came to me and proposed that I should replace O'Meara and become the Emperor's surgeon. This I declined. He then asked my reasons. I replied that it was an appointment I might have been ambitious to obtain had I not witnessed the persecution of O'Meara, which, according to him, was in consequence of his refusing to do the degrading duty of a spy. The Count left me, and no doubt went to Napoleon and reported the conversation, for he came back in about an hour with a paper containing eight articles, dictated, I presume, by Napoleon, and presented them to me for my acceptance.

Stokoe read the articles, which were as follows.

> (1) Mr Stokoe is considered as surgeon to Napoleon, and as filling the place of the French surgeon, mentioned in the decree of the British Government, dated the 15th of August, 1815.
> (2) He is not to be taken away without the consent of Napoleon, at least by a simple order of the Governor, and especially as long as the disease continues.

(3) During the time that he fulfils the function of Physician to Napoleon, he is not to be subjected to any military disruption or duty, but to be considered as an Englishman holding a civil employment.

(4) He is not to be obliged to render an account to any person of Napoleon's health. He will write every day, or oftener if necessary, a bulletin of Napoleon's health, of which he is to make two copies, one to be given to one of the officers at Longwood, and the other to the Governor whenever he desires it.

(5) No person whatever is to meddle with this medical function, and no restrictions upon his communications with Napoleon and the French, either by writing or verbally, by day or by night, are to be imposed upon him.

(6) He is not to be obliged to render an account of what he sees or hears at Longwood, unless anything which in his judgement might compromise his oath of allegiance to his country and his sovereign.

(7) Dr Stokoe engages to serve Napoleon in his profession, independent of all prejudice or party spirit, as if he were his own countryman, and not to make any bulletin or report of his complaints without giving him the original.

(8) In accepting these conditions, he is to preserve the integrity of all his rights as an English citizen and officer. He demands to receive from the Admiralty the same pay as his predecessor, and not to be assimilated in anything with the French prisoners. The whole of the above to be done with the permission of his chief, Rear Admiral Plampin.

Norwood Young, who is mostly unsympathetic to Stokoe and the French, claims that this document was very likely written at an earlier date. Napoleon would have given the matter considerable thought and there is no reason to believe that he did not dictate these articles while Stokoe waited in an adjacent room. He had maintained much of his mental sharpness and he was quite capable of producing complex instructions off the cuff; his voluminous correspondence is proof of this.

Stokoe was faced with three choices. He could reject the articles outright and leave Longwood without having consulted with Napoleon. His critics suggest this as the correct course of action but the doctor had been told that the Emperor was seriously ill and, if he had died shortly after, Stokoe would have provided a convenient scapegoat for Lowe and Plampin. He could have accepted the articles unconditionally. This would have been foolhardy and playing into the hands of his persecutors. The third option, which he chose, was to make his acceptance of the articles strictly conditional upon the subsequent approval of Plampin – this stipulation is actually included in the final article – and to only agree to revisit Napoleon if his senior officer gave consent. He was encouraged in this approach by the fact that he could see nothing in the articles 'incompatible with the honour of a British officer and a gentleman'. After stating to Montholon that he would accept the proposal only on this basis, he agreed to be taken to see the Emperor. The entirely conditional nature of Stokoe's acceptance and his determination to seek the approval of his seniors as soon as possible are issues of key importance and are confirmed unequivocally by the available British witnesses. Nicholls notes in his journal of 17th January that Stokoe told him that the articles were for the 'approbation' of Plampin; it would be the Orderly Officer's task to take a copy to Plantation House for Lowe's perusal. Verling uses almost the same words, 'Mr Stokoe had [later] gone to the Admiral to submit them for his approbation.' Only Bertrand differs, simply stating that the British doctor accepted the conditions of employment without appearing surprised.

On entering the Emperor's room, Stokoe found him lying on a sofa, his skin sallow and his features drawn. His description is very similar to Verling's earlier account of Napoleon's appearance. He still had the pain in his right side and the surgeon suspected an affliction of the liver.

> 'How long might a man live with such a complaint?' asked the Emperor, at the same time asking the doctor to answer him without evasion.
> 'There are instances of men living to an advanced period.'
> 'Yes, but is one as likely to live to that period in a tropical climate?'
> 'No.'
> 'What is the danger to be apprehended?'
> 'Inflammation and possible suppuration.'
> 'What would be the consequence of that?'
> 'If the matter formed, and it broke into the intestines, he might be saved; if it pointed externally, he might be saved by an operation; but if it burst into the cavity of the abdomen, death must ensue.'
> The Emperor clenched his hand and exclaimed, 'I should have lived to the age of eighty if they had not brought me to this vile place.'

Stokoe left his illustrious patient and sat down to write a medical bulletin, one copy of which he left with Bertrand. He concluded his report as follows:

From the evident tendency of a determination of blood to the head, it will be highly necessary that a medical man should be near his person, in order that immediate assistance may be afforded in case of recurrence of the above alarming symptoms, as well as for the daily treatment of chronic hepatitis which the above symptoms indicate.

Stokoe's critics say that he was coerced into expressing this opinion by Napoleon who wished a doctor of his own choice to be in permanent residence at Longwood. This is possible but we must remember that Stokoe, a lowly naval surgeon, had just acquired sole responsibility for the medical management of the greatest man of the age. His every decision would be analysed and very likely criticised. It is understandable that he adopted a cautious or even a defensive attitude. Few doctors would have behaved otherwise. The unexpected onset of Napoleon's more severe symptoms dictated the need for unbroken medical attendance as a commonsensical precaution. The Emperor's appearance suggested that he was genuinely ill and the surgeon had no reason to doubt the medical history given to him by the patient and his companions.[10]

Stokoe left Longwood at around 2pm and went straight to The Briars to seek Plampin's opinion on the document he had agreed to subject to his sanction. It is unclear exactly what was said at this meeting but the Admiral appears to have had no immediate objection to the articles and he did not criticise Stokoe's conduct. He probably viewed the surgeon's acts as reasonable under the difficult circumstances. If so, he was quickly to change his mind. Lowe had read the copy of the articles forwarded to him by Nicholls and he at once wrote to the Admiral. After complaining that Stokoe had not reported to him, he wished to know why the surgeon had given 'his assent to proposals of such a nature as those enclosed'. This had been done, according to Lowe, 'without any previous reference to or consultation with either your Excellency or me'. The Governor was always searching for an 'intrigue' but here he went a step further and distorted the facts to create one. Firstly it was correct for Stokoe to report to the Admiral, his rightful superior; later, the Governor contradicted himself by insisting that the naval surgeon was Plampin's responsibility. Secondly, he entirely ignored the conditional nature of Stokoe's acceptance, a proviso which had actually been inserted into one of the articles. With the Governor behaving in this manner, it was obvious that Stokoe's 'distress of mind' was fully justified.[11]

During the evening, the state of the Emperor's health gave continued cause for concern and Montholon decided to visit Plantation House to discuss the medical arrangements directly with Lowe. He set off in the dark in pouring rain accompanied by Nicholls and two men carrying lanterns. The Count opened the discussion by voicing his concern that Napoleon would have another attack in the night, that he dreaded '*un coup d'apoplexe*' or a rush of blood to the head, '*comme d'un coup de piston*'. He entreated the Governor to allow Stokoe, the only medical man acceptable to the patient, to remain at Longwood until a decision was made regarding his definitive appointment. Lowe agreed but then said that the surgeon was under the Admiral's jurisdiction and that he could not dispose of his services. Montholon, taken aback by Lowe's sudden lack of authority, questioned this but Lowe stood firm, insisting that he would have to confer with Plampin who was 'entirely independent of him'. He added that Stokoe would be at Longwood next morning, or at least his decision would be known by this time. The Governor was playing for time, probably trying to guess the severity of his prisoner's illness, unable to decide whether the urgent call for Stokoe was genuine or a charade. On the evening of the 17th, Lowe commented to Verling that 'it was by no means settled that Mr Stokoe should be allowed to accept the situation, that at all events many points remained to be discussed.' On their part, the French were determined to maintain the pressure on the Governor and a letter followed. This was in Montholon's handwriting but the Count confirms that it was dictated by Napoleon. It described the seriousness of his symptoms, the necessity for Stokoe's attendance, the delay in him arriving at Longwood, and the refusal to see Verling. Lowe was reminded that

> Even on the verge of death, the Emperor will receive care and medicines only from the hands of his own doctor; if he is deprived of him, he will receive no one and will consider himself to have been assassinated by you.

The letter was unhelpful to Stokoe as it simply stated that he had accepted the proposals presented to him.[12]

Before Montholon's return to Longwood, Napoleon was again seized by an attack of pain and, at 9pm, Bertrand sent a further urgent message to the Governor demanding Stokoe's help. Lowe has been accused of deliberately delaying the delivery of this note to the surgeon. Nicholls confirms that he met a dragoon carrying it later that evening, presumably heading from

Plantation House. When Stokoe finally arrived back at Longwood at 5.30am on Monday 18th, Bertrand says that the doctor was under strict orders from Plampin to discuss only medical matters. If so, this was a detailed resumé of the symptoms as the surgeon spent eleven hours with the French, much of the time in the company of the Grand Marshal. The second consultation with Napoleon lasted about an hour and took place just before Stokoe's departure at 4.30pm. The Emperor was reluctant to accept any treatment from the British surgeon until the Governor had consented to the conditions for his employment. Lowe was in no hurry to make a decision and had actually instructed Nicholls to return the documents to Bertrand. The officer dutifully did this only to find that the Frenchman had placed the papers back on his desk, commenting that it would be safer if he kept them. Life on St. Helena was as difficult for the Orderly Officers as it was for the doctors.

Stokoe wrote a second bulletin which, while being a frank medical opinion, only served to drag him deeper into the mire. He repeated his view that his patient had hepatitis and, although he believed him to be in no immediate danger, he added that the disease was worsening, that a prolonged stay in such a climate would surely shorten his life, and that a recurrence of the acute symptoms would require prompt medical attention. In response to this bulletin, Lowe requested Verling to return to Longwood without delay and to inform Montholon of his presence. We can only guess at Lowe's real thoughts, but Stokoe's blunt opinions must have irritated him as they forced him into a corner. He now had responsibility for a prisoner who had a serious illness caused in his opinion by the unhealthy climate, whose life would be shortened by long-term captivity and who required constant medical attention. French historians such as Masson agree that, in the eyes of the Governor, Stokoe's greatest crime was his diagnosis of hepatitis. Arnold Chaplin concurs that the surgeon's two unpardonable faults were to think that his patient had hepatitis and to believe that he was really ill. Such a lack of tact could not be endured.[13]

Just as after his previous consultation with Napoleon, Stokoe called on Plampin to give an account of his visit. The surgeon quickly sensed a change in the atmosphere.

> On being shown into the office where the Admiral was seated at his desk, I observed the secretary [Elliot] sitting in the middle of the room totally unemployed; the novelty of his presence at this time and under these circumstances struck me forcibly, and I realised that he was there as a witness. It

was natural that I should feel hurt at this treatment from an officer who I had hitherto looked up to as my patron and friend.

Plampin interrogated Stokoe as to the circumstances of his most recent visit to Longwood and the conversations he had had with the French. He made some notes regarding the surgeon's account of Napoleon's health and closed the interview by asking that the doctor not attend Longwood again without a pass. This implied that the doctor had originally attended Napoleon of his own volition whereas, in reality, he had responded to an order from the Admiral himself. Lowe and Plampin still had to make some response to the proposed employment of Stokoe as the Emperor's surgeon and, on Monday evening, Major Gorrequer wrote to Captain Nicholls.

> St. Helena
> Jan 18, 1819
>
> Sir,
>
> In reference to the verbal communication which Count Bertrand made to you yesterday, I am directed by the Governor to acquaint you, that having conferred with Rear-Admiral Plampin, in respect to the continuance of Mr Stokoe's medical attendance at Longwood, the Admiral has acquainted him, that he cannot dispense with Mr Stokoe's services in the squadron, so far as to admit of him being entirely excused from it; nor could he release Mr Stokoe from the obedience due to him, as Naval Commander-in-Chief, without the sanction of the Lords Commissioners of the Admiralty.
>
> The Governor himself will have no objection to Mr Stokoe affording his medical assistance to Napoleon Bonaparte, whenever so required; but he is desirous, in such cases, that Mr Stokoe's professional visits should be made in conjunction with the physician, who is at present in attendance at Longwood, following so near as possible, the instructions on this head.

This decision was made known to the French and it left Stokoe in limbo. The articles were not acceptable and he was not to be the Emperor's physician as O'Meara had been, but he was still to visit Napoleon as a doctor. He would almost certainly be unaccompanied as Napoleon was determined not to see Verling, a fact well known to the Governor and Admiral.[14]

On the next day, Tuesday 19th, Stokoe was again requested by Bertrand and he called at The Briars for the necessary pass. Plampin had just had a meeting with Lowe and he had been primed to subject the doctor to a thorough cross examination.

'When you signed your acquiescence to the proposal you gave me a copy of, did Count Bertrand or General Bonaparte demand any pledge from you that you would not repeat anything that passed in conversation, and did you give any such pledge?'

'I was not asked to pledge myself to anything of the kind.'

'Were you required to write out a bulletin?'

'Yes, by Count Bertrand, which I did, and the one you have is a copy of it.'

'Was the latter part of the bulletin put down at the suggestion of either General Bonaparte or Count Bertrand?'

The last question referred to Stokoe's comment that it was necessary to have a physician in constant attendance at Longwood in case the severe symptoms recurred. He indignantly replied that it was his own idea. Plampin now quizzed the surgeon as to why he had made a diagnosis of hepatitis and particularly asked a number of leading questions regarding the symptoms and how he knew of them.

This was ridiculous as Plampin had neither any contact with Napoleon nor any medical training and was in no position to question the doctor's opinion. Stokoe freely admitted that he had reached his conclusions based not only upon his immediate enquiries to Napoleon and a physical examination, but also on information provided by Bertrand, Montholon and a servant.

When Plampin, returning to the bulletin, wished to know why Stokoe had stressed the need for a permanent medical presence at Longwood when Verling was in residence, the doctor gave the obvious reply that Napoleon had refused to see his colleague. By now, the Admiral was becoming frustrated at his inability to fluster Stokoe and he resorted to questioning the surgeon's designation of his patient. Napoleon's proper title was a subject which greatly exercised the British authorities on St. Helena.

'Was the name of the patient omitted in the bulletin you left at Longwood at the suggestion of Count Bertrand, or your own act alone, and why did you omit the name of General Bonaparte?'

'I asked Count Bertrand what I should say with respect to the name, when he answered, '*Napoleon*' or '*the patient*', which was the reason of my not putting

down 'General Bonaparte'. I understood this was the proper way of beginning a bulletin.'

'I should have called him General Bonaparte and not the patient. Earl
Bathurst to Sir Hudson Lowe calls him General Bonaparte. Lord Melville
to me always calls him General Bonaparte, therefore on all occasions I call
him so, and I think the surgeon of the *Conqueror*, in making a report to his
Commander-in-Chief, ought to have thus styled him.'

The surgeon finally obtained his pass and set off for Longwood. In the
meantime, the Governor had been taking steps to ensure that his every
move was closely monitored. In a letter to Nicholls, he stipulated that
whenever Stokoe arrived at Longwood, the Orderly Officer was to carefully check his pass and was to 'inform himself as particularly as he can of
the footing on which the Admiral may have granted him permission to visit
General Bonaparte'. Any perceived deviation from these instructions was
immediately to be made known to Stokoe. In addition, Verling was to be
kept in a state of readiness to accompany Stokoe whenever the latter was in
the presence of Napoleon or any of his followers.[15]

Stokoe arrived at his destination at around 6pm. He first met with
Nicholls and Verling. Plampin had strangely forgotten to mention to
him the Gorrequer letter recommending that his visits be made in the
company of his medical colleague. The Orderly Officer now read the
relevant passage to Stokoe who commented to Verling that he would
much prefer that they see Napoleon together. This was wishful thinking. When he then accompanied Nicholls to discuss the matter with
Bertrand, the Grand Marshal said that it was futile to even broach the
subject with the Emperor – he would rather die than receive Verling.
This outcome remained possible as he was more ill, now unable to stand
without help.

The Orderly Officer retired and Stokoe was faced with a dilemma.
Nicholls had warned him that if he decided to again visit Napoleon,
the choice would be his alone. If he continued to act as the Emperor's
doctor, it was only a matter of time before the vultures in Plantation
House and The Briars swooped down on him. On the other hand, Lowe
had been careful to avoid definitively forbidding him to see Napoleon
in Verling's absence – the second surgeon's presence was 'desirable' but
not essential. If he walked away from Longwood and the Emperor was
to die without any medical intervention, he would equally be held

responsible. He had little faith that his superiors would shield him from the blame that would forever be attached to his name. He decided to see Napoleon; whatever the risks, this was the action one would have expected of a conscientious doctor.[16]

Stokoe was alarmed to find that the French had not exaggerated his patient's symptoms. He now had a fever and the doctor decided to spend the night at Bertrand's house in case the symptoms became exacerbated. He was roused by the Grand Marshal at 3am as the Emperor had developed a severe headache. He remained a bad patient but, after some persuasion, he allowed himself to be bled and to be prescribed a strong dose of Cheltenham salts. The doctor remained convinced of his diagnosis of liver disease but Napoleon refused a course of mercury treatment. Such was his concern, the surgeon would happily have stayed at Longwood all Wednesday but, at 11am, he received an order to report to Plampin. On arriving at The Briars, he handed the Admiral a report of his most recent consultation and his opinion as to the source of the disease. Plampin decided to overlook Verling's non-involvement and pursued a different angle of attack.

'Did you tell Count Bertrand that I said Lord Bathurst and Lord Melville called Bonaparte General Bonaparte and that I took them for my model and I should have thought that quite sufficient guidance for the surgeon of the *Conqueror*?'

'I daresay I did. It's most likely that I did.'

[To which the admiral replied] 'You are a very dangerous character, if everything that is said by your Commander-in-Chief is to be carried to them at Longwood.'

This conversation is quoted verbatim from the record produced by Elliot, the Admiral's secretary. Stokoe, now a 'very dangerous character' in the eyes of his commanding officer, must have been bewildered by this attack. Plampin was presumably embarrassed that his pettiness regarding Napoleon's title had been communicated to the French. Stokoe returned to his ship but, by late afternoon, he had received a fourth request from Bertrand to attend Longwood. He had now had time to deliberate on the events of the morning and he instead called at The Briars, handing the following letter to Plampin.

His Majesty's Ship Conqueror
St. Helena
20th January 1819

Sir,

The experience of today points out the necessity of my declining all further communication with Longwood. I therefore humbly beg leave that in case my services are again demanded in aid of General Bonaparte you will cause Count Bertrand to be acquainted with my wishes on this head.

I have the honour, etc.
John Stokoe

Plampin made a note on the bottom of the letter acknowledging receipt but refused an immediate answer, instead ordering the doctor to attend Longwood and to remain there overnight before returning to him the next morning by half past ten without fail. Stokoe had been late in arriving at The Briars that morning and one suspects that, in giving this very specific order, Plampin was hoping that the surgeon would again be delayed and thus guilty of another misdemeanour.

Stokoe reached Longwood at 8pm. The surgeon's frame of mind is well described in Bertrand's journal.

> He is afraid; he does not want to see the Emperor any more or to return to the *Conqueror*. He wants to go back to England. He has been treated most strangely; however, he cannot explain himself as he has been forbidden to do so by the admiral. In 20 years of service, he has never been treated like this before.

Napoleon remained adamant that Verling should be excluded and Stokoe saw the patient alone at 10pm for about half an hour. He spent the night in Captain Nicholl's room.[17]

On the next day, Thursday 21st, the surgeon reviewed Napoleon at 9am. Bertrand says that he was keen to leave; no doubt he was trying to comply with the Admiral's order. Unfortunately, he had a demanding patient. The Emperor wished the doctor to witness the therapeutic effects of a warm bath before his departure. Nicholls, in his usual watching brief, notes that Stokoe only left Napoleon at half past twelve and that he departed from Longwood at 12.50pm. Information disclosed in later years (to which we will return) suggests that both Napoleon and Stokoe knew that this was likely to be their final meeting. Harassed by his lateness, the doctor now fell from his horse on the crude road to The Briars. He suffered no serious injury but this served to delay him even more. He probably arrived at about 1.15pm and first gave the Admiral a brief summary of the Emperor's health. Stokoe was now determined to bring matters to a head, complaining that he was being placed in an invidious position that prevented him giving proper medical care.

> I beg that you will take into consideration that in this business, my reputation and honour being equally implicated, I cannot take upon myself the charge of a patient of such consequence and so seriously ill, in the disagreeable situation in which I am now placed, not at liberty to give my assistance at every moment. Hereafter, in the event of any sudden catastrophe which may occur, I beg that my name may not be mentioned unless I am placed in the situation of O'Meara, in accordance with the Articles offered for your consideration the other day. If not, I desire to remain as surgeon of the *Conqueror*, and to be relieved from that responsibility that now weighs upon my name, and of which I foresee the alarming consequences.

This heartfelt plea deserved a straight answer but the Admiral had a different agenda. Instead of dignifying Stokoe with a coherent reply, he attacked him for being late for his appointment. The doctor defended himself, saying that his patient was receiving treatment and that he had judged it advisable not to leave him earlier. Plampin relentlessly pressed his point, concluding that 'neither necessity nor humanity' justified Stokoe's late appearance and his failure to obey an order. The Admiral now decided to formally reply to Stokoe's letter of the previous day in which he had asked to cease his visits to Longwood.

Briars, January 21, 1819

Sir,
In answer to the letter you left with me yesterday evening I have only to observe it's of no consequence to me to know what experience you yesterday gained, nor do I conceive it requisite for you to ask my leave to decline your services in aid of General Bonaparte, *which I have never commanded*; and never having had any correspondence with Count Bertrand I cannot condescend

to commence one with him for the mere purpose of conveying your wishes on that head, more specially as you did not conceive any previous communication with me requisite before you gave your full consent to him to become General Bonaparte's physician, as has been stated from Longwood to His Excellency the Governor.

I am sir

Your most obedient servant

Robert Plampin

This is a typically slippery St. Helena letter. Plampin implies that Stokoe accepted the role of Napoleon's physician unconditionally – palpably untrue. Furthermore, he denies ordering the doctor to Longwood. This is a straightforward lie as the Admiral gave Stokoe an explicit order to attend the Emperor at the onset of his illness on the 17th. This directive was issued via Captain Stanfell of the *Conqueror* and Stokoe, realising that his behaviour was now being deliberately misrepresented, requested a second reading of the note sent by the Admiral to the Captain. He received no reply from Stanfell who was known to be a loyal supporter of all Lowe's policies.[18]

Notes

1. Chaplin, A, *The Illness and Death of Napoleon Bonaparte*, pp. 17–18; Richardson, F, *Napoleon's Death; An Inquest*, pp. 132–3; Markham, JD, *Napoleon and Dr Verling on St. Helena*, pp. 34, 39.
2. Stokoe, J, *With Napoleon on St. Helena*, pp. 5, 214–5; Young, N, *Napoleon in Exile*, Vol. II, p. 127; Richardson, p. 141.
3. Stokoe, pp. 9–17, 39–48, 69–70, 76; Marchand, *Mémoires de Marchand*, Vol. II, p.171; Chaplin, A, *A St. Helena Who's Who*, pp. 112–5; Balmain, Count, *Napoleon in Captivity*, p. 91; Gorrequer, Major G, *St. Helena during Napoleon's Exile*, p. 70; Lowe Papers 20133 f. 859.
4. Stokoe, pp. 48–50; Chaplin, pp. 198–9; Gourgaud, Général Baron, *Journal de Sainte-Hélène*, Vol. II, pp. 281, 289.
5. Stokoe, pp. 50–63; Young, Vol. II, pp. 128–30; Gourgaud, Vol. II, p. 280.
6. Stokoe, pp. 63–8; Marchand, Vol. II, p. 189; Forsyth, W, *History of the Captivity of Napoleon*, Vol. II, pp. 556–8; Bertrand, Général, *Cahiers de Sainte-Hélène*, pp. 147–8, 150.
7. Balmain, pp. 186–7; Lowe Papers 20125 f. 198; Stokoe, pp. 73–5; Malcolm, Lady, *A Diary of St. Helena*, p. 158; Gorrequer, p. 95.
8. Stokoe, pp. 75–9, 203–13; Forsyth, Vol. II, pp. 616–7; Korngold, R, *The Last Years of Napoleon*, p. 321; Masson, F, *Autour de Sainte-Hélène*, Vol. III, pp. 205–6; British Library, Eg. 3717 f. 120.

9. British Library Eg. 3717 ff. 161, 163; Stokoe, pp. 82–6, 217–9; Bertrand, pp. 245–6; Markham, pp. 44–5; *Journeaux de Sainte-Hélène*, pp. 146–7; Korngold, p. 321; Forsyth, Vol. II, p. 11; Young, Vol. II, pp. 131–2.

10. British Library Eg. 3717 f. 159; Stokoe, pp. 86–93, 221–2; Young, Vol. II, pp. 132–6; *Journeaux*, pp. 147–50; Markham, p. 47; Bertrand, p. 246; Korngold, p. 322–3; Masson, Vol. III, pp. 207–8.

11. Stokoe, pp. 93–5; Young, Vol. II, p. 136.

12. Stokoe, pp. 95–9; *Journeaux*, p. 147; Markham, p. 45; Forsyth, Vol. II, pp. 13–14; Marchand, Vol. II, pp. 206–7.

13. Stokoe, pp. 99–101; Young, Vol. II, pp. 136–7; Bertrand, pp. 246–7; *Journeaux*, pp. 147–8; Masson, Vol. III, pp. 213–4; Masson, *Napoleon at St. Helena*, p. 219; Chaplin, *The Illness and Death of Napoleon Bonaparte*, pp. 19–20; Markham, p. 47.

14. Stokoe, pp. 101–3; Young, Vol. II, pp. 137–8; Bertrand, p. 246.

15. British Library Eg. 3717 f. 167; Stokoe, pp. 103–7, 225; Young, Vol. II, pp. 138–40; *Journeaux*, p. 148; Markham, p. 63.

16. Stokoe, pp. 107–9; Young, Vol. II, p. 140; Bertrand, p. 247; *Journeaux*, pp. 148–9; Markham, pp. 49–50.

17. British Library Eg. 3717 f. 170; Stokoe, pp. 109–112; Young, Vol. II, pp. 140–1; *Journeaux*, pp. 148–9; Bertrand, p. 247.

18. Stokoe, pp. 112–6, 223–4; Young, Vol. II, p. 142; Bertrand, pp. 247–8; *Journeaux*, p. 149; Chaplin, *A St. Helena Who's Who*, p. 129.

5

COURT-MARTIAL

Stokoe's visits to Napoleon were now at an end. He remained under close scrutiny. Gorrequer wrote to Verling requesting any additional information he might have regarding his colleague. The Governor had denied Napoleon his chosen physician but he was not satisfied. He was now convinced that Stokoe had to be punished and, using Plampin as his willing accomplice, he started to construct a legal case. In a letter to the Admiral, he outlined his chief accusations against Stokoe. First, he deviously used French correspondence to undermine the doctor's assertion that he had only accepted the conditions of employment conditional to his superior's consent. In Montholon's letter of the 19th to the Governor, the Count stated that Stokoe had immediately approved the articles presented to him and, despite all the evidence to the contrary, this was the version of events Lowe chose to give credence to, commenting to Plampin, 'Mr Stokoe not merely, it appears, signified his acquiescence to these proposals, but further, without any reference to your Excellency's authority or mine, proceeded to act upon them.'

The Governor objected to Stokoe's perceived lack of consultation with Verling and also inferred that he had exaggerated Napoleon's symptoms. His medical bulletins, handed to Bertrand, were allegedly in contravention of a standing order issued in July 1817 forbidding officers of the squadron 'to hold communication of any sort, by writing or otherwise, upon any subject with any of the foreign persons upon the island'. Just for good measure, Lowe raked up the clandestine correspondence from Holmes, reminding

Plampin that Stokoe's name had been connected with this. He signed off with an invitation to the Admiral to seriously consider the naval surgeon's conduct and to take steps which he thought to be 'expedient'. If Stokoe was a pawn in the St. Helena game, then Plampin was a minor piece manoeuvred relentlessly around the board by Lowe.

The Governor's charge that Napoleon's symptoms had been talked up reflected continued British scepticism regarding the supposed illness. Marchand believed Lowe to be entirely dismissive of his master's medical problems and Bertrand noted acidly that French concerns would only be recognised when the Emperor was found dead in his bed. In this war of words, Baxter was enrolled to interpret Stokoe's bulletins, just as he had previously vetted O'Meara's script. He told Verling that Stokoe had 'attempted' to support O'Meara's diagnosis of liver disease but that he (Baxter) was sceptical that there was any significant illness. In a pencilled note found among the Lowe papers, Baxter tells the Governor what he wants to hear. He criticises Stokoe's diagnosis and his recommendation of a nourishing diet. 'Such articles ordered for a patient who is considered to be in danger of a determination of blood to the head would convey suspicion either of the sincerity or professional talents of Mr Stokoe.' He quibbles with the findings of both O'Meara and Stokoe, emphasising every inconsistency between the accounts of the two men. Lowe was presumably reassured by Baxter's words but he still could not be certain that Napoleon was out of danger. Indeed, on 24 January, three days after Stokoe's last consultation with the Emperor, he confided to Verling that he was considering sending Stokoe back to Longwood. The doctor would be confined to a cottage near the main house and would be forbidden any contact with the inhabitants of Longwood except to attend to Napoleon in an emergency. Lowe consulted Thomas Reade with his idea but, after discussion with the Admiral, it was dropped.[1]

Plampin had a more unpleasant fate planned for Stokoe. A few days later, the doctor was approached by Stanfell on the *Conqueror* and informed that it was the Admiral's intention to try him by a court-martial. When he asked the reason, he was told that it was for 'contempt and disobedience of orders'. Stokoe retorted that it was his obedience to the Admiral's demands that had landed him in trouble and that, left to his own discretion, he would not have attended Napoleon. Stanfell replied that in view of the proposed court-martial it would be improper for him to comment. The Captain returned to the shore and, after a period of grim reflection, Stokoe followed him to Jamestown. Here, he informed his superior that his health had deteriorated due to the climate and because of the fall from his horse and that he had been unable to attend to his duties for several days. He asked to leave St. Helena and to be invalided home. Stanfell promised to pass this request on to the Admiral but said that he was not optimistic as he understood that Plampin and Lowe were already preparing the charges against the doctor. Stokoe waited two days before Stanfell asked him to put his plea in writing, giving details of his ill health. After more procrastination, his application was granted and he departed St. Helena for England on the *Tricomalee* on 30th January. He poignantly writes, 'I thought all my sufferings at an end.'

Balmain was a perceptive witness of the infighting between the British and French, being a recipient of propaganda from both sides.

> The English have assured me that on the 18th, the day after that on which he was said to be dying, Napoleon had taken a walk round his new home in a red flannel dressing gown, leaning with his left arm on a billiard cue, holding in the other a field glass and that the ordinary officer had heard him singing Fra Martino in his bedroom.

On the day of Stokoe's departure, he writes,

> Here is the second English doctor dismissed from Longwood. With the exception of Baxter, who the French say is a poisoner, Verling, who they will not see, and Livingstone, who is an *accoucheur* (obstetrician), there is none other to give to them.[2]

After a second debacle involving Napoleon's doctor, Lowe was keen to distance himself from recent events. He did not want to be seen to have personally forced Stokoe off the island. In a letter from Gorrequer to Verling of 25th January, he stresses that Stokoe had been sent home because of his 'own particular desires'. While the Military Secretary was obediently transcribing Lowe's orders and opinions, in his secret journal he was contemptuous of the Governor's efforts to evade responsibility.

> Mach's [Lowe's] anxiety to turn off all the acts towards 2nd Magnesia Navale [Stokoe] being sent home upon the Polyphemes [Plampin] saying it was all his doing, and that he had no business to send him home; and that as for himself he had no hand whatsoever in it. It was very badly managed of Polyphemes.

What hypocrisy when everything was at his instance and active instigation. The next moment he was abusing Polyphemes for shrinking upon all and every occasion from any share of responsibility.

For the moment, Lowe and Plampin were apparently satisfied just to have removed Napoleon's favourite doctor from Longwood. On the Governor's direction, the Admiral wrote a long report detailing Stokoe's behaviour and this was forwarded to the Admiralty on the same vessel on which the surgeon of the *Conqueror* was returning home.[3]

Stokoe disembarked at Portsmouth on 14 April 1819. He first had to attend the Admiralty offices in London to submit himself for a medical examination. He had no qualms regarding this as he was confident that his state of health justified a period of leave and he was on friendly terms with the Principal Physician. When he entered the room he was surprised to find himself in the company of another medical man, Dr Weir, the medical member of the Transport Board, and also Sir George Cockburn and Sir Henry Hotham. Instead of performing a careful examination, Weir limited himself to a few peremptory questions and was dismissive of Stokoe's replies. The surgeon sensed that his senior colleague was acting under instruction. Cockburn concluded the brief proceedings by dismissing Stokoe with the comment that it was likely he would be sent back to St. Helena.

Stokoe's first reaction was to seek an independent medical opinion. Before leaving the building, he met Sir Pulteney Malcolm, a man who had little time for Lowe and his repressive regimen. When Stokoe complained of how unpleasant it would be for him to again serve under Plampin, Malcolm immediately reassured him.

> Stokoe, you are a surgeon. You are more independent than any of us so long as you do your duty, but I think you ought to view being sent back again as a proof that your conduct has been approved of.

Much cheered by this vote of confidence, the surgeon returned to Portsmouth believing that at least he was not returning to St. Helena in adversity. In fact, Malcolm was either not party to the views of his colleagues in the Admiralty or he was being duplicitous. On 7th August, a full week before Stokoe had arrived back in England, charges for a court-martial had already been drawn up from Plampin's report and signed by senior officials including Lords Melville and Cockburn. Henry Goulburn, the Undersecretary, wrote to Lowe on the following day confirming that the doctor would be sent back to St. Helena, 'in order to his being brought to trial for the offences to which he has been guilty'. Stokoe's first impression that his cursory medical examination was premeditated was correct. Melville and Cockburn and the other Lords of the Admiralty had had their fingers burnt in the O'Meara affair and they were going to take no chances with Stokoe. He was to be sacrificed to placate St. Helena's Governor.

The surgeon, oblivious of any betrayal, made preparations for his return passage. Being only a few months from retirement after twenty years of service, he had not anticipated another period at sea and had dispensed with items such as his cot, bedding and light clothing. His other belongings, including his medical instruments, were on their way to London. Accordingly, he asked the Admiralty officers for some extra time to make arrangements but they were surprisingly unsympathetic – he was to be rushed out of the country with no time to prepare for a warm climate or to take proper leave of his friends. The few comrades he did meet tried to raise his spirits, an old messmate congratulating him that his conduct must have been much approved of for him to be reappointed to the island. O'Meara also completely misjudged the reason for Stokoe's return; in his *Exposition* he writes, 'The universal burst of public opinion which has led to ministers sending Mr Stokoe back to St. Helena only proves that those principles of justice to which Napoleon Bonaparte continues to appeal are not extinct in the British nation.' Stokoe departed on 19th April and after a 'tedious and disagreeable' voyage on the *Abundance*, arrived at St. Helena four months later.[4]

The surgeon rejoined the *Conqueror* but was then unexpectedly forbidden to return to shore without further orders.

The following day at about one o'clock, the officer of the watch, Lieutenant Lloyd, received a letter from Captain Stanfell directing him to put the memorandum No. 22 into my hands on the quarter deck. It contained the first intimation I had of their Lordships' kind intentions towards me in sending me back again to St. Helena (a distance by the Cape of more than eight thousand miles), for the sole purpose of trying me by court-martial!

Placed under arrest, Stokoe now realised that he had been duped by Cockburn and his fellow Lords, who had already decided to court-martial him at the time of his medical examination in London but had withheld this information. To send him back without knowledge of his impending trial was unnecessarily cruel. More importantly, Stokoe was denied vital time to prepare his case. If he had known of his fate whilst in England, he could have collected the necessary papers and sought legal advice and the testimony of his friends.

Rumours of the surgeon's return had been circulating since early July. Two days before his arrival, on 19th August, Bertrand wrote to Lowe demanding that Napoleon should again have the vital assistance of 'his physician Stokoe'. The French made further similar requests in the following weeks but they were informed that he was not available because of the legal process. Napoleon was said to be ill again and he allegedly requested the doctor's help more each day, but this exacerbation of symptoms coinciding exactly with the return of Stokoe was designed to increase the scepticism of the inhabitants of Plantation House. Here, the surgeon's trial was a cause for celebration. Gorrequer writes in his diary for 21st August,

> The joy demonstrated by Nincumpoop [Reade] on opening the plichi by Abundance and finding that Magnesia de la Marina 2nd [Stokoe] was to be traduit [indicted] before Maritime Tribunal. How he jumped and raced all around the table, clapping his hands and shouting on Mach's [Lowe] telling him of it, and the ferocious grinning of the latter about it.[5]

The ten charges against Stokoe were as follows:

> 1st. For having on or about the 17th January last, when permitted by Rear-Admiral Plampin, Commander-in-Chief of His Majesty's Ships and Vessels at the Cape of Good Hope and the seas adjacent, etc., to visit Longwood for the purpose of affording medical assistance to General Buonaparte, then represented as being dangerously ill, communicated with the said General or his attendants upon subjects not at all concerned with medical advice, contrary to standing orders in force for the governance of His Majesty's naval officers on St. Helena.

Stokoe is accused of not limiting his conversation to entirely medical matters. Perhaps he mentioned the weather or indulged in other pleasantries with the Longwood residents. Young acknowledges that this charge was trivial.

2nd. For having on or about the same day, on receiving communication both in writing and verbally from some of the French prisoners at Longwood, taken notice of and given an answer to such communications previous to making the same known to the Commander-in-Chief, contrary to the said standing orders.

This refers to Stokoe's conditional acceptance of the 'articles', the proposals for replacing O'Meara as Napoleon's doctor.

3rd. For having in pursuance of such unauthorised communication signed a paper purporting to be a bulletin of General Buonaparte's health and delivering the same to the said General or his attendants, contrary to the said orders, and to his duty as a British Naval Officer.

Stokoe's medical bulletin is interpreted as being in contravention to the regulations outlawing 'correspondence' with Longwood.

4th. For having in such bulletin stated facts related to the health of General Buonaparte which did not fall under his, the said Mr John Stokoe's own observation, and which as he afterwards confessed were dictated or suggested to him by the said General or his attendants, and for having signed the same as if he himself had witnessed the same facts, which was not the truth and was inconsistent with his character and duty as a British Naval Officer.

Stokoe is charged for reaching a medical opinion based not only upon his own immediate observations but also on a history of previous symptoms related to him by the patient and his close attendants. It was transparent that some of the symptoms noted in his bulletin pre-dated his first consultation with the Emperor and there is no justification for the charge of subterfuge.

5th. For having in the said bulletin inserted the following paragraph, 'The more alarming symptom is that which was experienced in the night of the 16th instant, a recurrence of which may soon prove fatal, particularly if medical attention is not at hand,' intending thereby contrary to the character and duty of a British Officer to create a false impression or belief that General Buonaparte was in imminent or considerable danger, and that no medical assistance was at hand, he, the said Mr John Stokoe not having witnessed any such symptoms, and knowing that the state of the patient was so little urgent that he was four hours at Longwood before he was admitted to see him, and further knowing that Dr Verling was at hand ready to attend if required in any such emergency.

Stokoe, like O'Meara before him, is stated to have exaggerated the severity of Napoleon's illness. Without a second independent medical opinion, this charge could not be proven. Verling's presence was of little significance as the Emperor had repeatedly refused to see him.

> 6th. For having, contrary to his duty, communicated to General Buonaparte or his attendants information related to certain books, letters and papers said to have been sent from Europe for the said persons, and which had been intercepted by the Governor of St. Helena, and for having conveyed to the said General or his attendants some information respecting their money concerns, contrary to his duty, which was to afford medical advice only.

This refers to the 'Holmes correspondence affair'. Despite the evidence that Stokoe was innocent of any active involvement, a fact acknowledged by Bathurst in a letter to Lowe, his persecutors were unable to resist the temptation to add this slur to the list of allegations.

> 7th. For having, contrary to his duty and to the character of a British naval officer, communicated to the said General Buonaparte or his attendants an infamous and calumnious imputation cast upon Lieutenant-General Sir Hudson Lowe, Governor of St. Helena, by Barry O'Meara, late surgeon in the Royal Navy, implying that Sir Hudson Lowe had practised with the said O'Meara to induce him to put an end to the existence of the said General Buonaparte.

Stokoe is alleged to have discussed O'Meara's accusation against Lowe – that the Governor had plotted to shorten Napoleon's life – during his first visit to Longwood. He apparently admitted this to the Admiral. Lowe used Verling to obtain further information from the French but Montholon denied any knowledge of such a conversation with Stokoe and added that O'Meara's accusations were well known to them before Stokoe's arrival. Verling was an unwilling accomplice, pointing out to Lowe that it was O'Meara who should be held to account for the slander.

8th. For having disobeyed the positive command of his superior officer in not returning from Longwood on or about the 21st of January aforesaid at the hour especially prescribed to him by the Rear-Admiral, there being no justifiable cause for his disobeying such command.

This is perhaps the most cogent charge as Stokoe undeniably disobeyed Plampin's directive by delaying his departure from Longwood. Whether he was justified in remaining with Napoleon, partly at his patient's request and partly to observe the outcome of treatment, is a question at the heart of the medicine versus duty dilemma facing all the British doctors dealing with the Emperor. He was further delayed by the fall from his horse.

9th. For having knowingly and willingly designated General Buonaparte in the said bulletin in a manner different from that in which he is designated in the Act of Parliament for the better custody of his person, and contrary to the practise of His Majesty's Government, of the Lieutenant-General, Governor of the Island, of the said Rear-Admiral, and for having done so at the especial instance and request of the said General Buonaparte or his attendants, though he, Mr John Stokoe, well knew that the mode of designation was a point in dispute between the said General Buonaparte and Lieutenant-General Sir Hudson Lowe and the British Government, and that by acceding to the wish of the said General Buonaparte he, the said Mr John Stokoe, was acting in opposition to the wish and practice of his own superior officers, and to the respect which he owed them, under the general printed instructions.

This convoluted and petty charge – that Stokoe had referred to Napoleon as 'the patient' rather than 'General Bonaparte' – was also hypocritical. Gorrequer notes in his diary for 3rd May, 1819,

Dottore Great Gun [Verling] used the term Napoleon in speaking of our Neighbour in his report of Confab 1st same month. This was one of the charges against Stokoe. Humble Spine [Orderly Officer Blakeney] did the same also several times in his reports and so did O.O.Nick [Orderly Officer Nicholls], as Polyphemes 3rd [Plampin] observed to Ego [Gorrequer] one day pointing it out to him in one of the notes given before the Tribunal of Stokoe, saying: 'Better have it altered, for' said he, 'it is one of the very charges against Stokoe and here is O.O. doing the same.'

Two years later, Gorrequer catches Plampin referring to Napoleon as '*L'Empereur*' and Lowe himself eventually referred to his prisoner as Napoleon Bonaparte.

> 10th. For having in the whole of his conduct in the aforesaid transactions evinced a disposition to thwart the intentions and regulations of the said Rear-Admiral, and to further the views of the said French prisoners in furnishing them with false or colourable pretences for complaint, contrary to the respect which he owed to his superior officers, and to his own duty as an officer in His Majesty's Royal Navy.

This final charge adds little and was presumably included by way of a resumé or simply to inflate the total number of charges.

Forsyth's treatment of the case against Stokoe is revealing. He was a lawyer and his account of the St. Helena episode and Lowe's part in it is exhaustive – indeed exhausting. However, instead of simply listing the ten charges, he chose to include only the 'principal ones'. This allowed him to exclude the 5th, 8th and 9th charges. The reasons are not difficult to discern. Forsyth's work appeared in the mid-nineteenth century so the 5th charge, that Stokoe exaggerated the Emperor's illness, hardly reflected well on his accusers, particularly Lowe. Readers would have known of Napoleon's death less than two years later of a disease from which he was quite possibly already suffering at the time of the trial. Similar reasoning led Forsyth to omit the 8th charge – it would be unseemly to criticise Stokoe for remaining with his patient rather than attending an arbitrary meeting with Plampin. It was Forsyth's contention that the Governor was anxious to give Napoleon the best possible medical care; he did not wish him to appear grudging. The 9th charge referring to Napoleon's title was presumably omitted because it was overly trivial or because Forsyth was aware that many others on the island were breaking the regulations in their references to Napoleon.

Lowe's biographer was forced on to the defensive because the charges against the surgeon were contrived and specious. The regulations extant on St. Helena had been manipulated to render normal medical practice illegal. Stokoe was in the dock for crimes such as talking to his patient of non-medical matters, referring to his patient as 'the patient', for taking a thorough history of the symptoms, and for writing medical bulletins. Worst of all, he had suggested that the patient was actually ill. We have to agree with Ralph Korngold's words, 'To have a medical officer travel a total of 188 days to be tried on such charges must have been something novel in the annals of the Royal Navy.'[6]

The trial was initially arranged for 26th August 1819 but Stokoe obtained a postponement of a few days and the court-martial met on the 30th aboard the *Conqueror*. The members were as follows:

Captain Francis Stanfell of *HMS Conqueror*, and second officer in the command of His Majesty's ships and vessels in St. Helena Roads (President); Captain Wauchope (*Eurydice*); Captain Rennie (*Tees*); Commander Sir William Wiseman (*Sophie*); Commander James Hanwy Plumridge (*Sappho*); Mr George Nicholls, Purser of *H.M.S. Sophie* (Officiating Deputy Judge Advocate); Mr William Davies, Clerk of the *Conqueror* (Registrar).

Stokoe was keen to call Bertrand and Montholon as witnesses. This was understandable as they alone could confirm the truth of his account of events at Longwood. At first, Lowe objected on the grounds they were foreigners, prisoners, and attendants upon Napoleon. Nicholls wrote to Stokoe warning him that there were 'legal objections' to the French attending the trial. The Governor then relented but, for reasons that are obscure, neither attended the court-martial. Bertrand was allegedly stricken with dysentery and Montholon was necessarily detained at Longwood to perform the Grand Marshal's routine duties. In his journal, Bertrand makes reference to the court-martial and alludes to some correspondence with Nicholls on the subject but he gives no reason for his non-attendance. It was certainly a late decision – Nicholls records on 30th August that, in the early hours of the morning, Bertrand agreed to accompany him to the trial but that, at 8am when the horses were ready, he sent a note excusing himself. Perhaps the Orderly Officer was too tactful to document the precise nature of the Frenchman's indisposition.[7]

Robert Plampin was the first witness to appear. He was fired with a hatred of Stokoe and a fervent desire to please Lowe and he gave his evidence passionately. He commenced by producing written evidence of his various conversations with the doctor but then perjured himself by declaring that he had given Stokoe no command to attend Longwood on the morning of 17th January. The note written by his secretary to Stokoe, channelled via Captain Stanfell, clearly contained the words, 'you are to order Mr Stokoe to go directly to Longwood.' The surgeon had obtained this note and had refused to return it to the Admiral but he had left it among his papers in England. Already, his defence was being compromised by the failure of the Admiralty to give him proper notice of the proceedings against him. Plampin's account of events on the 17th was so confused that the court was forced to alter the wording of the first charge; instead of 'when permitted by the Admiral to go to Longwood' they decided upon 'permitted or ordered'. Abashed by his uncertain start, Plampin became more restrained and argued that Stokoe should not have agreed to the articles on a conditional basis. He then brought up the Holmes correspondence, claiming that this proved that the surgeon was a willing tool of Longwood. By now, he was fully into his stride again and his language became so violent that the court decided to suspend proceedings, requesting him to calm down.[8]

More witnesses were now called. Plampin's secretary simply confirmed the Admiral's statements. Stanfell declared that he had no memory of the word 'order' on the initial note to Stokoe. Verling and Nicholls told what they knew of Stokoe's relationship with the French. These were all wit-nesses called for the prosecution and, as the defendant could only call his own witnesses at the end of the trial, it was now time for him to speak in his own defence. The full transcript of the surgeon's speech is documented in the official minutes. Stokoe opened by reminding the court's members of his twenty-five years of faithful service and of his immaculate record up to the time of his arrival on St. Helena. He trusted that they would feel more pleasure in the acquittal rather than in the condemnation of a loyal officer who had been placed in such a trying situation. The doctor then questioned the sincerity of Plampin's evidence, pointing out that the pres-ence of a third person during his conversations with the Admiral and the fastidious transcription of every word suggested a premeditated attempt to incriminate him. When Stokoe invoked the absence of Bertrand and Montholon as another example of unfairness, he was brusquely reminded that they had been summoned but had refused to attend. He concluded this preamble with a declaration that he had been motivated only by a desire both to accommodate the wishes of his military superiors and to meet the needs of his patient; as he uttered these words, he must have reflected on the incompatibility of these objectives. He reiterated that he had not wanted to attend Napoleon and that, once this became unavoid-able, he had expressed a preference to be accompanied by his colleague Verling; hardly the actions of a man trying to comply with a secret French-inspired agenda.

Stokoe now dealt with each of the charges in turn, making many of the obvious objections already alluded to. For the first charge, he constrained himself to an appeal to the common sense of the members of the court-martial; how could he have only spoken of medical matters? With respect to the second charge, he stressed that any consent he had given to the articles was entirely conditional and that he had only gone so far as he believed that there was nothing in the conditions 'derogatory to my character as a British officer and a gentleman'. He refuted the third charge on the basis that he did not believe that any law should forbid a doctor writing a medical bulletin for his patient and the fourth charge because he had only taken a proper history of the symptoms and that these were not dictated to him but were the result of his own enquiries. The fifth charge, that he had exaggerated Napoleon's symptoms, could only be denied. He reminded the court that Verling's presence made little difference as General Bonaparte refused to see him.

Stokoe dismissed the sixth charge, saying that he had previously been exonerated from any involvement in the Holmes correspondence. He did not deny repeating O'Meara's accusations at Longwood, the substance of the seventh charge, but commented that this was 'a common topic of conversation'. His defence against the eighth charge was, he claimed, weakened by the absence of the French witnesses, as they could have testified that he was 'extremely anxious' to punctually attend his appointment with Plampin and that the delay was caused by both Napoleon's demands and his accident on the road. He expressed surprise at the ninth charge, stating that by using the purely professional term 'patient' he had judged that he would offend no one. The tenth charge was repetition and did not need to be answered.

Having done his best to nullify the specific accusations, Stokoe moved on to the attack. The charges brought against him were 'strained and coloured with all the art of legal ingenuity and backed by local power and prejudice, in order to accomplish the object of a prosecution instituted by an overwhelming authority'. It may have been unwise to remind the members of the court-martial of this 'overwhelming authority' as they were all naval officers with their own career aspirations and they will have been in no doubt as to the outcome favoured by Plampin and Lowe. Having risked antagonising the court, Stokoe now requested its indulgence and sympathy, listing the difficulties he had faced. Firstly, there was the unprecedented nature of his employment as Napoleon's doctor. If he had erred, it was not because of any preconceived design, but because he had been placed in 'circumstances of peculiar delicacy and embarrassment' with no clear guidance from the Governor as to his correct behaviour.

Secondly, that he had been denied the attendance of the only witnesses who could refute the charges (Bertrand and Montholon) and, thirdly, that the trial had been kept secret from him until the last moment, depriving him of vital documents. He could not resist a dig at Plampin. Although he intended not even 'the most distant disrespect' to his Commander-in-Chief, he was surprised at his demeanour during his testimony and would have been much alarmed by this did he not have complete confidence in the justice of the court. He regarded the members as being his advocates as well as judges.

> I therefore submit my character, my honour, and everything that is dear to me into your hands, and shall rest perfectly satisfied with your decision whatever it may be.

The surgeon called Plampin as his first witness. He wished to know whether his interviews had been documented at the time or written from memory at a later date. This question demanded a simple 'yes' or 'no' but the Admiral was allowed to wriggle out of a straight reply, launching into interminable digressions. The court was clearly influenced by the rank of the witness. He did, however, acknowledge that Holmes had written to Stokoe without approval to use his name – a tacit acceptance that the charge pertaining to the recent correspondence was meaningless.

The defendant then called more witnesses. Verling recalled that Stokoe asked him a few questions of 'no importance' but he and Nicholls both agreed that it would have been very difficult for the surgeon to limit his conversation to purely medical matters; both had discussed all kinds of things with the French prisoners. Although Stanfell had no memory of the word 'order' on the note he gave to Stokoe he accepted that he would have regarded the doctor's refusal to attend Napoleon as an act of disobedience. Lieutenants James Hay and William Clark testified that Stokoe had fallen from his horse and had sustained severe bruising to his shoulder. All these witnesses deserved credit as any statement favouring Stokoe required courage.

On paper, the surgeon's self-defence is coherent and persuasive. He successfully undermines all the chief charges against him. We have less knowledge of his demeanour; we cannot know whether he presented his

1. Saint Helena in 1816

2. Napoleon on St.
Helena

3. The Emperor dictating his memoirs

4. View of Longwood in 1820 by Marchand

5. Bertrand

6. Montholon

7. Gourgaud

8. Las Cases

9. Madame Bertrand

10. Sir Hudson Lowe

11. An unflattering
French depiction of
Lowe

12. Rear-Admiral Sir George Cockburn

13. Earl Bathurst

14. Rear-Admiral Robert
Plampin

15. Major Gideon Gorrequer

16. View of Plantation House

17. William Warden

18. Alexander Baxter

19. Barry O'Meara

20. John Stokoe

21. James Verling

22. Francesco Antommarchi

23. Archibald Arnott

24. Thomas Shortt

25. Francis Burton

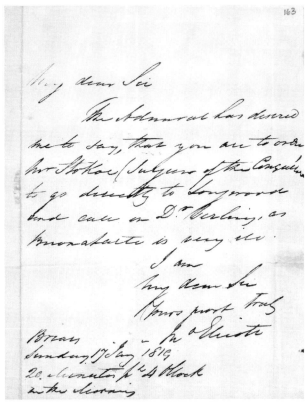

26. Original note of 17th January 1819 ordering Stokoe to attend Napoleon (British Library).

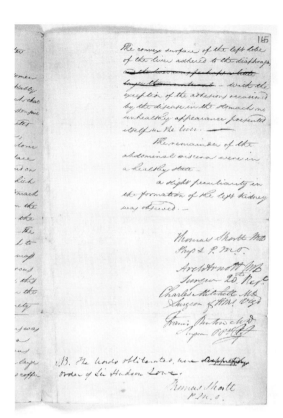

27. Final page of the first post-mortem report showing the change forced on Shortt by Lowe and the doctor's footnote implicating the Governor (British Library).

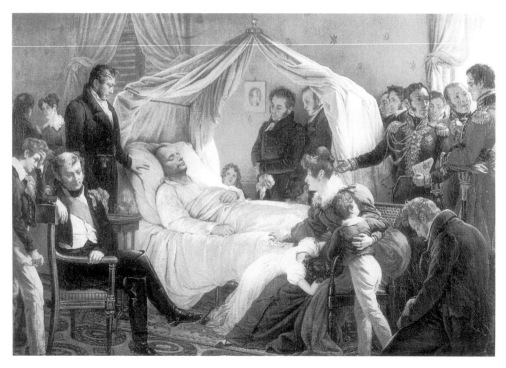

28. Napoleon's death bed. Antommarchi is standing with his hand on the pillow and Arnott is standing second from the right near the foot of the bed.

29. Napoleon after death

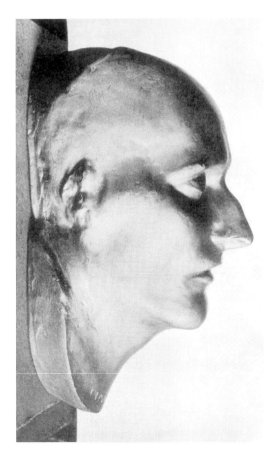

30. Napoleon's death mask

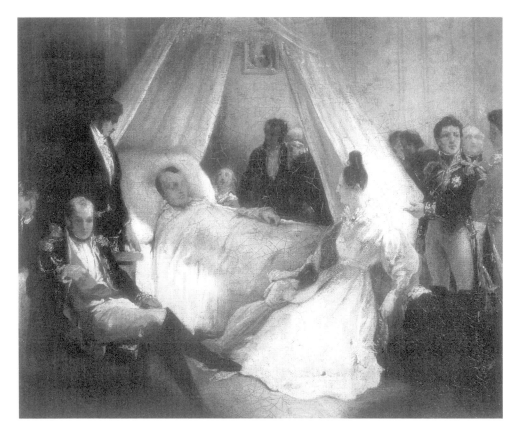

31. A less crowded 19th-century interpretation of the death bed scene by Von Steuben.

32. An early photograph of Longwood House.

case with confidence or whether he was diffident. Verling thought that his colleague managed his defence 'indifferently'. Bertrand notes in his journal that Stokoe's case was well written but ultimately 'feeble'. None of the French entourage attended the trial and he is probably just repeating Verling's opinion. Major Charles Harrison, an eyewitness to the whole trial, thought the doctor's defence to be 'bad, irritating, and disrespectful'. Balmain is more positive.

> [Stokoe] had to conduct his own defence which he did with considerable skill and presence of mind; acknowledged that he had been insubordinate, confessed being the dupe but not the accomplice of the enemies of Plantation House and moved all who heard him to compassion ...

The trial records do not suggest that the surgeon acknowledged 'insubordination' at any stage. It is very unlikely that the Russian actually attended the trial on the *Conqueror* and he was probably expressing the popular view on the island.[9]

The trial lasted four days, from 30th August to 2nd September. Stokoe may have had his sympathisers on St. Helena but the members of the court-martial knew what was expected of them and, after six hours of consideration, they found him to be guilty and ordered that he be dismissed from the service. All charges except the ninth – that pertaining to Napoleon's proper title – were proved. Chaplin comments, 'It is difficult to understand why Stokoe was treated so harshly, unless partisanship on the part of his judges is admitted.' The trial members were biased, and it is also transparent that the action against the doctor was carefully planned by his commanding officers. Charles Harrison was impressed with Plampin's testimony.

> I shall not forget the firmness, perspicuity, and force (added to which a little bitterness) with which the old Admiral went through the whole of the evidence, and he not only astonished the doctor by producing documents he could have had very little idea were in the Admiral's possession but he made a certain Knight [Thomas Reade] stare with all eyes, when he produced every note, every letter, and also minutes of every syllable of conversation that had taken place, from the very commencement, between himself and Mr Stokoe relative to his visits to Longwood.

That which Harrison interpreted as thoroughness, others may have regarded as persecution.

A number of procedural irregularities made the trial at least unfair and, at most, illegal. Stokoe should not have been deemed fit to return to St. Helena on the word of a single doctor. He was entitled to review by a full Medical Board which would have had proper authority to invalidate his leave. He should, of course, have been informed of the court-martial prior to his departure from England to allow him good time to prepare a proper defence. Once on St. Helena, he was forced to act as his own advocate. Harrison says, 'Mr Stokoe could not get any one to assist him in his defence; none of his friends would come forward.' Acting for himself, he could not tell the whole truth. He was unable to raise sensitive issues such as the grudge that the Admiral held against him or the closeness of the compact between Admiral and Governor. Captain Stanfell both presided over the trial and played a role as a key prosecution witness, a clear conflict of interest. Finally, Plampin was guilty both of perjury and of attempts to suppress the evidence of this. The Admiral had denied on oath that Stokoe had asked him to return the original note of the 17th ordering him to attend Napoleon, but the Admiral's secretary admitted that he had heard the doctor make the request. Caught in the act, Plampin had the wording of the trial minutes altered to conceal the fraud.

Word of Stokoe's fate spread quickly. Balmain, whose support for Stokoe greatly irritated Lowe, wrote:

> The authorities of the island naturally made a great sensation of this affair and almost persuaded people that he would be hung … Everyone is wondering why Surgeon O'Meara, who Sir H. Lowe says is much guiltier, is not likewise tried either before an ordinary jury on board the *Conqueror* or before an extraordinary tribunal at London.

The feeling that Stokoe had been unfairly singled out and dealt with was not confined to the Russian Commissioner and not restricted to the inhabitants of St. Helena. Lowe, realising that he had to defend his actions, wrote to Bathurst on 1st September expressing the views of Sir William Wiseman.

> He [Wiseman] told me after the court-martial was over, he believed that there had never been a court-martial assembled where the deliberation had been more full and impartial or where the members had taken more pains to

inform themselves on every point, and to form the judgement without any motives of prejudice. He had been a very short time here. He expressed his astonishment at the infamous falsehoods, as he termed them, which had been circulated in England respecting the system observed here.

These words are quoted in several works to justify the treatment of Stokoe but they are meaningless. Wiseman was himself a member of the court-martial and he was bound to applaud a legal process in which he was one of the most senior participants.[10]

Stokoe left St. Helena for England on 12th September 1819 but he was not quickly forgotten by the French. Napoleon had great confidence in him. When the doctor had returned to the island for his court-martial, the Emperor dictated urgent letters on three occasions asking for his renewed care. Napoleon tried to send the physician a letter of support and sympathy following the guilty verdict and before his final departure but this was ruthlessly intercepted by the British authorities and it did not reach him. During the delirium in the later stages of his disease, it was Stokoe's name he called out.[11]

Stokoe would not meet Napoleon again but he did have the opportunity to confront Plampin. The Admiral returned to England during 1820 and the doctor was waiting for him on the quay at Portsmouth. We have no record of exactly what passed but it seems that Stokoe expressed his opinion of his adversary's conduct in no uncertain terms. The doctor later claimed that the Admiral made a complaint to the Admiralty regarding this meeting but the authorities denied this. Indeed, Plampin remained uncharacteristically quiet about the incident. Perhaps he understood that any legal action would highlight his unpopularity within the service. It was not only Napoleon who disliked him. When the Admiral clumsily applied for the Order of the Bath in early 1821, Lord Melville dismissed his application in a superficially polite but clearly ironic letter. 'I feel it my duty to state that I do not consider myself at liberty to submit to His Majesty the name of any naval officer to be a Knight Commander of the Bath for any services except such as were performed during war against the enemy.'[12]

The details of Stokoe's punishment suggest that he commanded more sympathy among his naval peers than his former Commander-in-Chief. Although removed from the service, his judges recommended to the Admiralty that, in consideration of his long and previously unblemished service, he should be granted half pay. This was not possible for a dismissed officer but he was allowed a civil list pension of £100 per year with £300 extra pay for the St. Helena period of service and eleven-twelfths of full pay from the time he was invalided to his return to the *Conqueror*. This financial settlement was more than was necessary and it indicates that there was official unease at Stokoe's treatment. The surgeon was heartened. 'This spontaneous generosity', he says, 'spoke volumes and was gratifying to me. It showed that I was not regarded as a culprit; it evinced milder feelings towards me, and encouraged the hope that, after the lapse of a few years, I might be restored to my rank.'

Public opinion was largely, but not entirely, in his favour. The *Morning Chronicle*, a newspaper that was mostly critical of Britain's management of Napoleon's exile, detected a scandal and was quick to turn on Lowe. In a leading article, the Governor was accused of forcing the doctor from his patient's bedside at the hour of greatest need. The trial was deemed to be unfair. 'The system of terror so powerfully operating in St. Helena that a military officer declined giving Surgeon Stokoe his countenance and assistance on a plea of ill-health: and a writer in the Admiral's offices begged he would excuse him from attending to take notes for fear of incurring displeasure.' Regional papers, such as the *Liverpool Mercury*, joined in the clamour. The charges against the doctor were pronounced to be 'frivolous and vexatious'. The *Western Luminary* referred to Stokoe's 'excellent character'. On the other hand, *The Times* sided with authority, stating that the sentence had been both 'proper and humane'. Stokoe visited the newspaper's editor but could get no redress for the views expressed except for an undertaking to publish the minutes of the trial.[13]

The doctor had brought back a faithful clerk's copy of the proceedings of the court-martial from St. Helena and when he compared this with the official copy, which he only obtained twelve months later, he discovered the change to the wording that had been made at Plampin's instigation. Realising that the Admiral had committed fraud and that this in itself ought to lead to the verdict being overturned, Stokoe wrote a detailed letter to John Barrow, Secretary to the Admiralty, on 4 November 1820. He describes the Admiral's misdemeanours and ends with a heartfelt plea for justice.

> Such conduct in a man [Plampin] to whom I had been endeavouring to recommend myself by every attention in my power, and to whom I looked up as my friend and protector, excites feelings in my mind that cannot be described, and might, in the opinion of many, justify a spirit of recrimination

on my part where facts are not wanting to prove that those who have been chiefly instrumental in depriving me of the fruits of twenty-five years' service, degrading me by a public trial, were not always the most strict observers of those laws and regulations for the alleged violation of which I have experienced so much real suffering and endless anxiety.

This was not only a vigorous defence of his own position but also an attack on the probity of Plampin and Lowe. It is a measure of the disquiet at the Admiralty regarding the surgeon's plight that he received no admonition for this daring letter but only a polite rejection. Their Lordships were unable to comply with his request to reconvene the members of the court-martial to consider any alleged mistake. Stokoe had also referred to Plampin's communication with the Admiralty following the contretemps on the quay at Portsmouth but Barrow denied that the Admiral had made any such complaint.[14]

If the British authorities were keeping the surgeon at arm's length, he was being lauded elsewhere. The Bonapartes were highly appreciative of his sympathetic treatment of Napoleon and were well aware of the sacrifice which had been forced upon him. They not only made efforts to ensure his financial security but they showed him friendship and trust, involving him in the most intimate parts of their family life. The initial introductions – to Madame Mère, Cardinal Fesch (Napoleon's uncle) and Louis Bonaparte – were made by Las Cases who had probably been instructed to do so by the Emperor. Las Cases also connected the doctor with his fourth and greatest benefactor, Joseph Bonaparte, Napoleon's elder brother. Joseph had sought refuge in Philadelphia and had quickly become accustomed to the American way of life. In 1816 he wrote to his sister-in-law: 'I am growing more and more attached to this country every day. It is the land of liberty, peace and happiness.' He was a womaniser and his wife, Queen Julie, preferred to stay in Europe with her two daughters, moving from Frankfurt to Brussels.

Towards the end of 1821, the youngest of the girls, Charlotte, who was only eighteen years, decided to join her father, and Stokoe was asked to accompany her. They embarked at Antwerp and endured a difficult voyage of two months during which the doctor vigilantly watched over his charge. Joseph showed his gratitude by treating Stokoe as a personal friend and the surgeon remained in America until 1823 when he re-crossed the Atlantic to fetch the other daughter, Princess Zenaide. The following year, a third and final mission was entrusted to him as he returned Princess Charlotte, who was betrothed to Prince Napoleon Louis Bonaparte, to France. From this time he only saw Joseph occasionally but he maintained a warm correspondence with Napoleon's brother and other family members up to Joseph's death in 1843.

In the early years of the nineteenth century, Frédéric Masson discovered a note which Napoleon had handed to Stokoe at their last meeting at Longwood on 21st January, 1819. It was addressed to King Joseph.

> I would be obliged if you would pay Doctor Stokoe £1,000 sterling which I owe him. When he sends you this note, he will give you all the information you might desire regarding me.

> Napoleon

Bertrand makes a reference to this payment in his journal entry for the 21st but, rather confusingly, says that the letter was addressed to Denzel Ibbotson, the commissary who served the French after the departure of Balcombe. According to the Grand Marshal, Stokoe was also presented with a letter of recommendation to Marie-Louise and all her family and instructed to write a work favourable to the Emperor. There is no evidence that he produced any written record beyond his memoirs. Marchand gives a muddled account of Stokoe's demise but does allude to the doctor being accused of being bribed by Napoleon's money which suggests that he also knew that payment had changed hands. The note is conserved in the *Bibliotheque Thiers* and was obviously cashed – on the reverse, William Holmes has written, 'Received the sum of the with mentioned order'. O'Meara was probably also involved in this deposit into Stokoe's account.

It is unlikely that Stokoe gave his care to Napoleon expecting such a reward. His determination to distance himself from Longwood as quickly as possible was not the behaviour of a man who had accepted a large bribe to fulfil the role of Napoleon's doctor. More likely it was a spontaneous gesture by Napoleon, an attempt to recompense the surgeon for the damage to his career that had resulted from performing his medical duties. Nevertheless, it is questionable that Stokoe should have accepted the gift. Whatever the moral implications of his decision, his action was unequivocally against regulations. He was extremely fortunate that the British authorities on the island, particularly Lowe and Plampin, were unaware of the transaction at the time of his court-martial.[15]

Stokoe never lost hope of clearing his name and he continued to seek advice from his friends and lawyers. There were many legal mistakes in the trial proceedings against him but British law at this time was inflexible and there was little hope of retrospectively changing the outcome of a naval court-martial. When Sir George Cockburn became First Lord of the Admiralty in 1842, Stokoe made a final effort to gain reinstatement to the service. Cockburn was an active participant in the injustice and perhaps he would now show generosity. The doctor received the following prompt reply.

Leamington, Warwicks
October 15, 1842

Sir,

I beg to acknowledge the receipt at this place of your letter of the 10th instant, and I am sorry to learn from it that circumstances have caused me to appear so much connected with the misfortunes you have mentioned. It must, I hope, be quite unnecessary for me to assure you that I have never entertained any adverse feeling towards you personally, and though the jealousy which prevailed relative to all the St. Helena transactions seems to have pressed so hardly upon you, I have always considered the errors attributed to Dr O'Meara and you to have proceeded from your having been placed in so trying a position, rather from any real intention on your parts to oppose and counteract the orders and intentions of the Governor and of your immediate commanding officers. I do not recollect, nor can I here refer to documents to inform me, why you were ordered to be tried by court-martial on your return to St. Helena, nor what description of complaint, if any, was made to the Admiralty relative to the imprudent transaction at Portsmouth of which you speak; but I will inform myself on these points when I return to town, and you may rest assured of my disposition to view the whole as little unfavourably as the facts set forth in the official documents may permit, and, at all events, I cannot but much lament your having experienced such severe misfortunes.

Cockburn's lapse of memory with regard to the court-martial charges was convenient but his admission that Stokoe and O'Meara had been victims of difficult circumstances was as close to an official apology as either ever received. If he consulted the documents as promised, he decided to let the matter rest. Lowe and many of the officers of the court were still alive and to give amnesty to Stokoe would have been to impugn their original decision and their reputations.[16]

The passage of time had not diluted the virulent nature of much of the literature pertaining to the Emperor's exile. Two years later, an anonymous article in the *United Service Magazine* criticised Stokoe and O'Meara, implying that they were largely responsible for Napoleon's death by misdiagnosing his illness as hepatitis. Stokoe was moved to collect his papers and to write his memoirs. Their publication would be his self-defence against any more attacks. On the other hand, he had by now married and had a family to support and, despite the help he had received from the Bonaparte clan, he remained dependant on his government pension. He feared that publication of such a controversial memoir might result in a charge of libel and threaten his financial security. In the same situation, O'Meara would have published, but Stokoe was of a more cautious disposition.

Stokoe died of a stroke in September 1852. His last years were overshadowed by the loss of his wife and his two children, a son and a daughter. He was buried at Kirk Merrington near Durham – his gravestone can still be found in the yard of St. John's Church. His property was sold at auction in London in the summer of 1853. The catalogue is a poignant reminder of his closeness to Napoleon's family. Items include cutlery from Longwood's silver service, a lock of the Emperor's hair, a cameo ring presented to him by his famous patient, and a number of valuable presents from Joseph and his wife. Stokoe's memoirs were finally published by the French historian Paul Frémeaux in 1901. He found them almost by chance in a drawer during a visit to London and was given permission to publish them in France by Edith Stokoe, the doctor's great-grand-niece. She produced an English version a few years later. Frémeaux found Stokoe's writings to be diffuse and repetitive and he felt obliged to edit and annotate the work to render it more intelligible for the average reader. As he notes in the introduction, 'A simple recital would not be possible without notes which, being almost as voluminous as the text, would soon exhaust the reader's patience and make him throw the book on one side.' This heavy handed approach left the work open to criticism and it was less well received in Britain than in France. Even so long after the events, the narrative of Stokoe's misfortunes was controversial and it was no coincidence that the most critical reviews were penned by Lowe's apologists, notably Seaton, who referred to it as a 'murky compilation compiled from scanty material'. Frémeaux in turn attacked Seaton's sycophantic account of Lowe, accusing him of producing 'a scanty book from abundant materials'. Some of the documents used by Frémeaux, including the crucial note ordering Stokoe to attend Longwood, are now contained in an enormous Grangerised version of Forsyth's *History of the Captivity of Napoleon* held in the manuscripts section of the British Library.

Compared with O'Meara, Stokoe has been ignored by British historians of the exile. A number of major accounts were written prior to the appearance of his memoirs but even those writing after their publication often only mention him in passing. No definitive interpretation of the surgeon's fate is possible but he was very likely sacrificed to clear the conscience of the chiefs at the Admiralty. Men such as Lord Melville and Sir Pulteney Malcolm had been disloyal to Hudson Lowe in their support of O'Meara and their treatment of Stokoe was opportunistic. By overreacting to the surgeon's minor improprieties they were able both to assuage Lowe and to publicise the fact that the subversive encouragement that they had given to O'Meara, another naval surgeon, was never to be repeated.

In his Hunterian lecture of 1913, Sir Arthur Keith declared that O'Meara and Stokoe were 'dismissed from the Navy by ignorant laymen because they were competent and trustful physicians'. With respect to Stokoe, this remains a reasonable conclusion.[17]

Notes

1. Stokoe, J, *With Napoleon at St. Helena*, pp. 116–20; Marchand, *Mémoires de Marchand*, Vol. II, p. 208; Bertrand, Général, *Cahiers de Sainte-Hélène*, p. 295; Chaplin, A, *The Illness and Death of Napoleon Bonaparte*, pp. 21–2; Markham, JD, *Napoleon and Dr Verling on St. Helena*, pp. 51–3.

2. Stokoe, pp. 120–3; Young, N, *Napoleon in Exile*, Vol. II, p. 143; Balmain, Count, *Napoleon in Captivity*, pp. 202–3.

3. Stokoe, p. 124; Markham, p. 57; Gorrequer, Major G, *St. Helena during Napoleon's Exile*, p. 135.

4. Stokoe, pp. 124–8; Markham, p. 132; Young, Vol. II, p. 144; Forsyth, W, *History of the Captivity of Napoleon*, Vol. II, p. 66.

5. Stokoe, pp. 128–30; Young, Vol. II, pp. 144–5; Bertrand , p. 385; Montholon, Comte de, *Lettres du Comte et de la Comtesse de Montholon*, p. 32; *Journeaux de Sainte-Hélène*, p. 181; Gorrequer, p. 139.

6. Lowe Papers 20126 ff. 61–4; Stokoe, pp. 130–41; Young, Vol. II, pp. 144–7; Markham, pp. 51–4, 86; Gorrequer, pp. 133, 242; Forsyth, Vol. II, pp. 72–3; Richardson, F, *Napoleon's Death: An Inquest*, p. 139; Korngold, R, *The Last Years of Napoleon*, p. 328.

7. Stokoe, pp. 141–3; Young, Vol. II, p. 145; British Library Eg. 3717 f. 128; Bertrand, pp. 386–7; *Journeaux*, pp. 183–4.

8. Stokoe, pp. 143–6.

9. Stokoe, pp. 146–56; Markham, p. 91; Richardson, p. 140; Bertrand, p. 387; Balmain, p. 221; Glover, G, *Wellington's Lieutenant Napoleon's Gaoler*, p. 281.

10. Stokoe, pp. 156–60; Young, Vol. II, pp. 150–1; Chaplin, A, *A St. Helena Who's Who*, p. 129; Glover, pp. 282–3; Balmain, p. 221; Forsyth, Vol. II, p. 74.

11. Stokoe, pp. 161–2, 175; Chaplin, *A St. Helena Who's Who*, p. 49; Bertrand, p. 391; Ganière, P, *Napoléon à Sainte-Hélène: La mort de L'Empereur L'Apothéose*, p. 71.

12. Stokoe, pp. 183–5; Richardson, p. 142.

13. Stokoe, pp. 185–6; Young, Vol. II, p. 150; Richardson, pp. 141–2.

14. Stokoe, pp. 186–92.

15. Stokoe, pp. 192–4, 226–8; Seward, *Napoleon's Family*, p. 183; Masson, F, *Autour de Sainte-Hélène*, Vol. III, pp. 212–3; Young, Vol. II, pp. 142–3; Bertrand, pp. 247–8; Marchand, Vol. II, p. 208; Ganière, p. 361; Gonnard, *The Exile of St. Helena*, p. 83; Korngold, p. 327.

16. British Library Eg. 3717 f. 143; Stokoe, pp. 195–7, 239–40.

17. Stokoe, pp. 194–9, 241–2; Frémeaux, *The Drama of Saint Helena*, pp. 2, 311–2; Richardson, pp. 141–4; Young, Vol. II, p. 151; Ganière, pp. 364–5.

6

A MISSED APPOINTMENT

James Verling was the official British doctor at Longwood from January 1818 to September 1819 but he had hardly any contact with the house's most famous occupant. When he sighted the Emperor it was an unusual enough event for him to report it immediately to George Nicholls who, in turn, passed the information on to Lowe. Despite his lack of intimacy with Napoleon, Verling's story is of great interest as it provides a unique insight into the politics of St. Helena and further proof of the scheming of the French and the malevolence of the Governor. The doctor kept a meticulous journal commencing at the time of his appointment to Longwood and continuing up to the time of his departure from the island. The manuscript was originally handed down in his family but then was carelessly lost at sea by Verling's nephew. In an unlikely sequence of events, it turned up in the hands of the British Consul to China who passed it to Napoleon III, the nephew of Napoleon Bonaparte. It was then preserved in the French national archives where it remains today. A French translation appeared in the respected military periodical *Carnet de Sabretache* in 1921 and it was reprinted in 1998. For English readers, there has been a transcript of the original in the Bodleian Library in Oxford since 1915 and the diary has recently been made entirely accessible in David Markham's fine book, *Napoleon and Doctor Verling on St. Helena*, published in 2005. There has been a tendency for historians to portray Verling's experiences on St. Helena in a favourable light, contrasting his fate with that of O'Meara and Stokoe. On reading his journal, it is obvious that if Verling did escape St. Helena unscathed, it was only by the skin of his teeth.[1]

James Roche Verling was born at Cobh in Ireland in 1787 and he spent his early years studying medicine in Dublin. He must have disliked his middle name because he had dispensed with it by the time he obtained his Doctorate of Medicine in Edinburgh in 1809. This degree, a thesis on jaundice, meant that he was more highly qualified than most of his medical colleagues on St. Helena. A year later, he entered the army as a Second Assistant Surgeon in the Artillery (the so-called Ordnance Medical Service). He served with distinction in the battles of the Peninsular War during 1812–1813, returned to England in 1814, and was promoted to First Assistant Surgeon in the weeks after Waterloo. This was his rank when, in August 1815, he proceeded to St. Helena in medical charge of the Artillery Department. He sailed on the *Northumberland* with Napoleon as a fellow passenger and had opportunities to converse with him. Marchand later recalled, 'The Emperor considered Dr Verling to be a perfectly honest man; he had spoken to him several times on the *Northumberland*, either at the table when he was invited or during his walks on deck.' The tone of his journal and the testimony of others suggest that Verling was not only honest but easy to like. Walter Henry certainly thought so.

> Dr Verling is an esteemed friend of mine; and I know that he was well quali-
> fied in every respect for the duty in which he was employed; being a clever
> and well educated man of gentlemanly and professional manners and long
> military experience.[2]

When O'Meara was forced out of Longwood, Verling was the obvious choice open to Lowe as his replacement. He would have preferred Baxter but he knew him to be unacceptable to Napoleon. It would surely be more difficult for the French to object to Verling who was well qualified, understood their language, and who had already met them on the voyage to the island. The surgeon was verbally ordered to his new accommodation on 25th July 1818 and he arrived in the early hours of the morning just as O'Meara was leaving. Lowe had not given Verling a written order, a recurrent theme in his treatment of the doctor, and over three months later Verling was forced to write to him requesting a proper written command to leave his artillery post for his new duty. The Governor complied and his order was worded such that Verling had to give medical attention to

Napoleon and the other 'foreign persons' and was to remain at Longwood until the Governor received further instructions from the Government. The doctor forwarded the letter to the Ordnance Medical Department in England and the unexpected detour in his career was formalised.

In reality, there was only a remote possibility that he would attend Napoleon. The Emperor, as we have seen, objected on principle to any doctor selected by Lowe. He wished his physician to be his own choice and he wanted them to be autonomous of the British authorities. They must be able to act without constraint, as would be the case for their attendance on any other private individual. He declared his own version of the Hippocratic Oath: 'A physician was to the body what a confessor was to the soul, and was bound to keep such confessions equally sacred, unless permitted to divulge it.' This plea for medical confidentiality was not designed to impress the Governor, who remained cynical regarding French intentions. Only a couple of weeks before Verling's introduction, he wrote to Charles Ricketts of the East India Company.

> Nothing would satisfy but that the medical man should be delivered over to them [Napoleon and his followers] tied hand and foot – his mouth hermetically sealed, with my consent as well as his own so that he could never open it on subjects of his profession except on permission given, and then what he was permitted to say to be taken as official and exclusive.

Despite these entrenched positions there was a polite dialogue between the French and Lowe regarding the stipulations pertaining to any doctor who might be acceptable to both sides. In April 1819, Montholon, presumably with his master's authority, had written to the Governor listing seven articles which would have to be complied with before the Emperor received a British doctor. These were a re-run of the conditions presented to O'Meara and Stokoe. The physician was to be Napoleon's alone; he was to act as Napoleon's personal doctor and was not to be summarily removed; the normal rules of medical confidentiality were to apply; he was to write medical bulletins, of which the original was to remain in French hands; that he would also be able to communicate, verbally or in writing, with the French at any time of day or night; and that he would not repeat conversations heard at Longwood unless they were interpreted as a threat to his country's security.

Lowe's response to these proposals was measured. He accepted that Napoleon could choose his own physician but pointed out that any British doctor would still be considered a British officer and would be employed and paid by the British Government and would not be 'in any wise dependant upon, subservient to or paid by Napoleon Bonaparte'. The doctor would only be removed if a suitable French medical person became available or if the British Government directed it. There was no question of the doctor concealing details of any illness the Emperor might suffer – this would have to be reported, but only to the Governor. Lowe did not require routine medical bulletins but he would need access to a copy if there was any 'serious indisposition'. Medical attention would be available at Longwood at all hours but the Governor demanded to see any written communications. Finally, he did not wish to know the content of conversations at Longwood but the physician, as a British subject, would be bound to pass on to him any discussion referring to the Governor's duties or anything relating to a breach of security or infraction of the regulations. The studied reasonableness of this exchange belies the poisonous nature of the relationship between Longwood and Plantation House and the remoteness of a mutually acceptable solution.[3]

Although Verling may not have been fulfilling his role as Napoleon's British doctor he was nevertheless popular with the French entourage. Saint-Denis commented approvingly of the surgeon's caring attitude to his new companions and confessed that he had soon gained 'the confidence of us all'. The Montholons particularly liked him; when Madame Montholon wrote to her husband from Europe after her departure from St. Helena, she reminded him to give 'a thousand thanks' to Verling and added that she wished the doctor could have been with her during her most recent illness. This fondness for the British surgeon was manifested in the form of gifts. On New Year's Day in 1819, he received a breakfast service of plate from Madame Bertrand and a gold watch, chain and seals from Madame Montholon. Napoleon probably encouraged this generosity. Verling was understandably concerned that he might be compromised by such valuable presents and, after consulting the Governor, he tactfully refused them. Madame Montholon was phlegmatic but Madame Bertrand took offence and launched into a violent tirade against Lowe who, she predicted, would soon be replaced.

Verling found the Bertrands trickier to handle than the other prisoners. Madame was inclined to be sulky and was easily upset. Count Bertrand had allegedly told her that he thought Verling blamed him for Napoleon's refusal to see the physician. Verling tried to accommodate them while avoiding over-familiarity. On 1st February 1819, he wrote in his diary, 'It appears to me evident that the less communication I have with the Bertrands the better, as they are very strongly, and I believe very justly suspected by the Governor.' In reality, he could hardly avoid them, particularly Madame Bertrand, who constantly sought his medical opinion.[4]

The Governor was determined to make it explicit that Verling was available to be Napoleon's doctor; all that was required was French unconditional acceptance. On more than one occasion during his stay at Longwood, he was ordered by Lowe to present himself to Bertrand and formally offer his medical services to the Emperor. Bertrand rejected the offers, referring Verling to the conditions contained in the earlier correspondence with Montholon; in essence, *'L'Empereur ne prendra qu'un medecin de son choix.'* The irony of the situation was that both the doctor and patient were reluctant parties. Verling, no doubt mindful of the misfortunes of O'Meara and Stokoe, wrote to Lowe as early as June 1819 requesting his removal from Longwood. By September, his resolve not to be Napoleon's medical attendant had hardened. In conversation with the French, he declared that he was only there because he was 'a military man and obliged to obey orders'. His anxiety to escape his situation led him to write to Lowe making a formal request to be relocated.

Napoleon's resistance to the appointment was not attributable to any antipathy to Verling as a man. In Saint-Denis's words, 'It was enough that the doctor had been stationed at Longwood by the Governor for the Emperor to refuse to receive him or see him.' Marchand agrees. 'This refusal was not directed at the doctor himself but at the Governor who in this doctor had a man of his own choice.' It was a touchy subject for the valet's master. When Marchand found the Emperor vomiting, he 'very carefully avoided suggesting the help of Dr Verling'. Despite this stand off, there was real hope in both British and French camps that Verling might, at some stage, take the place of O'Meara. Baxter wrote to Verling towards the end of 1818.

I am glad that you have had sight of the man or ghost, but could have wished you were a little nearer. The time approaches when I think you will be in daily attendance upon him and it would not be surprising if I was also to be of the party ... I like the proceedings of Montholon and it appears to be the wish of all parties to come to an understanding. I trust you entertain no doubt of B. selecting you as his immediate medical attendant ...

This was all rather optimistic, particularly with respect to Baxter's own part. The allusion to Montholon's activities is more meaningful. Both Montholon and Bertrand retained hopes of Verling eventually becoming Napoleon's doctor. They knew that the Emperor had a high opinion of British doctors. When it later became known that a Corsican physician was bound for St. Helena, Madame Bertrand acknowledged to Verling that 'he [Napoleon] did not like the coming of the foreign surgeon and would prefer an English one.' As the Emperor's health worsened, the need to achieve a resolution intensified. Marchand comments that the Grand Marshal and the Count pressurised the ailing patient to accept Verling. Napoleon was stubborn. If Verling was to be his physician, it would have to be on his terms. The doctor would have to accept conditions similar to the articles presented to John Stokoe.[5]

Thus it was that in the course of 1819, Bertrand and Montholon made concerted efforts – a mixture of coercion and charm – to persuade the British doctor to become '*l'Homme d'Empereur*'. We must presume that they had Napoleon's authority for their proposals although they may to some degree have acted independently in their enthusiasm to seek a solution. The first serious approach was made by Bertrand in January. Verling was taken aback when the Grand Marshal paid him an unexpected visit in the morning. The Frenchman appeared to be in a jovial mood.

> He then professed to feel sentiments of good will towards me and expatiated
> upon the praise I was entitled to from everybody <u>at the present moment</u>.

The last words are underlined in Verling's journal, implying that either Bertrand or the doctor or both believed this state of affairs not to be inevitable. After some prevarication, Bertrand came to the point.

> Our influence has been repeatedly used to induce him to see you, and in
> vain, even when he thought he was going to die. The Governor now recedes
> from Lord Bathurst's letter [a letter of May 1818 in which it is stated that
> Napoleon should be able to select his own doctor], Napoleon has made a
> choice; obstacles are thrown in the way, he is about to refuse him. The corre-
> spondence is becoming more warm (the Governor is a man who never feels
> a blow until he is knocked down). He [Lowe] perseveres in wishing to force
> you upon him, and I warn you that motives will soon be attributed to him for
> this line of conduct in which your name will unavoidably be implicated, and

in a manner in which your name ought not to appear. I therefore advise you to retire immediately from the situation.

Verling replied that as a military medical man, it was his duty to remain at his post and that he felt able to resist any false imputations. Was this a genuine attempt to get rid of Verling? Forsyth believed so and he describes the surgeon's dismissive response as 'spirited'. It is more likely that the Grand Marshal was deliberately raising the stakes and trying to force Verling to make a concession to Napoleon without the consent of the Governor. This interpretation is supported by Madame Bertrand's behaviour. It is improbable that she was acting without her husband's approval when, a few weeks later, she tried to involve the doctor in a discussion of his role at Longwood. She expressed her anxiety that he should become Napoleon's physician and asked him directly if he would be prepared to accept the conditions offered to Stokoe. Verling tactfully declined to give a straight answer and subsequently informed Lowe of the approach. The Governor advised him to keep his distance from the Grand Marshal.

On 1st April, Montholon made a much more detailed proposal to Verling. The surgeon, fearing that he might be entrapped in a new French intrigue, made the following verbatim record of the Count's offer and copied it to the Governor in the form of a memorandum.

Having had a reason to visit at Count Montholon's he took an opportunity when we were alone of introducing the subject of Napoleon choosing a surgeon. He said, I must be aware that he had long endeavoured to fix Napoleon's choice on me, and how flattering it would be to me should I now be chosen notwithstanding that I was the person selected by the Governor, as this must be attributed to the favourable impressions made by my conduct during the 8 months I had been at Longwood. He informed me that propositions which the Governor might perhaps accept, had this morning been made, and if accepted Napoleon would instantly choose a Surgeon, but that he could not think of having near him *l'homme du Gouverneur*; by this, he meant he said any person whose views of promotion and of self interest might prompt him to act under the Governor's influence.

If, on the contrary, I was willing to become *l'homme de l'Empereur*, to attach myself, *comme le sien propre* [as his very own], the Count Montholon was authorised to make a proposal to me, which he advised me to accept, as I should at once obtain a degree of his confidence by avowing the motives of making my fortune, a motive much more intelligible to him than any vague declaration of admiration of the Man.

He said that Napoleon was willing to give me an allowance of 12,000 Francs per annum, to be paid monthly and he [Montholon] had represented to him the danger I might incur of *de perdre mon état* [losing my position], pointing out the examples of Mr O'Meara and Mr Stokoe, he would at once advance a sum to my practice in Bills upon the house of Baring, the interest of which should be equal to my present pay from the British Government.

He asked the amount of my pay and I told him nearly £1 per day on this Island. He told me Napoleon would not require from me any thing which should compromise me with Government or with any tribunal, or even in public opinion – that Mr O'Meara had never been required to do any thing of this nature – I should be able when I saw him to judge the state of his liver which he himself thought was much diseased; that in my Bulletins my report might lean rather to an augmentation than a diminution of the malady. That I might draw the line rather above than below, as he was still in hopes that *la force des choses* [the force of circumstances] might summon him from St. Helena.

He [Montholon] however was much more in dread of apoplexy [a stroke] attacking Napoleon, to which they all thought he had a strong tendency, but advised me to be guarded upon this subject as it was one on which he [Napoleon] would not converse and from which he wished to avert his thoughts. To this proposal I replied that I considered it totally incompatible with my duty to enter into a private agreement with Napoleon Bonaparte.

Frédéric Masson believed that Montholon's attempts to win over Verling revealed the Frenchman's poor judgement and lack of morality. The offer of money was mercenary and the hint that Napoleon's illness might be exaggerated was crude. The Count realised that he had gone too far and returned to the doctor a few days later, telling him that the suggestion that he should play up the Emperor's symptoms was entirely his own and had not been approved by Napoleon who only required that his surgeon should conduct himself faithfully (*loyalement*) towards him. Verling continued to play a straight bat, saying that he could not be expected to enter into any secret arrangement or make any promise without the Governor's permission. Montholon enquired what he would do if Napoleon were suddenly to become very ill. The doctor replied that he would be prepared to see him under these circumstances, as an emergency consultation did not equate with an agreement to be the patient's normal medical attendant.

The French were not to be deterred by Verling's repeated refusals to engage in clandestine negotiations. Count de Montholon made further attempts to win him over in August and September 1819. On the first of these occasions, Montholon was in bed due to illness. He was surrounded by papers which included communications with Napoleon. He told Verling that it was 'his own fault' if he did not become the Emperor's physician and offered him a document to sign. This contained the same stipulations as contained in Montholon's previous correspondence with the Governor. The Count made every effort to sugar the pill. By signing the document, he explained, Verling would only be showing himself to be an 'honest man' willing to see Napoleon in an emergency. The surgeon's acceptance would be wholly conditional and the British Governor would be able to confirm or annul it. His acceptance would surely be viewed as a formality and would be perceived to arise from a 'laudable desire' to give medical assistance to a patient with an illness requiring urgent attention. Furthermore, if the surgeon was willing to sign this preliminary agreement, he would immediately receive 3,000 Louis which he would keep irrespective of the nature of his future employment. If Verling remained some time at Longwood as the Emperor's doctor he was guaranteed an income of 500 Louis a year for life.

The doctor was not deflected by this circumlocution and he replied that he could not consider signing any paper however conditional it might be. No doubt, he remembered that Stokoe had agreed to proposals made under similar terms. He asked the Count to put himself in his place and to imagine how he would react. Montholon assured him that he would readily accept if in Verling's situation as it would resolve the immediate 'crisis' and that when another doctor arrived to replace him, perhaps the return of Stokoe or a new foreign surgeon, he would be able to depart Longwood on good terms with Napoleon. Verling commented that this was all just repetition of the previous proposal; he again stressed his unequivocal rejection of every part of it and left the bedroom. He quickly informed the Governor of the latest attentions paid to him and that the financial inducement had been increased.

The final attempt to procure Verling's services was made a couple of weeks later. Montholon had recovered sufficiently to be walking back to his house from Bertrand's and he invited the doctor to accompany him. He had convinced Napoleon to employ Verling without any conditions and without any signed documentation. All that the Emperor required was that his new physician would give his word of honour not to make any written report of his health without him receiving a copy and that he should not repeat any conversation he might hear at Longwood. Indeed, Napoleon would not need his doctor to write any health bulletins so only the second point was relevant. As Verling records in his journal, Montholon could not prevent himself introducing a hint of subterfuge.

> He added there were engagements which every medical man took tacitly, such as to conceal any little disease or infirmity to which his patient was liable. Upon my looking at Montholon, he said that he had replied to Napoleon that this was a matter of little consequence since he had none, to which he [Napoleon] replied, but suppose it possible I should get *la chaude piss* [the hot piss – the urethritis of venereal disease] you would not have it inserted in a bulletin.

The Count had assured his master that Verling was a man of honour. When the doctor repeated his refusal of any secret compact, emphasising the vital role of the Governor, Montholon expressed his regret. He was sorry that Verling was missing such an opportunity. His wife, the Countess de Montholon, had made it her last wish before leaving the island that Verling should become the Emperor's doctor and Madame Bertrand was also 'warm in his interest'. The steadfast surgeon reaffirmed that his mind was made up and wished Montholon good evening. An entry in Bertrand's journal for 7th September reveals that Montholon was, on this occasion, the mouthpiece for the Emperor and his retinue, who still hoped to convert Verling to their cause. Napoleon wished the surgeon to be sounded out; was he prepared to sign secret guarantees and to write bulletins for the eyes of the French only? Walter Henry was aware of the pressure being exerted on his medical colleague. He confirms that Verling 'indignantly rejected' the bribes offered to him and also that he reported the facts immediately to Sir Hudson Lowe.[6]

Verling's prompt communication of all the French efforts to subvert him was designed to placate the Governor and to remove him from any suspicion. Lowe, as has already been amply demonstrated, was a man who was suspicious of all his subordinates. In the face of Verling's irreproachable conduct, he laboured to find a reason to distrust and despise him beyond the fact that he was liked by the French. In the spring of 1819, Bertrand asked Verling about his family and connections in Ireland. The question was probably innocent but the anxious surgeon decided to inform Lowe of the conversation and the fact that he had friends in Ireland who were Catholics. In an act of maliciousness which is ignored by Forsyth and reluctantly acknowledged by other pro-Lowe historians, the Governor immediately wrote to Bathurst to bring this to his attention and to imply that Verling was therefore worthy of suspicion. Fortunately for the doctor, Bathurst was actually in favour of Catholic emancipation and he delivered a snub to the Governor. In his reply, sent on 8th April via Goulbourn, he ordered Lowe to inform Verling that the Governor's reference to his Roman Catholic relations could 'make no impression on his Lordship's mind'. He added:

> Whatever may be his connections in Ireland or the religion either of himself or them, Lord Bathurst cannot permit any circumstance of that nature to invalidate the confidence to which his uniform, discretion, and propriety of conduct, up to the date of your late communication so justly entitle him.

This deserved slap of the wrist must have been distasteful for Lowe, particularly as he had little choice but to pass on the content of the letter to Verling as directed. The doctor notes that Lowe personally read him the relevant extract on 21st August.[7]

Having lost this skirmish and having been humiliated in the process, Lowe was now gunning for the Artillery Surgeon. A week later, Verling reported to the Governor that Montholon's health was deteriorating and that the Count had attributed this to the number of letters and messages he was forced to receive by the British authorities. Lowe was annoyed and demanded a subsequent meeting at which he angrily accused the doctor of implying that he had personally caused the Count's illness by treating him inhumanely. Verling riposted that he had only stated that Montholon's health was worse, and that the comments regarding the correspondence came from the patient and not from him.

When Verling added that Matthew Livingstone, a surgeon of the East India Company, had also called to see Montholon, Lowe again tried to find fault, complaining that he was unaware of this. The surgeon said that he had informed the Governor's staff of the visit of his medical colleague. Lowe persisted, accusing Verling of not obeying instructions issued to him earlier in the month to report 'anything extraordinary' which occurred at

Longwood. Verling agreed to read this letter again but pointed out that he believed it improper for him 'to come forward every moment obtruding my opinion'. He continues in his journal.

> He [Lowe] observed that in my capacity as a British officer that he thought that I might assist and forward the views of the Governor. I told him that I conceived it my duty to deviate as little as possible from my medical capacity and that in this instance especially I saw nothing further to be required of me than a declaration of the actual state of Count Montholon's health.

Lowe's initial distrust and subsequent growing dislike of Verling is well demonstrated in Gorrequer's diary. The references to Verling become more frequent in April 1819. On the 4th, Gorrequer writes;

> 3rd Magnesia [Verling] soon after came in where we both were and after speaking to him some time, on going away he [Lowe] said to me: 'Didn't you observe his manner of speaking, how short he breathed as if frightened' and again expressed himself very doubtful of his being trustworthy.

Two days later, the secretary reveals that the Governor was 'displaying hostility' towards Verling and that he believed the doctor to be concealing his knowledge of events at Longwood. And again on the 7th;

> Great Gun Magnesia [Verling] came and Mach [Lowe] asked afterwards 'Did you see a man in your life so embarrassed.' Finds a great deal of faults with him for having indulged Veritas [Montholon] ...'

Five months later, in September, the entries suggest that Lowe's antipathy to Verling had increased.

> Mach said Magnesia Great Gun [Verling] had played a double part. The rancour he showed against him. His jealousy. He said that any other should be chosen in his place.

At the same time, Lowe was writing to Verling approving his conduct; the charge of playing a 'double part' was not only unsubstantiated but also hypocritical.[8]

Despite this constant questioning of his loyalty, Verling was ordered to stay at Longwood. As he was not fulfilling his intended role as the Emperor's personal physician, there is the question of how he spent his time and also to what extent he became involved in the day-to-day affairs of the exiles. Was he another O'Meara or did he really keep his distance from the French, as he protested in his communications to Lowe? There is scant evidence that he enjoyed his residence at Longwood and, in his journal, he often moans about duties which he believed to be inappropriate and demeaning for a medical man. Lowe pressurised him to act as a British spy. This was particularly the case during the Stokoe affair. In late January 1819, Gorrequer writes a note to Verling that demonstrates both the Governor's obsession with detail and the demands made on the doctor.

> Can you inform him [Lowe] whether Count Montholon was with General
> B. [Napoleon] before he saw Mr Stokoe on the morning of the 17th, or if
> Count Montholon only saw General B. after Mr Stokoe had left him. Also, if
> Count Montholon and Count Bertrand were together that morning.

Further questions are posed regarding the exact times at which various individuals arrived and departed Longwood. Verling was also resentful of being used as an interpreter. He was fluent in French so this was expedient but, in the event, he found it difficult to fulfil this duty without complications. In August 1819, he writes in his journal:

> Having more than once thought that no good could arise to me from any
> interference however indirect in the unpleasant communications that
> occasionally go on at Longwood, I had expressed to the Governor my unwill-
> ingness to act as an interpreter and he fully agreed with me.

Lowe acquiesced to this request saying that there should be no need for the surgeon to do any further translation.

Bertrand confirms that the French asked Verling to read English dispatches to them and, in the Grand Marshal's journal, there are some hints that the doctor, at least in his early days in residence, was willing to run certain errands for the prisoners. There is a cryptic note made during August 1819 that '*le médecin*' had been very helpful in handling some papers belonging to O'Meara who was just about to depart the island. The Grand Marshal is probably being intentionally vague but it is very likely that he was referring to Verling. A few months earlier, in March, '*le docteur*' had similarly informed the French of reports of growing support for the Emperor in their homeland. Bertrand implies that he did this with much enthusiasm, relating the conscripts' cries of '*Vive Napoléon!*' Verling makes no reference to these incidents in his journal.

Less contentious is Verling's role as Longwood's 'General Practitioner'. This was quite separate from his potential attachment to Napoleon – a fact that Madame Bertrand, his most demanding patient, was keen to remind him of. She was concerned that her favourite doctor would be forced out of Longwood and that she would be abandoned. Verling tolerated her but the following journal entry for February 1819 suggests that it was not an ideal doctor-patient relationship.

> Madame Bertrand, having been tormented and tormenting me with a thousand chimerical complaints arising from a tendency to hysteria and from the want of any force of character to support the monotony of her situation, has latterly taken it into her head that the womb must be affected with some organic disease, as she went ten months without conceiving. This had been the topic of conversation for the last 3 weeks between her husband, herself and me …

Verling also cared for others in Napoleon's retinue. The Emperor took a keen interest in the health of his companions and usually had an opinion regarding the optimal treatment. When he learned that the doctor was giving mercury to Marchand, who had an intestinal disorder, he said to Saint-Denis, 'these devils of English doctors treat their patients as they treat horses. Well, if Verling cures him, that is all I ask.' The valet was sick for twenty days but then recovered. The surgeon also tended to Madame Montholon, who had liver problems, and to her husband who had a similar affliction. It was Verling who recommended that Madame Montholon return to Europe as the St. Helena climate was impeding her recovery. His administrations were greatly appreciated. Count Montholon wrote to the Countess in June 1820, reassuring her of his good health which had been restored by Dr Verling's 'perfect treatment'.[9]

If Verling had any concerns as to the health of his Longwood patients, he had the option of calling in his medical colleagues for a second opinion. During his stay on St. Helena, he had direct contact with a number of other Anglo-Irish doctors who were either serving in the Army, the Navy, or the local civilian services. He had relatively little contact with O'Meara as his arrival at Longwood coincided with his countryman's departure. Furthermore, Verling held no illusions as to the dangers of fraternising with his disgraced predecessor. When O'Meara wrote him a harmless note regarding the ownership of some volumes of Byron's works, Verling 'conceiving it prudent that no communication, however trivial, with Dr O'Meara should be private', immediately showed it to the Governor. This determination to appease Lowe soured his relationship with Stokoe who believed that Verling could have done more to help him in his one-sided fight with the Governor's regime. In his memoirs, Stokoe refers to his colleague as 'Lowe's puppet'; Verling's ungracious description of Stokoe's performance at his court-martial confirms antagonism between the two men. Archibald Arnott, Surgeon to the 20th Foot, who was to play such a vital part in Napoleon's final days, first visited Longwood in August 1819 when Verling acted as translator. There is no record of any disagreement between Verling and Arnott, although the Governor's preference for the latter was a possible cause of friction.

The fellow doctor with whom Verling had most dealings, Matthew Livingstone, acted as both Surgeon and Superintendent of the East India Company's medical establishment. Unlike his military peers, he had a specialist medical interest, being an '*accoucheur*', an obstetrician. As Madame Bertrand had suffered a miscarriage and a number of symptoms relating to her later pregnancy, it was natural that Verling should call for Livingstone's help. The obstetrician was, however, a reluctant visitor to Longwood. Verling notes in his journal that he was 'not desirous of being called in' and Count Bertrand says that he was so frightened of paying visits that he neglected his wife. Livingstone's dread of being involved in a French plot led to him falling out with Verling. For once, it was not Napoleon's health that was in question. The circumstances are described in a letter written by Thomas Reade, who obtained the facts directly from Livingstone.

Dr Verling stated to him [Livingstone] that Count Montholon was affected with a spitting of blood, a pain on the right side, supposed to be the liver complaint, and also an intermittent fever. That upon all the occasions of his, Dr Livingstone's visits to Count Montholon, he never could perceive any of the slightest symptoms of the above complaints. That particularly on his last visit, where Dr Verling stated that the Count had a violent fever upon him, he was very much surprised to find a large fire in the Count's room, hot enough to increase the heat to 90 degrees. He instantly mentioned this to Dr Verling, stating his surprise that he, as a pupil of Dr Gregory's of Edinburgh, would have permitted such a thing, and at the same time told him that he believed it had been designedly done, and that he was convinced nothing was the matter with Count Montholon. That he was sure that there was something improper in all this.

Verling wished Livingstone to write a certificate detailing Montholon's illness but the latter refused. Such a document might have been used by the Count to justify his departure from St. Helena and his return to Europe to join his wife. This difference of opinion, and Livingstone's suspicion that Verling was in some way playing a part for the French, led to a serious quarrel.[10]

In his writing, Verling is often disarmingly frank respecting the difficulties he faced. He probably did not intend the contents of the diary to be disseminated. He wrote the following after an awkward confrontation with Lowe in May 1819 during which the Governor berated him for his role in 'delicate communications' at Longwood.

> Upon the tenor of this conversation, which I have not fully detailed, I have to remark that it has left upon my mind the impression that the situation of Physician to Bonaparte is one which cannot be held by a British officer without the certainty of sacrificing his peace of mind for the time he holds it and with more prospects of ultimate injury than benefit. All the pains I had taken to obtain the good will and good word of the people about Napoleon, the only mode I knew of obtaining his, and of which the Governor was aware, seem now to throw a shade of suspicion upon any conduct and the mere idea of an approach to Count Bertrand seems to have cancelled anything that might have appeared praiseworthy.

Verling fully understood that it did not require a wrong action to incur the wrath of Lowe; only the slightest hint that a false step might be taken. The dilemma he faced was a 'Catch 22' scenario for all the British doctors connected with Napoleon. He had to reside at Longwood and had to make himself constantly available to the Emperor and his followers; were he to do otherwise, the Governor might be accused of depriving Napoleon of a doctor and Verling would certainly pay the price. On the other hand, by liaising so closely with the French he risked attracting the suspicion of

Lowe who remained convinced that Longwood was a hotbed of intrigue. When Verling refuses the New Year present of Madame Bertrand, her husband comments in his journal that the surgeon apologised to her and said that he could not accept because the Governor was a man 'so suspicious that he would believe him won over [to the French]; that there were not two men like the Governor; that being a humble officer, he dare not risk the Governor's disapproval and the loss of his post'. In another conversation with Madame Bertrand, the doctor gloomily asserts that he will leave Longwood on bad terms with both the French and Lowe.[11]

Verling consoled himself with the thought that his attachment was not indefinite. He was, he explained to Madame Bertrand, 'a mere locum tenens, till the arrival of a French surgeon'. The appearance of the Corsican physician, Francesco Antommarchi, on St. Helena on 20th September 1819, must have seemed a prayer answered. Antommarchi, as will be explained in the next chapter, had been summoned to be Napoleon's private doctor. In Lowe's words to Baxter, 'matters became changed'; there was 'no longer any motive for keeping an English medical person in habitual unrestrained communication with General Bonaparte and his followers'. The Governor was also pleased at this development as he was tiring of the endless negotiations concerning Verling's suitability as Napoleon's surgeon. He wrote to Bathurst:

> The arrival of Professor Antommarchi put a stop however to all discussion on the matter. The experience I had had of the arts practised with every British medical person who had been admitted to Longwood, did not lead me to encourage their views on this point. I was decided in my opinion that a foreigner subject to the same regulations as themselves was the proper person.

Verling, pleased at no longer having to endure these 'arts', arranged to give up his quarters in the house on the day after Antommarchi's arrival. He had just packed his belongings and sent off his baggage when he was called to a meeting with Montholon, Bertrand and the Corsican physician. Both the Grand Marshal and Count expressed their regret at his sudden departure and requested that he stay longer; they would write to the Governor on the subject. Bertrand pressed the point, observing that the surgeon, in Verling's own words, was 'wanted on the spot, etc, etc'. Antommarchi also exhorted the surgeon to stay on to share with him the details of Montholon's ongoing treatment.

Colonel Wynyard was informed of French dismay at Verling's loss and he communicated this to Lowe, who wrote a short note to the doctor permitting him to remain until Antommarchi was established in his new situation. Verling, understanding that nothing on St. Helena was quite what it seemed, decided to visit Plantation House, 'conceiving it better to learn the Governor's sentiments from his own mouth, as his approval did not appear to me to be what was necessary and his positive wish was what I required'. In the resulting discussion, it became obvious that Lowe was still dubious of the motives of Bertrand and Montholon and that he would prefer Verling off the scene. The surgeon agreed to leave the following day and the Governor advised him to inform the French of his departure at the last moment.[12]

Having finally escaped from his forced employment, Verling decided to cool his relations with the exiles. This cannot have been a surprise to the Governor as Verling had expressed his disquiet at his situation and Thomas Reade had also informed him of the surgeon's anxiety to get away from Longwood. A month following his change of quarters, Verling wrote to Wynyard stating that he intended to confine himself to his military duties and that he would only visit the French if he was particularly directed to do so. He was apparently determined on this course of action as, a few weeks later, he penned a further letter in much the same vein; 'The idea of attending at Longwood on any footing than by direct orders of my superiors never occurred to me, and even of this situation, I was not desirous.'[13]

The logical culmination of Verling's strategy of estrangement was his departure from St. Helena. This ambition was reinforced by an absence of five years from his family. On 27th September, only a week after his removal from Longwood, the surgeon first broached the issue with Lowe.

In the morning, I had mentioned to the Governor that I had long been anxious to get home, that my family affairs required it, and I had spoken more than once on the subject to Sir T. Reade, and I believed had mentioned it to Major Gorrequer, that as I had now left Longwood, and from what had passed was not anxious to continue my intercourse with it, I should feel obliged to him to give me leave to go to England. He observed that no relief had come for me, but I told him that I certainly should have been relieved had I not been sent to Longwood; he said however that the number of medical men on the Island would not permit him to allow me to go. Before I left Plantation

House, I took an opportunity to urge the point again and requested him to take it into consideration.

So Verling was desperate to leave and Lowe was reluctant to let him go. Within days, the situation appeared entirely the reverse. Reade reassured the doctor that he thought that the Governor would relent and when Verling made a formal application for twelve months leave of absence to the Commandant of the Royal Artillery on St. Helena, Major James Power, this was quickly approved. The frigate *Eurydice* was on the point of departure for England and Lowe assumed that Verling would benefit from the 'real favour' he had gifted him by making his escape. Unexpectedly, the surgeon chose to defer his leave and to delay his departure, informing both Reade and Lowe of his decision. He does not elaborate the reasons for this in his journal and we have only the words of Power and the Governor to explain his *volte-face*. The senior artillery officer commented to Reade that the doctor wished to put off his passage until March or April of the following year because of the inclement season, his desire to spend the following winter in Edinburgh, and the expectation that his successor would soon arrive on the island. In a letter to Bathurst, Lowe says that Verling justified his prolonged stay by quoting 'pecuniary matters and fear of giving offence to the Director General of the Ordnance Medical Department'.

There is some sense in all these reasons but, in the hyper-charged atmosphere of St. Helena, Verling's sudden change of heart was bound to create suspicion. Major Power informed Verling of a conversation he had had with Reade in which the Deputy Adjutant-General had asked him why the surgeon had not taken advantage of his leave. The Governor was much surprised and Reade enquired of Power if he did not think it strange that Verling should apply for leave and then decline to take it. There was only one certainty: Lowe and Reade were seeking a sinister motive.[14]

Verling's last days on St. Helena were to prove difficult. Under the circumstances, it would have been politic for him to avoid any contact with Longwood but, surprisingly in view of his avowed determination to shun Napoleon's household, he continued to make visits to Madame Bertrand. Initially, he claimed that this was a matter of 'professional duty' but then he adds in his journal, '... as I had several times visited, politeness required that I should make another [visit], and acquaint Madame Bertrand, that she might act accordingly in case of future illness in her family'. Verling's attentions to the Grand Marshal's wife may not have been entirely altruistic. She was a hypochondriac but also a beautiful woman who could be charming and witty. The young surgeon may have been flattered by her dependency upon him. Whatever his motivation for continuing the liaison, he obtained permission from Lowe to see her whenever his 'medical attendance' was required and 'occasionally to enquire after her health and that of the children'.

Verling had been accommodated but he remained nervous that his reasons for maintaining his connections with Longwood might be misconstrued and he decided to obtain more explicit permission from the Governor. On 12th October he wrote to Gorrequer.

> As my stay may be protracted somewhat longer than was at first intended, I request you will make known to His Excellency my anxiety to have clear instructions for my guidance in any intercourse which may take place with Longwood should such be deemed necessary.

This simple request triggered a prolonged and increasingly antagonistic dialogue between doctor and Governor in which the former sought clarification of his role and the latter steadfastly refused to spell out his requirements.

Neither man emerges with credit. Verling is playing with fire whilst Lowe is at his most obdurate and opaque. The Governor replied to the surgeon (via Wynyard) pointing out that now that Antommarchi was at Longwood, Madame Bertrand had easy access to a doctor.

> He [Lowe] has not the slightest objection to the continuance of your visits – but he sees no motive for ordering them or conveying any more particular instruction to you on the occasion, than what he might incidentally think is necessary to give to any Professional Person, not belonging to the establishment at Longwood, who might occasionally be called in or who might have obtained his permission for paying visits there.

Later, Lowe adds that had Verling become Napoleon's physician, he would have given written instructions for his guidance but that as this had not happened, he felt that there was no need. He did, however, attempt to explain his views on the matter to the confused surgeon. Unfortunately, Lowe's prose style is remarkably obtuse. A single example, again written through the channel of his Secretary, Wynyard, on 16th October 1819, will suffice.

Your application for leave of absence rendered it unnecessary to enter into consideration of the more formal demand made for you being directed or ordered to attend her, and the Governor's desires or suggestions (not his directions) for your continuing your attendance upon her so long as you remained here (the protraction of your stay on the island being wholly unforeseen when the Countess's demand was made) he certainly did not conceive could have been regarded in any other light, than as a simple act of attention towards her, or at most, as an accommodation to the service, in the sphere of which you had been acting.

Faced with such classical Lowe obfuscation, Verling was unsure which way to turn. He understood enough of the Governor's correspondence to believe that he was now part of an unequal battle of wills. He was later to observe to Thomas Reade that it was unfair that he 'should be obliged to enter into anything like a contest' with Lowe and that, in effect, he was forced to regard any suggestion made by the Governor as a command. The surgeon admitted that he was bewildered.

He [Lowe] has kept me totally in the dark as to his wishes; in a word, did he wish me to go to Longwood or did he wish me to stay away and why did he not send another?

When, in late October, Madame Bertrand was again unwell and sent a groom and horse to fetch her favourite doctor, he decided to try and force Lowe's hand. Instead of proceeding to Longwood, he approached Reade and said that he would not attend the Countess without definite orders from his superiors. Later the same day, he called at Plantation House and informed Lowe of this personally. The Governor expressed surprise at Verling's unwillingness to attend his patient and declared that he was not interested in discussing the surgeon's motives. Verling remarked that he still did not know Lowe's own views on the matter, to which the Governor angrily replied that he had none. Lowe ended the exchange by suggesting that the surgeon should go to Longwood to explain to Madame Bertrand in person why he was reluctant to treat her. He believed this necessary to prevent the French making capital of the doctor's non-attendance. This led to an awkward meeting between the surgeon and Countess. Madame Bertrand was distraught at his refusal to attend her unless ordered to do so and she asked that he at least remain her friend.

The doctor was unable to resist the pull of Longwood and his former patient and in the months of late 1819 and early 1820 he made several social visits. He informed Lowe that he was acting out of politeness and respect. Livingstone, who was willing to administer medical help to the Countess and her child without specific guidance, had by now taken over the role of her private physician.

Verling's continued attachment to the French despite the lack of any medical objective only served to heighten the suspicions of Lowe and his associates. Reade, always sniffing around for a conspiracy, commented to Nicholls that he thought it 'odd' that Verling still socialised with Madame Bertrand. Nicholls helpfully warned the surgeon of Reade's curiosity and told him that it would be prudent to make no more visits. Lowe had already advised Verling that he did not believe the Countess to be a free agent. Although she might not be always aware of it, the Governor thought her to be often the 'instrument' of indirect attacks upon him. His distrust of both doctor and patient is well illustrated in a private letter to Bathurst written in November 1819. He admits that, 'It was not easy for me to judge what were the views of the persons at Longwood and what were those of Dr Verling'. Was it all innocent or was the doctor hatching plots with his confrères? Lowe comments acidly that Verling gave him no information about events at Longwood beyond the bare minimum required by his professional duty – 'he could not have maintained a greater degree of secrecy in regard to them.' The Governor implies that the surgeon is scheming and manipulative.

> If Dr Verling was sincere in his desire of breaking off all relations with the persons at Longwood, there was a natural and obvious way of doing so, by simply acquainting Madame Bertrand of it, without involving me in any discussion on the subject, but his perfect readiness to attend upon her, and the persons at Longwood in general, if he <u>obtained an order</u> from me, is hardly reconcilable with the desire of breaking of all relations with them and rather betrays a secret inclination to have become the medical attendant upon them, <u>on the same footing as he was before</u>, if he could cover the renewal of his visits as a duty forced upon him by me, and not as an act of his own free will.

Lowe concluded that the doctor's behaviour was 'very extraordinary'. As for his own conduct, he assured Bathurst that he had tried to give Verling as much freedom as possible at Longwood. He had not issued restrictive instructions as this might have given Bonaparte an additional pretext to refuse to see the British surgeon. 'The latitude enjoyed by Dr Verling and the persons at Longwood themselves left no cause of objections, or dissatisfaction, either on his part or theirs.' By giving the surgeon free rein, or plenty of rope, he could not himself be blamed for French disapproval. In a heated discussion at the end of November, the Governor criticises Verling for again demanding his orders. 'You would not act upon your own responsibility.' The doctor must surely have immediately thought of O'Meara and Stokoe, medical colleagues who had dared to hold their own opinions.[15]

Verling left St. Helena on 23rd April 1820 (the date usually given is the 25th but references in his journal suggest two days earlier). He made his final farewells at Longwood a few days before his departure. Madame Bertrand had accepted that the surgeon was not to blame for the difficulties of the previous months and that he was acting according to the force of circumstances rather than from inclination. He sat with her for an hour and a half. Bertrand and Montholon also came to say goodbyes. Historians have singled out Verling as one of the few men who left St. Helena on good terms both with the French and the Governor. They were persuaded of his healthy relationship with Lowe by the evidence of the official correspondence in which the Governor praises the doctor on more than one occasion. Indeed, Lowe had the decency to acknowledge to Verling in conversation that his position at Longwood was an extremely disagreeable one and that he knew that it required great delicacy. In May 1819, the Governor had written to Bathurst,

> I do not hesitate to submit Dr Verling's name to your Lordship as a person whose conduct hitherto has given every reason to suppose he is activated by right principles and who is in other respects fully competent to the discharge of all the duties required of him.

Lowe goes on to compare Verling favourably with O'Meara and to stress that, unlike his predecessor, he had resisted designs from Longwood. Six months later, Lowe communicated with Verling directly, telling him of his 'fullest approbation' and again applauding him for rejecting French proposals. He asked his secretary to assure the doctor of 'the favourable sense he entertains of the general line of your proceeding' in a situation which he believed to be 'irksome and painful'. In a letter of the same month to Bathurst, he expressed the view that the surgeon was 'entitled to every consideration' and he confessed that he would miss his professional services following his departure. Entries in Gorrequer's diary show that Lowe was not averse to discussing additional pay or even a promotion for Verling.[16]

This was all a smokescreen. We have seen that, in reality, the Governor was highly suspicious of the surgeon and that he had missed no opportunity to smear him, even lowering himself to question Verling's family connections. His true opinion of Verling is confirmed in a conversation with Reade in early August 1820. Gorrequer is the ever-present fly on the wall. After a volley of invective directed at Nicholls, who had not seen Napoleon for three days, the Governor suddenly redirected his fire.

> He bewailed his unfortunate choice in him [Nicholls] and Great Gun Magnesia [Verling] who the moment he had found he could not become our Neighbour's [Napoleon's] attendant, became perfectly indifferent to anything else, particularly towards him, besides his being 'orbo' [blind].

Lowe sensed that the dislike was reciprocated. The Governor was not intuitive but, following a meeting with Verling in November 1819, he conceded to Bathurst that there appeared to be 'a gleam of dissatisfaction' in the doctor's manner. Verling was more than unhappy – he feared the destruction of his career. After a meeting with Lowe and Reade in March 1820, he writes ruefully in his journal, 'It is evident that I have made a powerful enemy.' Frustrated by the surgeon's repeated requests for orders relating to his attendance at Longwood, the Governor had stamped his foot on the ground in a characteristic attack of temper. That the two men parted company on anything other than good terms is proved by Verling's final journal entry for Sunday 23rd April 1820, his last day on St. Helena.

> I rode to leave my card at Plantation House; on my return I met Sir H. Lowe. He stopped me and asked when I sailed, I said in the evening, and that I had just called at Plantation House. He paused for some time and then informed me that he had just been writing to Lord Bathurst such a letter as would be sure to do away with any unfavourable impressions, which might have been made upon his mind, by my remaining upon the Island; to which I could not avoid replying that if such existed they must have arisen from erroneous views of my conduct. A long and angry conversation in consequence ensued which terminated however by my saying that since he had thought proper to

declare his opinion of the correctness of my conduct, I begged once more to return him my thanks for his former recommendations. He observed in parting, 'Well sir, I shall send my letter to Lord Bathurst.'

I saw Sir T. Reade in Town, who asked me if I had seen the Governor, and told me he had desired him to mention the letter to me. I asked him if he had seen the letter and he said that he had copied it, and that it was of such a nature as to remove every unfavourable impression. I made no further remark and we parted.

In the conversation with Sir H. Lowe, on my observing that I had not been treated with the confidence I expected, he remarked that I had not sought his confidence but had endeavoured to fill the situation in as independent a manner as possible. To this I made no answer, and do not conceive it any imputation on my conduct.

Verling's later affidavit in favour of Lowe in the legal proceedings against O'Meara was very likely provided out of expediency rather than because of any sympathy for the Governor's cause. This interpretation is justified by a comment in Gorrequer's journal for 1st February 1823, the time at which Lowe was canvassing support.

Mach [Lowe] speaking about the letter he had read a day or two before from Great Gun Magnesia [Verling] said it was a mean, low, vulgar, piece of cunning to elude giving him a direct answer to that from himself to him …

Verling had contrived to give Lowe as little ammunition as possible and the Governor erupted into one of his rages; 'He had himself behaved with the greatest candour and openness with him and that was the return he received; but he would yet make him answer the whole; he had not done with him.' According to Gorrequer, he ranted on for some time in a similar strain.[17]

Fortunately for Verling, the persisting rancour of the discredited ex-Governor did him no harm and, on his return home, he pursued a successful career in the army, rising to the rank of Inspector-General of the Ordnance Medical Department in 1850. He retired in 1854 and died at Cobh in 1858 in his seventy-first year. Verling has left no writings from his later years but there are clues that he still carried scars from St. Helena. It was common knowledge that the old doctor disliked discussing his time at Longwood. When Forsyth asked for his help in compiling his history of the captivity, Verling refused.[18]

Notes

1. Markham, JD, *Napoleon and Dr Verling on St. Helena*, p. viii; *Journeaux de Sainte-Hélène*, pp. 9–10, 64.

2. *Journeaux*, p. 9; Chaplin, A, *A St. Helena Who's Who*, pp. 131–2; Drew, R, *Commissioned Officers in the Medical Services of the British Army*, Vol. I, p. 209; Marchand, *Mémoires de Marchand*, Vol. II, pp. 197–8; Henry, W, *Trifles from my Portfolio*, Vol. I, p. 239.

3. Markham, pp. 15, 26, 36; Richardson, F, *Napoleon's Death: An Inquest*, pp. 132–3; Lutyens, E, *Letters of Captain Engelbert Lutyens*, p. 73; Kemble, J, *Napoleon Immortal*, p. 244; Gregory, D, *Napoleon's Jailer*, p. 149; Forsyth, W, *History of the Captivity of Napoleon*, Vol. II, pp. 621–4; Montholon, CJT de, *Récits de la Captivité*, Vol. II, pp. 345–8.

4. St. Denis, LE, *Napoleon from the Tuileries to St. Helena*, p. 217; Montholon, Comte de, *Lettres du Comte et de la Comtesse de Montholon*, p. 37; Markham, pp. 42–3, 47, 58, 73; Bertrand, Général, *Cahiers de Sainte-Hélène*, p. 216.

5. Markham, pp. 81–98, 64, 34; Bertrand, pp. 381–91; Masson, F, *Autour de Sainte-Hélène*, Vol. III, p. 200; Young, N, *Napoleon in Exile*, Vol. II, p. 124; St. Denis, p. 217; Marchand, Vol. II, pp. 196–8..

6. Masson, pp. 216–7; Markham, pp. 48–64, 130–1, 82, 143, 95; Forsyth, Vol. II, pp. 15, 51–2; Young, Vol. II, pp. 154–9; Bertrand, p. 391; Henry, Vol. I, p. 239.

7. Young, Vol. II, pp. 155–6; Markham, p. 109, 132, 85; Korngold, R, *The Last Years of Napoleon*, pp. 318–9; Gregory, p. 165.

8. Markham, p. 90; Gorrequer, Major G, *St. Helena during Napoleon's Exile*, pp. 125–7, 140–1.

9. Markham, pp. 56–9, 75, 48; Bertrand, pp. 314–8, 150; St. Denis, p. 194, Marchand, Vol. II, pp. 197–8; Montholon, *Lettres du Comte et de la Comtesse de Montholon*, p. 46.

10. Stokoe, J, *With Napoleon at St. Helena*, p. 82; Markham, pp. 113, 37, 91, 83, 135, 60–7, 165; Chaplin, p. 95; Bertrand, p. 377; Young, Vol. II, p. 157.

11. Bertrand, pp. 220–1; Markham, pp. 62, 96–7.

12. Markham, pp. 61, 155–9, 100–1.

13. Markham, pp. 107–113.

14. Markham, pp. 103–6, 117, 153.

15. Gonnard, P. *The Exile of St. Helena*, p. 100; Markham, pp. 102–15, 148–58; Young, Vol. II, pp. 160–1.

16. Forsyth, Vol. II, p. 82; Markham, pp. 118, 103, 128–9, 150–2; Chaplin, A, *Thomas Shortt*, p. 58; Gorrequer, pp. 144–6.

17. Gorrequer, pp. 123, 266; Markham, pp. 117–8, 155.

18. Chaplin, *A St. Helena Who's Who*, p. 132, Drew, Vol. I, p. 208; Chaplin, *Thomas Shortt*, pp. 56–7.

7

CORSICAN UPSTART

From August 1818, when O'Meara left St. Helena, until September of the following year, Napoleon saw no doctor except for the few visits by Stokoe. This was, of course, largely his own choice, but the British Government remained wary. The Liberal opposition might make political mischief, claiming that ministers had deliberately deprived the Emperor of proper medical supervision. Earl Bathurst was keen to end the impasse and, as early as the summer of 1818, an unexpected opportunity arose to solve the problem of Napoleon's physician once and for all.

Cardinal Fesch, Napoleon's uncle residing in Rome, had applied to The Prince Regent for permission to procure and send out a Roman Catholic priest to give spiritual succour to the exiles. This was prompted by the death of Cipriani – Napoleon's *maitre d'hôtel* had had to be buried in a Protestant ceremony overseen by a minister of the same religion. Bathurst had no objection to the appointment and he asked Lowe to inform the Emperor that permission had been given for the priest to reside at Longwood. In his letter to the Governor, Bathurst added that, as Napoleon had expressed his wish for a French surgeon of reputation and a cook, he had asked Fesch to also select 'proper persons' for these posts.

So it was that the selection of Napoleon's new doctor was left in the hands of a man of the Church. It was soon apparent that Cardinal Fesch was not up to the task. His choice of appropriate persons was compromised by his irrational belief that Napoleon had already escaped from St. Helena. The Cardinal and his sister were under the influence of a

German visionary who informed them that the Emperor had been miraculously removed from the island by angels; she was less certain where he was. Distracted by his supernatural leanings, Fesch made only laboured efforts to find his priest, doctor and cook. There was, however, an obvious candidate for the medical post. Las Cases, now in Europe, proposed Fourreau de Beaurégard (see Chapter 1). The French physician was still anxious to go to St. Helena to join his former patron and there is no doubt that Napoleon would have been delighted to have him at Longwood. Fesch now showed himself to be also influenced by earthly matters. Several members of Napoleon's family – Madame Mère, Jerome, Pauline, Lucien and Louis – owed their security to the Cardinal's reputation. He was under the control of a Church which was antagonistic to the ex-Emperor. If the Cardinal were to send a Frenchman of Napoleon's choice he could be accused of Bonapartism. There were elements in Paris who remembered that it was Napoleon who had given the priest his Cardinal's hat. Fesch extricated himself by rejecting Fourreau on the spurious grounds that he was not a surgeon and that he had made unreasonable demands for remuneration and assistance. The doctor had asked for a salary of 12,000 francs – the same pay as the humble naval surgeon Barry O'Meara – and to be accompanied by a valet and a pharmacist to prepare medicines.

Fesch now decided upon Francesco Antommarchi, a Corsican doctor, as the most suitable candidate. This was an astonishing rise from obscurity for the young man who was connected to Madame Mère through his friendship with a certain Simon Colonna di Leca who had attached himself to the Bonaparte family. It was Colonna who first suggested Antommarchi; Napoleon's mother supported him as he was Corsican and Fesch because he was not Fourreau. Also he was cheap. He settled for a salary of only 9,000 francs and asked for no servants or medical assistance. He appeared willing to exile himself on St. Helena indefinitely.[1]

Antommarchi was born in 1789 at Morsiglia, a small village in the extreme north of Corsica. All aspects of his life and all facets of his personality have been rubbished by historians. No other in the St. Helena saga has attracted so much odium; even Lowe has had his staunch supporters. Many attacks have started with the assumption that his medical qualifications were bogus; in Norwood Young's words, he was unsuitable for his unexpected promotion because he was 'neither a physician, nor a surgeon, nor a Frenchman, nor had he ever been in medical practice at all'. This statement is strictly correct only in the reference to his nationality. In recent times, Antommarchi has attracted a more sympathetic press and unbiased research has confirmed that he did have a respectable medical education. He first studied at Pisa and, in 1808, at the age of nineteen years, he obtained a diploma as a doctor of philosophy and medicine. This was not a high flying qualification but, in an age when many 'doctors' had no certificate at all, neither was it an insignificant achievement. He then moved to Florence to continue studies in surgery at the hospital of *Santa Maria Nuova*. Here he attended lectures in subjects such as physiology, pathology, operative surgery, obstetrics, chemistry and botany. His great passion was anatomy and he made the acquaintance of Professor Mascagni, one of the most renowned anatomists of the era.

The Napoleonic Wars were raging around him but he avoided conscription as an army doctor and, in 1812, the year of the Russian Campaign, he successfully submitted his surgical thesis on cataracts of the eye. It might have been expected that he would now pursue a career in surgery, but the prestigious post of Prosector was created at *Santa Maria Nuova*. This was what we would term an 'Anatomy Demonstrator', an essentially academic attachment in which the incumbent was expected to make the dissections, give lectures, and instruct the medical students. Supported by his patron Mascagni, Antommarchi successfully applied for the new position. This was a feather in his cap but it meant that the young doctor's practice was now composed of corpses rather than patients.[2]

Those who opposed Antommarchi's surprising appointment to St. Helena were quick to decry his lack of real experience. Planat de la Faye, Napoleon's old *officier d'ordonnance* from the Hundred Days and a friend of Fourreau, wrote to King Louis in protest. Antommarchi, he said, was 'a man without knowledge and was no more than a preparer of dissections in the Florence hospital amphitheatre'. News of the newcomer's shortcomings reached St. Helena before him and, shortly after his arrival, Bertrand interrogated him as to his actual experience of practical medicine and surgery. Amtommarchi, to his credit, made no attempt to exaggerate his achievements, giving the Grand Marshal an honest account of his training and his particular attachment to anatomy. It was soon common knowledge on the island that the Emperor had been sent an odd choice of doctor. Walter Henry comments in his memoirs, 'Signor Antommarchi had been a pupil of the celebrated Mascagni at Florence and was a good anatomist but not remarkable for a profound knowledge of the other therapeutic sciences.' Captain Charles Harrison wrote home that the new man 'had not had sufficient experience in the world'.

Antommarchi was hampered by more than just a lack of medical acumen. He was out of his depth in the corridors of Longwood. One historian has claimed, with some exaggeration, that he 'had not even the social qualities required, being merely an ignorant provincial from a village in a wild and remote corner of savage Corsica'. Napoleon believed that the inhabitants of Antommarchi's part of his homeland were conceited and headstrong. The young man was indeed vain and pompous and, despite his qualifications, quick to misunderstand. His lack of insight into his own professional and personal deficiencies, and his determination to further himself at all cost, meant that he sorely tested the patience of all around him. In Masson's words, 'He questioned nothing and considered himself everyone's equal'. Not only had the Emperor been sent a man who was more trained to perform his post-mortem than to keep him alive, but his new doctor trampled over the precious protocols that he carefully preserved at Longwood.

His loyal servant, Marchand, quickly realised that there was a problem.

It only took me only a few days after Dr Antommarchi's arrival to judge, if not his medical knowledge, at least his character. Never in his life having approached an eminent and powerful man such as the Emperor, he was ignorant of the ground on which he trod. When he arrived, he discussed the Emperor's health with me often and, every morning, he asked me about the night's events. I went so far as to warn him of things which might annoy the Emperor. 'Be more serious in front of the Emperor,' I told him. 'When you answer his questions; and be careful when you speak to Count de Montholon and the Grand Marshal, not to refer to them as Bertrand and Montholon; the Emperor addresses them so but you are not permitted to.'

Antommarchi thanked Marchand for the advice but did not necessarily act upon it.

His behaviour prior to his arrival on St. Helena suggested an unscrupulous side to his character. When his mentor Mascagni died in 1815, he left several posthumous works including *Prodromo della Grande Anatomia*, a fine collection of anatomical plates which had been produced at great expense. A local society of friends of the arts, including several Englishmen, undertook the task of publishing this great book in conjunction with the Mascagni family. Antommarchi, as a favoured pupil, was entrusted with the checking of the proofs. When he left Florence, he took a few copies of the first edition with him and, by now having assumed the title of

'Editor', he was determined to make a personal dedication of the work to the Prince Regent. The learned society in Florence believed him to be taking disproportionate credit, and one of the society's members, Sir John Webb, thought it necessary to write to the British Government to warn ministers that Antommarchi might be heading for England and that he was up to no good.

> The circumstances have led me to inform myself regarding Mr Antommarchi and I have it from reliable sources that he possesses more talent for intrigue than he does medical knowledge … he generally gives the impression of being more capable than he is.

It has been postulated that the Corsican was mentally ill; having 'some sort of delusional disturbance arising from a sense of persecution – that he was an incipient schizophrenic of the paranoid type'. Diagnoses of mental illness, particularly forms of paranoia, have been suggested for a few of the personalities on St. Helena but there is no need to invoke this in Antommarchi's case. His failings are too commonplace to require a psychiatric explanation.[3]

In January 1819, Cardinal Fesch had finally assembled his 'little caravan for St. Helena' in Rome. It was made up of Antommarchi, the Corsican priests Buonavita and Vignali, the valet Coursot, and a cook, Chandelier. Vignali, the younger of the two clerics, had attempted a short course of medical study. Fesch hoped that he might also act as Antommarchi's assistant but this ludicrous suggestion was ignored as the priest proved to be semi-literate, only able to read or write with great difficulty. Their departure from Rome was delayed and the time was used to hold a meeting to discuss Napoleon's health and particularly to devise a treatment plan which Antommarchi could implement upon his arrival. Scrutinising O'Meara's medical reports, five eminent professors from the university decided that the Emperor had both a liver disorder and scurvy, a disease caused by a poor diet lacking in vegetables. Antommarchi was not included in the discussions but he received the learned recommendations – 'the law, the prophesies…' – from which he was determined not to deviate. A copy was also given to Vignali, a circumstance that considerably annoyed Antommarchi.

In his memoirs, the doctor portrays himself as anxious to reach St. Helena, but Fesch, still convinced that Napoleon was a free man, was in no hurry and the party only left Rome on the first leg of the journey to

London on 25th February. They reached the English capital on 19th April, and Antommarchi used his connections with Mascagni and Napoleon to open every door available. He obtained John Stokoe's medical reports made during January and sought the advice of a number of respected British physicians regarding the most likely illness of his patient; it was agreed that it was probably hepatitis. He took the Mascagni work to Earl Bathurst who promised to pass it on to the Prince Regent. Antommarchi had also paid a visit to O'Meara – this was understandable but it was also bound to raise suspicions. The Corsican claimed that he was under surveillance by the police. The anatomical plates which he intended to take with him to St. Helena were seized by the British authorities and minutely inspected at the Colonial Office. Were the tendons and nerves secret escape routes? Could the lymphatic system be spelling out a secret message in hiero-glyphics? Antommarchi tends to exaggerate but his allegations that he was harassed and offered incentives not to proceed to St. Helena are credible.[4]

A further two and a half months elapsed before the party embarked at Gravesend; Jamestown was reached on 20th September 1819. Their first steps on the island were not auspicious. Cardinal Fesch had neither given the travellers a suitable letter of recommendation nor written to Napoleon about them. After all, he believed the prisoner to have broken his chains. Their decision to first dine with the Governor also created a poor impression at Longwood. Irate at not being given immediate news of his family in Europe, Napoleon initially refused to see any of them, and he ordered Bertrand to give them a grilling. Each had to submit a written statement of their name, age, family background, previous employment and current intentions to the Grand Marshal of the Palace. Only after he had subjected them to the indignity of providing this information did the Emperor deign to see them.[5]

The decision to attend the Governor before Napoleon was clumsy but it also reflected the reality that it was crucial for the newcomers to form a good relationship with the British authorities. The Corsican doctor must have been aware that Lowe was a prickly character with the capacity to make his life very uncomfortable. What was the attitude of the British Government to Antommarchi? We have seen that he was closely observed while in London but he appears to have convinced ministers that his loyalties were not mis-placed. In a letter to Lowe of 12th July 1819, Bathurst advises the Governor to 'avoid a scene' with Bonaparte. As for the new arrivals; Buonavita was 'very harmless' and 'The surgeon is reckoned very intelligent but I think will not be disposed to be troublesome, as he is apparently inclined to make advances to the Government by proposing to dedicate the work he is completing to the Prince Regent.'

Antommarchi may have satisfied the Colonial Secretary but his behaviour on the island was not designed to please Lowe. Either out of naivety or cussedness, the doctor railed against the restrictions imposed on all those who resided at Longwood. He airs his various grievances in his memoirs. He especially resented the Governor's intrusion into what he considered to be his private affairs. Shortly after their arrival on the island, Lowe insisted that the newcomers be searched and that their papers should be examined; this was a sensible precaution to prevent subversive material being smuggled into Longwood. The Governor would have been heavily criticised for not instituting such an elementary security measure if any such effort had later come to light. But Antommarchi is shocked: 'He even has the right to undress us!'

Once in residence at Longwood, he continued to test the Governor's patience by exploring the limits of the regulations. He accepted with ill grace the stipulation that he be accompanied by a British Officer when entering Jamestown or visiting the British military hospital on the island. In his later writings, he professes to be bewildered by these regulations and resorts to sarcasm. 'I had to be under the surveillance of an officer because there might have been an uprising among the sick, and a man as belligerent as me was capable of conquering England with a few dying men.' His illegal excursions brought him into conflict with the troops around Longwood. One evening, just before Christmas 1819, he remained in the wood near the house until long after dark and then attempted to pass the sentry who refused to allow him back in until the Orderly Officer permitted it. This incident culminated in a long letter of complaint from Antommarchi to Lowe in which the doctor claimed that he had been threatened by the sentry and moaned that was being treated as a common criminal. He was out so late simply because he wished to avoid the oppressive heat of the day, '... the force of the sun which shoots its rays perpendicularly upon our heads'. In Forsyth's words, Antommarchi was 'an apt pupil in the art of grumbling'.

The Governor replied with a placatory letter to the physician, promising to investigate the affair but also expressing surprise that he and the priests had not been made aware of the regulations pertaining to all the exiles. Thomas Reade undertook the enquiry and concluded that the sentry, a soldier of the 66th Regiment, had not threatened to attach his bayonet or charge his firelock but had only told the doctor that it was against his orders to let him pass. Lowe must have hoped that Antommarchi would now adopt a more dignified tone, but he was to be disappointed. The Governor informed Bathurst that Antommarchi had shown 'a disposition to complain from the outset'. He later noted that the 'Professor' appeared better reconciled to his situation but Lowe's intolerance and Antommarchi's self-pity were incompatible. When the doctor complained that his rooms were not properly furnished, Gorrequer recalls that the Governor reacted in a 'violent brutal way' and that he then 'kept raving for a while'. A puzzling entry from the secretary's diary for 15th January 1820 is of little significance in itself but it illustrates perfectly the pettiness of much of the sniping between the occupants of Longwood and Plantation House.

> The cunning turn given [by Lowe] to the desire in Foreign Magnesia's [Antommarchi's] letter, not to send him *pantalons d'été*, viz, that this was too cool a climate, when probably it was because he could have them so much cheaper; at the same time mentioning in his dispatch to Big Wig that thermometer never had been, since that Magnesia's arrival above 71, when it must have been certainly above 74 at least frequently here and at our Neighbour's [Longwood], and I have no doubt 75 or 76.

With even his choice of pantaloons being questioned, it was unthinkable that Antommarchi could escape a conspicuous role in the Governor's conspiracy theories. At the end of 1820, we have, again in Gorrequer's characteristic words, 'Mach's observation about the Jack Corse Magnesia [Antommarchi] being *vergognoso* [abashed] at meeting with Mach, and having a guilty look'. There followed the usual tirade by Lowe, in which the physician was accused of hatching some yet undiscovered plot, possibly involving the exaggeration of Napoleon's illness.[6]

It was understandable that Antommarchi should seek society outside the limits of Longwood and natural that he was drawn towards the other doctors on the island, particularly the Anglo-Irish Army and Navy medical staff who were in close proximity. He made a reasonable first impression on Verling who describes him as appearing about thirty years of age and as being 'rather a gentleman-like man, mild and talkative'. Antommarchi was keen to maintain his professional contact with the artillery surgeon and he urged him to stay on at Longwood. However, when the Corsican tried to socialise with his fellow doctors, he was snubbed.

In early December 1819, he sent out a number of dinner invitations. These were delivered via the Governor's office. Archibald Arnott pleaded a prior engagement, Matthew Livingstone was unwell, and James Verling had a reason to extricate himself. Walter Henry received a verbal invitation but he too was unable to accept. Either the doctors' excuses were genuine, or they were averse to spending time with their foreign colleague, or they had been warned off by Lowe. Antommarchi decided it must be the latter and he sent the Governor a stinging letter in which he attributed the surgeons' refusal to the 'universal terror impressed on the minds of the inhabitants of this island'. The young physician had his faults but he was observant and not entirely stupid. Lowe rebuked him for his 'unprovoked and indecorous attack' and accused him of naivety. 'You can, Sir, have had no opportunity to trace the real causes which influence the conduct of individuals on this island.' The affair perturbed the Governor enough for him to relate the details to Bathurst. He concluded his account as follows.

> By the letter which was addressed to Dr Antommarchi, dated 4th October, a great facility was afforded him of communication with the medical gentlemen on the island, in matters relating to his own profession. From this moment he appeared to cultivate their acquaintance with great assiduity – and although I saw no objection to the ordinary relations of society between him and them, yet, the attempts to form a particular society with them alone, evidenced a disposition to wander from the principle upon which I had granted each facility for communication with them.

So Antommarchi's professional contacts were condoned but any attempt by him to befriend the other doctors was viewed with deep suspicion. Lowe may not have actually forbidden the doctors to attend the dinner party but they knew that accepting the invitation would do them little good. From this point on, Antommarchi's contact with his fellow medics was largely of a professional nature. Livingstone spoke no Italian and found him difficult to communicate with anyway. The Corsican was accompanied by Arnott during his visits to the hospitals and was to become more closely linked with him in the final days of Napoleon's life. The two men disagreed over the diagnosis of the Emperor's illness but there was no real antagonism.[7]

Antommarchi's plan for a convivial dinner was more likely prompted by boredom than by any ulterior motive. Marchand comments that the young doctor was the man who had most difficulty adjusting to the monotony of life at Longwood. Once the novelty of his situation had worn thin, St. Helena must have been remarkably dull compared with London and Florence. The Emperor urged him to travel around the island and Antommarchi took him at his word, spending long hours exploring on horseback or on foot. His restlessness was such that he was rarely at Longwood but was more likely to be found on the streets of Jamestown or elsewhere. To help relieve the ennui, he also indulged himself in a number of what one Victorian author terms 'sentimental diversions'.

At first, the other exiles took a sympathetic view of the new arrival. Montholon thought him a 'fine young man' whose only problem was that he was ten years too young for his position. Familiarity bred contempt and Montholon's later opinions are less flattering. He thought the doctor to be frivolous and presumptuous and wrote to his wife that he found Antommarchi's behaviour inexplicable; 'Nothing can put him right … the smell of a skirt attracts him so much that he ignores everything else.' Bertrand also became exasperated with the physician's immaturity. In early 1821, Antommarchi unnecessarily involved himself in a contretemps between the Grand Marshal and Napoleon – tension had been created by the suggestion that the Countess and the children might leave the island. Bertrand confronted the doctor and recorded his reaction in his journal. 'Antommarchi then became offensive and called me names. When I asked for an explanation, he refused to say anything further and merely whistled.'[8]

It was most important for Antommarchi to make himself acceptable to Napoleon. In fairness to the doctor, the Emperor was probably prejudiced against him before his arrival on St. Helena. Despite his apparent isolation, Napoleon was surprisingly well informed and was aware of Antommarchi's lack of worldliness and real medical experience; it is possible that friends of Fourreau had written letters to the island. His initial contact with the young physician gave him no reason to change his opinion. At their first meeting, the Emperor quizzed Antommarchi about his family in Corsica and his medical studies. He appeared satisfied with the doctor's replies but he revealed his true thoughts to Bertrand.

> I am very unfortunate not to have a doctor … If Madame Mère had spent two, three, or six thousand livres, she could have sent me Vacca or Locatelli [two famed Italian physicians]. Vacca was brought up in France and speaks French. But Antommarchi is uneducated. He is a most unreliable man. He repeats what he hears which is a violation of the first principle of his

profession. He puts Madame Bertrand's back up. If I should say to him: 'How is the Grand Marshal?' he would at once repeat it in such a way as to make it sound an insult. Besides, it is his misfortune, poor man, to be an indifferent doctor. Also, he fails to grasp any of the finer points of a conversation, and he doesn't know French.

The Emperor remarked to Montholon that his family had sent him savages.

Napoleon was driven to distraction by Antommarchi's unfortunate combination of ignorance and conceit. Walter Henry claims that when the Emperor discovered that he had a better grasp of chemistry than his doctor, he curtly dismissed him from the room, '*Va-t-en … bête!*' He also exploded when Antommarchi responded to his advice that the doctor should discuss the management of tropical disease on the island with his British colleagues by saying that he knew more than them and that they could tell him nothing. From the French perspective, Antommarchi's redeeming feature was that he had not been selected by Lowe. Probably mainly for this reason, added to the fact that he had no serious alternative, Napoleon agreed to employ his countryman as his personal doctor. Antommarchi was to reside in O'Meara's old quarters.[9]

The true state of Napoleon's health at this time is uncertain as we only have the reports from Longwood and these tend to exaggerate any minor indisposition. He was certainly not acutely unwell. At times, he was cheerful, whistling or singing, but he was also pale and he was becoming increasingly unfit and flabby. O'Meara had previously raised concern as to the prisoner's sedentary lifestyle. To encourage him to leave his room, Antommarchi and others suggested that he take exercise on horseback but the Emperor was unenthusiastic. The doctor then proposed gardening; this was not a new idea as Montholon had made a plan for enlarging the garden earlier in the year. In large part due to Antommarchi's persuasion, Napoleon decided to suspend his game of hide and seek with the Orderly Officer and, from early October 1819, he spent much of his time working out of doors. Captain Nicholls was delighted by this turn of events.

The General was in his morning gown amidst the people at work, directing them. Takes a spade sometimes and begins to potter – sends messages to me for carts, shovels and spades. God send he may always continue in this humour during my residence at Longwood.

Hudson Lowe and his allies strained to find something sinister in this burst of physical activity. When the Marquis de Montchenu, the only Foreign Commissioner left on the island, was offered some haricot beans from the garden, he had a choice of the green or white varieties and accepted a mixture. Lowe later advised, in all seriousness,

> Whether the *haricots blancs* and *haricots verts* bear any reference to the *drapeau blanc* of the Bourbons and the *habit vert* of General Bonaparte himself, and the livery of his servants at Longwood, I am unable to say; but the Marquis de Montchenu, it appears to me, would have acted with more propriety if he had declined receiving either, or limited himself to a demand for white alone.

Whatever the political significance of the vegetables, Napoleon benefited greatly from all the spadework in the fresh air. His morale was boosted by the end result; a well watered and well planted garden on three sides of the house. Although his gardening suggestion was not original and had not required any medical expertise, Antommarchi was keen to take all the credit for the improvement in his charge's health and mood, writing to Colonna in July 1820.

> It is ten months since I arrived on this island and I can assure you that I have not passed one day or night without providing my famous patient with all the help which my zeal and my knowledge have made possible. I found him affected by chronic hepatitis of a most serious nature; the care that I have given him appears to have been crowned with success.[10]

Shortly after Antommarchi sent this exaggerated and self-congratulatory letter, the health of the Emperor did start to cause real concern. The physician felt obliged to write a more pessimistic note to Colonna speaking of a 'very grave relapse' and referring to the appearance of symptoms including pain in the liver and the leg.

Napoleon remained highly sceptical of his doctor's abilities and was very reluctant to receive any treatment from him. When, in October, Antommarchi proposed the placing of vesicatories, a sort of blistering plaster, on his arms, Napoleon refused, commenting that he was already torturing him enough. Bertrand and Montholon talked him into it and he eventually allowed Antommarchi to apply the plasters, although Marchand describes him as holding out his arms in repugnance. Napoleon's reservations were fully justified as the doctor botched the procedure, failing to shave the skin and then forming shapeless vesicatories which were uncomfortable and left the patient without the use of his hands. The Emperor's mood deteriorated as he was first unable to eat his dinner and then was told that the perpetrator could not be found. When Antommarchi belatedly returned to Longwood, Napoleon laid into him, complaining that he had been treated worse than 'the poorest man in a hospital'. Why had the doctor blistered both arms at once thereby completely disabling him? When Antommarchi tried to interrupt, the Emperor cut him short; 'Go away. You are an ignoramus and I a greater one for having let you do this.'

According to Marchand, the vesicatories actually had some good effect, at least restoring his appetite, but the damage had been done. The incident had confirmed Napoleon's worst suspicions regarding his doctor and it was the start of a deterioration in their relationship well summarised by Saint-Denis.

> During the first phase of his illness, the Emperor frequently sent for Antommarchi. When one of us went to his quarters to tell him that the Emperor wanted him, he was most often away from Longwood or at Madame Bertrand's. When it was reported to the Emperor that Antommarchi was out, he would show his dissatisfaction. As soon as the doctor was informed that they had been looking for him he would hurry back and the Emperor would not fail to give him a dressing down. He would very often go to Madame Bertrand's in the evening, and that was precisely the time the Emperor would send for him. Once, the Emperor, very irritated at having to wait for him for a long time, said to him, 'you come to me as though you were paying a thirty-sous visit. You are here in my service and at my order. If Larrey were here he would not leave the head of my bed; he would sleep there, on the carpet. When I send for you it is because I need you. You ought to be at home, and not somewhere else,' etc. Antommarchi, after such a scolding, ought to have paid attention to it, but, whether he was bored by remaining in his room or for some other reason, he still continued to go away, which was the case the whole time the Emperor's illness lasted, and so this conduct, which was wholly unreasonable, increased the Emperor's ill humour more and more.

Napoleon's reference to Dominique Larrey, his senior military surgeon who he once described as 'the most virtuous man that I have ever known', is poignant. It must have been incredible to him that he was now being attended to by a recalcitrant young man with virtually no clinical acumen. When Antommarchi's mind was turned to medical matters, it was usually more with comic than with therapeutic effect. Engelbert Lutyens, the Orderly Officer, recalls the doctor wandering around Jamestown looking for ivory balls. Well aware of Antommarchi's penchant for play, the British presumed that he wanted billiard balls whereas it later transpired that he required smaller spheres to insert into a wound.[11]

At the start of 1821, Napoleon was deeply depressed both by his illness and his doctor. He now walked in his garden leaning on Antommarchi's arm; 'Put away your pills. Let us cease to grope our way blindfold, and trust to nature; that is much better ... The devil take your medicines. If I can perspire and the wounds in my thigh open anew, I am cured.' The Emperor still had the scar of the thigh injury he received at Toulon as a young man. He vented much of his frustration on his doctor. When Antommarchi visited him in the early hours of the morning, there was a 'scene' lasting two hours. Napoleon informed Bertrand that the surgeon was 'nothing but a great rogue, a rascal, a good-for-nothing'. The Grand Marshal, he cried, should appoint Antommarchi as 'first lackey' to his wife – Napoleon was irritated that the physician was conscientiously attending the Countess, who had a miscarriage around this time.

Demoralised by this constant stream of invective, Antommarchi approached Thomas Reade at the end of January and announced his desire to return home. He almost certainly took this step without confiding in the Emperor or the other Longwood residents. Lowe communicated the request to Montholon who informed Napoleon. Although he cannot have been much distressed at the prospect of losing his incompetent physician, he was irritated that Antommarchi had grasped the initiative and he immediately dictated a note to Montholon for Lowe's attention. In it, he complained of Antommarchi's shortcomings and demanded a doctor from Paris, preferably one of the older experienced army doctors, men such as Desgenettes, Percy or Larrey. He did not want Cardinal Fesch to be involved again – the choice could be left in the hands of the British and French governments.

On the following morning, Antommarchi formally submitted his resignation to Montholon with an expression of regret that he had been unable to win the confidence of the Emperor. Napoleon dictated the following withering response for the Count to give to the doctor.

> Monsieur, The Emperor, taking into consideration the wish which you have expressed to me [Montholon] in your letter of 31st January, authorises you to present yourself to the English officer commanding at St. Helena so that he can facilitate your departure. If it is possible that he could place you on the same vessel as the Abbé Buonavita, your assistance will be of great help to this disabled elderly man during such a long hard voyage. During the fifteen months that you have been on the island, you have given His Majesty no confidence in your moral character; you can be of no use to him with respect to his illness, and your staying here for a few more months would be without object.

The priest was returning to Europe because of ill health.[12]

Montholon describes Napoleon's response to Antommarchi as 'hard' but there is evidence in Bertrand's journal that, despite the uncompromising tone of the letter, the Emperor still retained some affection for the young doctor.

> He [Napoleon] told Antommarchi that he could go back with Abbé Buonavita. The doctor replied that he would do whatever the Emperor desired, but that he felt that he had done nothing for which to reproach himself. The Emperor then patted him and gave him a slap on the shoulder.

Neither the Grand Marshal nor the Count had much faith in Antommarchi but, as there was no immediate prospect of recruiting a new doctor from Europe, they now faced the alarming prospect of the Emperor having no medical assistance at all. They decided to launch a charm offensive on both patient and doctor to ensure Antommarchi's retention until some other arrangement was in place. This seemed to work as, at the beginning of February, Napoleon had mellowed enough to inform Antommarchi that, although he had asked for another physician, he could stay on if he wanted to; he would have to make up his own mind. The Emperor advised the doctor that he must improve his behaviour, as it was this rather than his potions which had caused the unpleasantness. He gave Antommarchi a few hours to make his decision.

Montholon and Bertrand coaxed the physician to accept this olive branch by appealing both to his ego and his mercenary instincts. The Count flattered him, telling him that he had actually behaved rather well. The Grand Marshal confided to him that he had behaved 'honourably' and pointed out that the sacrifice he was making would bring him great rewards. If the doctor stayed on St. Helena the Emperor would ensure him a brilliant future, all the more so when he returned to private practice.

Antommarchi was swayed by this intense courtship and Montholon helped him to draft a letter to the Emperor stating that he had resolved to remain in his post until a suitable replacement was found. Although he had achieved the desired result and averted a crisis, Bertrand remained cynical regarding the doctor's true motivation.

> He will soon be leaving. He will have benefited from the situation. He says that fundamentally one is forced to be a slave here; that he prefers a little more happiness and peace of mind to honours, and that he will write his book in Europe.[13]

During March there was another worrying development. The Emperor was becoming progressively weaker. Antommarchi remained elusive and Montholon expressed disgust that the doctor still failed to take his patient's symptoms seriously.

Napoleon, the Count wrote to his wife, could not live much longer. 'I have never seen anybody so much like a corpse as he now is.' Yet, when the doctor did put in an appearance, he was apparently unperturbed. On 20th March the Emperor had been ill during the night but he only agreed to see Antommarchi with reluctance. The physician felt his pulse and indicated to Montholon, with 'a smile of incredulity' that it was normal. The clear implication was that the nocturnal symptoms had been exaggerated and that there was little to worry about.

In fact, Antommarchi was playing a double part. He fully appreciated the seriousness of the situation but he had decided on a strategy of concealment. This attempt to hide the severity of the disease from the patient and his companions was misguided but it was not a practice unique to Antommarchi. Many doctors of the time advocated this paternalistic approach as the best policy. Antommarchi's real opinion of the Emperor's state was contained in a letter to Colonna which he handed to Buonavita. He believed him to have worsening chronic hepatitis.

> In order to exculpate myself from all responsibility, I declare to you, to all the Imperial Family, and to the whole world, that the disease under which the Emperor is labouring is an effect of the nature of the climate, and that the symptoms it exhibits are of the most serious kind.[14]

Unfortunately for Antommarchi, it was not so easy for him to evade accountability; he was still Napoleon's personal physician and he could hardly watch him die without attempting some form of medical treatment. On the other hand, he was impeded not only by his lack of therapeutic experience but also by the awkwardness of his patient and the uselessness of almost all of the drugs in the early nineteenth-century pharmacopoeia. The Emperor was convinced that many drugs, mercury for instance, did more harm than good and we now know that he was right. Antommarchi needed courage to write a prescription.

Napoleon started to vomit and also developed a fever. His doctor suggested an emetic. It appears strange that the remedy should be designed to make the symptoms worse but emetics were a vital part of the so-called 'antiphlogistic regimen' which was purported to rid the body of impurities causing disease. Other commonly used agents included laxatives and drugs designed to increase perspiration. Napoleon remained dubious and he initially refused the medicine before allowing himself to be talked into it by Bertrand and Montholon. On 22nd March, a quarter of a grain of tartar emetic was administered in a glass of lemonade. The patient immediately became violently sick and rolled about on the floor in agony. Antommarchi insisted that it was the correct treatment but that the dose had been too strong. Unsurprisingly, Napoleon refused any repeat performance; instead he resorted to his own favourite cure, liquorice in water. Showing it to Montholon, he commented astutely, 'If it doesn't do me any good, it will do me no harm.' Marchand says that Antommarchi was present and that he smiled at the Emperor's words, and restated the case for another emetic. 'Why don't you go for a long walk and take the emetic yourself!' Despite this rebuke, the doctor was intent on imposing his treatment on his patient and he later whispered to Marchand that he intended to smuggle the emetic into the Emperor's drinks. The loyal valet was horrified and refused to take part in the scheme. Napoleon, as usual, was alert to all possibilities and he had ordered his butler, Pierron, to check that his drinks were not doctored. Montholon relates what happened next.

Confident he had taken adequate precautions, he was going to drink some lemonade, when, stopping with the glass between his lips, he said to me, 'But there seems to be a strange smell. Are you really sure that nothing has been mixed with this lemonade?'

– I am sure of it, I responded; but it is better for me to check. Your Majesty must not drink it. I am going to drink it; we will soon see.

He gave me the glass and I drank. Ten minutes later, I was struck by a feeling like sea-sickness and I only just had time to get to my room.

Napoleon was furious and he tore a strip off Marchand who was almost certainly innocent. He then called for the real culprit but Antommarchi was not at Longwood. When he returned in the evening, the Emperor had cooled a little but he still called him an assassin. The surgeon tried to redeem himself by saying that by refusing medical help the Emperor was endangering his life.

Well, Sir, do I owe you an account? Do you not believe that for me death would be a blessing from heaven? I do not fear it, I will do nothing to hasten it but I will not grasp at straws to survive.

The doctor was curtly dismissed with a threat that he would not be consulted again. In fact, his ostracism lasted only forty-eight hours. Marchand was ordered to throw the remaining drinks out of the window.[15]

Napoleon was more disenchanted than ever by Antommarchi's incompetence and slyness. In a deliberate slight to the Corsican physician, he asked Vignali to feel his pulse. After urgent solicitations from his entourage, he agreed to see another British doctor, Archibald Arnott. Antommarchi, who had encouraged this second opinion, met with Arnott on 25th March and discussed Napoleon's case, giving him details of the symptoms and the treatments used. On 1st April, the Emperor gave his consent for the British surgeon to see him in person – we will return to Arnott.

Having a more experienced medical colleague at his side must have been a considerable relief to Antommarchi but, as he continued to pay his own visits, he was still in the firing line. A week later, an incident occurred which discredited both doctor and patient. Since Madame Bertrand's miscarriage, Antommarchi had been seeing her regularly. It is unlikely that there was anything improper in their relationship but Napoleon, whose own advances to the Countess had been rejected, suspected an illicit liaison and he resented it. When Antommarchi attended him at 7.30 in the morning, the Emperor flew into a rage, shouting that he should have been there much earlier and that he should pay less attention to the Grand Marshal's wife. Whilst Antommarchi was still in the room, Napoleon turned to the newly arrived Bertrand and continued his diatribe against the doctor.

> Very well, let him spend all his time with his whores,' Napoleon said. '*Qu'il les foute par devant, par derrière, par la bouche et les oreilles*, but get rid of that man for me, he is stupid, ignorant, pretentious, and utterly devoid of any sense of honour … I'll have no more of Antommarchi … I have made my will: in it I have left Antommarchi twenty francs to buy himself a length of rope with which to hang himself.

The Emperor repeated five or six times that Madame Bertrand was a whore and again slated Antommarchi for never being available when he was needed. After the shaken doctor had left, Napoleon informed Bertrand, in front of Marchand and Saint-Denis, that he was wrong to allow his wife to be Antommarchi's lover. The Grand Marshal listened to this obscene drivel without comment.

Antommarchi later informed Bertrand that he was not prepared to remain in his room for long periods and that he would not act as a 'nurse'. He had decided to leave St. Helena and he was going to Plantation House to request permission whether Napoleon liked it or not. When he informed Lowe of his wishes, the Governor was unenthusiastic, expressing his regret that Antommarchi was not able to continue his work with Arnott's help. The physician protested that he was in complete accord with his colleague and that the problem was the Emperor himself, who treated his doctor as a menial and abused him. Lowe replied, 'But Signor Professor, it is necessary always to consider the temperament of the patient and circumstances of the case.' Unimpressed by this insight, Antommarchi again begged to be allowed to leave but the Governor stalled, commenting that the matter required careful deliberation and that he would have to refer it to England. The doctor returned to Longwood where he lied to Bertrand that he had the approval he required.

Napoleon's violent rages were often followed by a desire for instant reconciliation. As soon as he had tired of insulting Madame Bertrand, he suddenly declared to her husband that he wished Antommarchi to continue to attend him; indeed, he ordered it. The Grand Marshal and Count were by now well used to these paroxysmal changes of mood and, after some cajoling and exhortations that he show a little more devotion, Antommarchi was once more brought back into the fold. Keen to maintain the status quo, the

Grand Marshal defended the physician, pointing out to Napoleon that he had attended him several times in the night and that he had only overslept because his Chinese boy had forgotten to wake him at six. Bertrand, who must have been distressed himself, explained that the doctor had been particularly upset by the invitation to buy some rope to hang himself. 'He has been in a great hurry,' replied Napoleon.[16]

The Emperor may have resigned himself to Antommarchi's presence but he was ever vigilant, suspecting new malpractice by his doctor. The patient was ill and tetchy and the young man's clumsy manners were the perfect catalyst for his temper. When Napoleon gave Vignali instructions that he wished to be treated as a Catholic at the end of his life, Marchand and Antommarchi witnessed the scene. Suddenly, the ill man noticed that his doctor was smiling and he sent him from the room with an admonition for being heartless. 'Has anyone been worse cared for than me by him?' he asked his valet. On another occasion, Antommarchi was unable to suppress a laugh when Napoleon presented a book to Arnott with an expression of his admiration for 'brave men of all nations'. The Emperor shot him a disapproving glance and, on the following day, attacked him again for his incivility. The physician squirmed and made the feeble excuse that he had been reminded of a childhood nursery rhyme. There were also rumours that Antommarchi was being indiscreet, making irreverent comments regarding his patient's toilet to the Longwood servants. Napoleon took the matter seriously enough to force the doctor to sign a declaration that he would repeat nothing of what he heard or saw during his consultations.

It is remarkable that Napoleon tolerated Antommarchi right up to the end. Marchand notes that his master had a 'habitual spirit of generosity which allowed him to forgive'; this attribute was sorely tested by his countryman. Although Antommarchi was not banished, in the last few weeks of his life the Emperor increasingly looked to others, notably Arnott. He was also sidelined by his medical peers. He was allowed to accompany the regimental surgeon to the patient's room but when, on 21st April, Arnott consulted with two other British doctors as to the best course of action, the Corsican was excluded.[17]

Napoleon had only two weeks to live. Probably feeling remorse at his earlier behaviour, Antommarchi moved his bed to the library next to the Emperor's room, keeping a constant vigil. Montholon and Bertrand, not for the first time, pleaded with the dying man to allow his physician to attend him. He relented with ill grace. 'What am I to do? He may not possess a bad soul but he is an imbecile.' On the 26th he offered his arm to Antommarchi for the first time in several days. By the following day, the doctor's rehabilitation appeared complete as the Emperor, detecting the regret in his face, was suddenly friendly towards him. 'You will be pleased with what I do for you ... I shall leave you 100,000 francs and I shall recommend you to the Empress.' Marchand witnessed Antommarchi's profound appreciation.

As the Emperor's energy ebbed away, he became less lucid and more inconsistent in his demands. On the 29th, he angrily refused Montholon's attempts to call Antommarchi. The physician was then allowed back at the death bed with Arnott. Saint-Denis describes the scene.

> The two doctors, the Grand Marshall, General de Montholon, Marchand, the members of the household were ranged in great part before the bed, and some on the opposite side; they all had their eyes fixed on the Emperor's face, which had no other movement than the spasmodic motion given by the hiccoughs. It was Antommarchi who, standing by the head of the bed, gave him a little water to moisten his mouth, first with a spoon, then with a sponge. He would frequently feel the Emperor's pulse, either at his wrist or at the jugular vein [in the neck].

Montholon claims that, in his last moments, Napoleon preferred that he should wet his lips and not the doctor. When the Emperor died on 5th May, it was Antommarchi who closed his eyes.[18]

The death of his patient did not mark the end of Antommarchi's part. He was embroiled both in the post-mortem and in the creation of a death mask. He departed the island on 13th May 1821. Napoleon's final judgement on the only non-British doctor to tend him during his exile was contained in his will. This was dictated to Montholon and completed in mid April. To the members of his household, he left the following: Montholon 2,000,000 francs; Bertrand 500,000; Marchand 400,000; Saint-Denis, Noverraz, Pierron, Vignali 100,000 each; Archambault 50,000; Coursot and Chandelier 25,000. The only Longwood resident to receive nothing was Antommarchi.

As he lay on his death bed, Napoleon continued to think over his legacy and he made a number of codicils involving additional bequests. One of these was a recommendation to Marie-Louise to pay Antommarchi a pension of 6,000 francs. This was a concession to the doctor but it was still a snub when one considers that Vignali, the uneducated priest who arrived on the island at the same time as Antommarchi, had received a lump sum of

100,000 francs. The will and the additional codicils proved difficult to enact as the Emperor had made promises beyond the funds available to his banker Laffitte. The decision of the arbitrators, made two years after Napoleon's death, was that the sum should be divided up with varying reductions; the Longwood domestics were paid almost in full and most others around two thirds of the original amount.

Antommarchi had not forgotten the Emperor's promise to award him 100,000 francs and he obtained a note from the executors of the will – Montholon, Bertrand and Marchand – confirming that the verbal offer had been made. As even those included in the formal will were not in receipt of the amounts specified, Antommarchi was fighting a lost cause and he neither received any lump sum nor any pension from Marie-Louise. His only reward was expenses to allow his return to Tuscany and a smaller pension of 5,000 francs payable annually from the remaining Laffitte funds. He had obtained something but his ambition to leave St. Helena a rich man had been dashed.[19]

This was not the end of his misfortune. On his return to Europe, he was immediately in conflict with Mascagni's family who believed that he had no right to publish the *Grande Anatomia*. Its appearance brought him further criticism. The death mask of the Emperor that he claimed to have fashioned on St. Helena was thought to be either a fake or of poor quality. Depressed by the failure of his various projects, he sought a way out by volunteering his medical services to the forces of the Polish Insurrection in 1831. He was appointed Head Surgeon in a hospital for officers and then Inspector General of Military Hospitals in Warsaw but he soon quarrelled with his Polish surgical colleagues and with the Medical Faculty and his resignation was promptly accepted. After an unsuccessful period in Paris, he left for America in 1836 to seek his elusive fortune and he died at Santiago in Cuba two years later at the age of forty nine.

Antommarchi's reputation was tainted and the obituaries and subsequent biographical entries were not kind. Some of the press was unfair. In Hoefer's *Biographie Générale* it is insinuated that two of the works that he was supposed to have written, one on cholera and the second on lymphatic vessels, had never been seen. More recent research has shown that these writings do exist. To a large degree, Antommarchi contributed to his poor reputation by leaving an account of his experiences on St. Helena – *Les derniers moments de Napoléon* of 1825 – which was conceited and dishonest. It is uncertain whether the book was actually written on the island or produced from notes that were edited following his return to Europe. The account is confusing, often given with no reference to chronology. There is general agreement that it is a very poor historical record. Philippe Gonnard comments acidly that 'It is impossible to put much faith in a witness who does not appear very intelligent and has so little regard for the truth.' Masson dismisses the book as 'pure fiction' and Lord Roseberry describes it as 'worthless and mendacious'.

The only consistent theme in the work is Antommarchi's determination to portray himself in the best possible light. With his innate love of theatrical effect, he alternates contrived monologues with flowery prose. There are innumerable discrepancies with other more reliable contemporary accounts. It is strange that during the periods when Napoleon refused to see him, the doctor is nonetheless able to give a detailed relation of the progress of the disease and the conversations of the patient. Gonnard generously suggests that Antommarchi had muddled up his dates. This does not excuse the frequent omissions of fact. Among the tedious record of the single-minded devotion of the author and the unceasing gratitude of his patient, there is nothing of the arguments with Napoleon nor of his attempts to leave his employment. On a day on which it is well documented that the Emperor refused to see Antommarchi, the physician blithely informs us that the patient accepted one of his remedies with the words, 'You can measure by my resignation the gratitude I feel for you.'

Napoleon was very likely resigned to his fate; Antommarchi was crass enough to interpret this as a sign of gratitude and dishonest enough to insert words into the Emperor's mouth. To pad out his work to two volumes, he also borrowed from the writings of others, notably from O'Meara and Las Cases. Antommarchi's book was not a great success at the time and it is rarely quoted now. In using the doctor's own writings sparingly in telling his story, I have followed Gonnard's pithy advice: 'The historian need not therefore count on Antommarchi's book for obtaining any information.'[20]

Notes
1. Masson, F, *Autour de Sainte-Hélène*, Vol. III, pp. 214–232; Forsyth, W, *History of the Captivity of Napoleon*, Vol. I, p. 628; Young, N, *Napoleon in Exile*, Vol. II, pp. 166–9; Ganière, P, *Napoléon à Sainte-Hélène: La Mort de L'Empereur L'Apothéose*, pp. 80–1; Korngold, R, *The Last Years of Napoleon*, p. 346; Paoli, F, *Le Dr Antommarchi ou le Secret du Masque de Napoléon*, pp. 86–8.
2. Young, Vol. II, p. 167; Paoli, pp. 56–60, 67–72; Chaplin, A, *A St. Helena Who's Who*, pp. 49–50.
3. Masson, Vol. III, pp. 230–1; Bertrand, Général, *Cahiers de Sainte-Hélène*, p. 397; Glover, G, *Wellington's Lieutenant Napoleon's Gaoler*, p. 288; Young, Vol. II, p. 167; Gonnard, P, *The*

Exile of St. Helena, pp. 108–9; Marchand, *Mémoires de Marchand*,
Vol. II, pp. 300-1; Masson, F, *Napoleon at St. Helena*, pp. 89–90; Richardson, F, *Napoleon's
Death: An Inquest*, p. 147; Kemble, J, *Napoleon Immortal*, pp. 248–9;
Henry, W, *Trifles from my Portfolio*, Vol. II, p. 4.

4. Young, Vol. II, p. 169; Masson, *Autour de Sainte-Hélène*, Vol. III, pp. 232–3; Antommarchi, F,
Les Derniers Moments de Napoléon, Vol. I, pp. 11–14, 23–33; Richardson, p. 148.

5. Paoli, p. 99; Ganière, p. 87; Masson, *Autour de Sainte-Hélène*, p. 234; Young, Vol. II, p. 171.

6. Forsyth, Vol. II, pp. 630, 93, 83–4; Antommarchi, Vol. I, pp. 56, 107–8, 239; Bertrand, pp.
402–4; Markham, JD, *Napoleon and Dr Verling on St. Helena*, p. 159; Gorrequer, Major G,
St. Helena during Napoleon's Exile, pp. 142, 155, 187.

7. Markham, pp. 99–100; Lowe Papers 20128 ff. 491–4; Forsyth, Vol. II, pp. 93–4; Kemble, p.
250; Korngold, p. 389.

8. Marchand, Vol. II, pp. 279–80; Masson, *Autour de Sainte-Hélène*, Vol. III, p. 238;
Montholon, CJT de, *Récits de la Captivité*, Vol. II, pp. 428, 360, 482–3; Gonnard,
p. 108; Montholon, Comte de, *Lettres du Comte et de la Comtesse de Montholon*, p. 78;
Bertrand, General, *Napoleon at St. Helena*, p. 1.

9. Paoli, p. 99; Bertrand, *Napoleon at St. Helena*, p. 33; Montholon, *Lettres du Comte et de la
Comtesse de Montholon*, p. 61; Richardson, pp. 147–8; Henry, W, *Surgeon Henry's Trifles*, p.
178; St. Denis, LE, *Napoleon from the Tuileries to St. Helena*, p. 258; Bertrand, *Cahiers de
Sainte-Hélène*, p. 398; Marchand, Vol. II, p. 234.

10. Lowe Papers 20145 ff. 34, 82; Young, Vol. II, pp. 177–87; Korngold, p. 349; Masson,
Autour de Sainte-Hélène, Vol. III, p. 237.

11. Marchand, Vol. II, p. 280; Young, Vol. II, p. 189; St. Denis, pp. 258–60; Lutyens, E, *Letters
of Captain Engelbert Lutyens*, p. 74.

12. Kemble, pp. 258–61; Bertrand, *Napoleon at St. Helena*, p. 20; Montholon, *Récits de la
Captivité*, Vol. II, pp. 479–82; Masson, *Autour de Sainte-Hélène*, Vol. III, pp. 241–2.

13. Bertrand, *Napoleon at St. Helena*, pp. 20, 35–7; Montholon, *Récits de la Captivité*,
Vol. II, pp. 482–3.

14. Montholon, *Lettres du Comte et de la Comtesse de Montholon*, p. 75; Montholon, *Récits de
la Captivité*, Vol. II, pp. 488–9; Ganière, pp. 152–3; Kemble, p. 260; Antommarchi, Vol. II,
pp. 28–9; Young, Vol. II, p. 207.

15. Richardson, F, p. 151; Roseberry, Lord, *Napoleon The Last Phase*, p. 24; Montholon,
Récits de la Captivité, Vol. II, pp. 490–9; Marchand, Vol. II, pp. 288–9.

16. Lutyens, p. 104; Young, Vol. II, pp. 210–14; Kemble, pp. 262–3; Bertrand, *Napoleon at St.
Helena*, pp. 148–52, 218; Paoli, p. 152; Forsyth, Vol. II, p. 15; Korngold,
pp. 375–7.

17. Marchand, Vol. II, pp. 309–10; Masson, *Autour de Sainte-Hélène*, Vol. III,
pp. 249–50; Montholon, *Récits de la Captivité*, Vol. II, 516; Roseberry,
p. 25.

18. Roseberry, p. 26; Marchand, Vol. II, p. 313; Masson, *Autour de Sainte-Hélène*,
Vol. III, pp. 252–3; St. Denis, pp. 273–7; Montholon, *Récits de la Captivité*, Vol. II, p. 549.

19. Young, Vol. II, pp. 278–96; Paoli, p. 189; Gonnard, p. 106; Antommarchi, Vol. II, pp.
144–6, 155–65; Masson, *Autour de Sainte-Hélène*, Vol. III, pp. 255–6.

20. Gonnard, pp. 106–11; Roseberry, pp. 26–7; Chaplin, A, *The Illness and Death of Napoleon
Bonaparte*, pp. 24–5; Masson, *Napoleon at St. Helena*, p. xvii.

8

A MISTAKEN DIAGNOSIS

Gideon Gorrequer was in the habit of dining with Sir Hudson and Lady Lowe. The Governor's wife, engagingly referred to as 'Sultana' by the secretary in his secret diary, was well known for speaking her mind.

> He [Lowe] broke out at pratzo [dinner], before Sultana, observing Longwood had been fatal to all medici [doctors], Sultana observing 'Yes, to four viz: O'Meara, Stokoe, Verling,' and adding, 'Dr Baxter fell away in disgrace at least with you.'

Baxter had shown the Governor unswerving loyalty in all his schemes but the relationship between the two men soured with time. The long-suffering doctor was unable to tolerate Lowe's moods indefinitely and matters had come to a head in April 1819 when he summoned up enough courage to berate the Governor for compromising his reputation and overlooking him for promotion. Baxter complained that his name had been slandered because of the part he had been forced to play in the O'Meara medical bulletins. Lowe retorted that if his senior doctor were to be suddenly sent home, ministers would want to ask him a lot of questions when he reached England. The doctor ignored the veiled threat and said that he planned a peaceful retirement and that, anyway, he knew nothing of what had passed on the island. Baxter left St. Helena for England with a detachment of the 66th Regiment only a few days later but the resentment simmered on. Gorrequer records the Governor abusing the doctor and Reade chipping in that he would 'repent all his life going away'. According to family legend, Baxter remembered Lowe as a good man but a 'rough diamond'.[1]

Baxter was never acceptable to the French as Napoleon's physician. The Scotsman is maligned in all the Longwood memoirs although much of this was not personal. Whilst he accused him of being a spy and a poisoner, Napoleon admitted to O'Meara that he believed his reassurance that Baxter was an upright man; he would never allow the doctor to treat him because he had been imposed by Lowe. With other candidates for the post – men such as O'Meara, Stokoe, and Verling – all gone from St. Helena, in the early months of 1821 it was far from clear who the Emperor would be able to turn to if his disease continued to advance and Antommarchi remained useless. There were, however, a number of competent doctors still on the island, notably the experienced British army surgeons attached to the regiments of the garrison. One of them was to play a controversial part in the last month of Napoleon's life.

Archibald Arnott was born in Dumfriesshire in 1772 and was educated in medicine at Edinburgh. He joined the 11th Light Dragoons as Surgeon's Mate and was promoted to Assistant Surgeon in 1799. Eighteen months later, he was appointed Surgeon in the 20th Regiment of Foot and it was with this unit that he saw active service in many of the theatres of the Napoleonic Wars. His Peninsular Medal, now in the museum of the Royal Regiment of Fusiliers, has ten clasps – Egypt, Maida, Vimeiro, Corunna, Vitoria, Pyrenees, Nivelle, Orthez, Nive and Toulouse. He also gained valuable experience in the ill-fated expedition to the Scheldt where many of the troops died of the notorious 'Walcheren fever'. Arnott contracted the disease and needed two years of home service to recover. After a posting in Ireland, the 20th departed for St. Helena. At this time he was 46 years old, just three years younger than Napoleon. He was, by all accounts, a well respected army doctor and a kindly and likeable man.[2]

Because of his regimental seniority and undoubted experience, Arnott was immediately appointed as Principal Medical Officer on the island. This gave him some authority over the other medical officers and it was logical that Lowe should regard him as a possible solution to the stalemate at Longwood where Verling continued his futile vigil. Arnott was to enter centre stage in the spring of 1821 but he made a brief appearance much earlier. On 20th August 1819, Bertrand wrote to the Governor stating that the Emperor had fallen sick in the night; Lowe responded by sending Arnott to offer his services. He simultaneously assured Verling that this was not meant to interfere with his attendance – Arnott's visit was 'one of duty as well of attention'. On arrival at Longwood accompanied by Verling, Montholon directed the two doctors to the Grand Marshal's house. As Arnott was unable to speak French fluently, Verling explained to Bertrand that his colleague was *'chef des officiers de santé'* and was offering his medical help.

The conversation that followed between Arnott and Bertrand is well documented by Verling in his journal and the Frenchman in his diary. Both men are largely in agreement with Arnott's own version of the discussion, which is contained in an incomplete memorandum written for Lowe's attention.

I communicated to him [Bertrand] the object of my visit; that I had been ordered by you [Lowe] to offer my assistance in a medical capacity to General Bonaparte, in concert with Dr Verling, to which Count Bertrand replied that the Emperor was very ill, and that although he [the Emperor] entertained a very high opinion of the English Faculty, yet he had refused to be visited by any British surgeon, unless he would accede to certain conditions. The Count also said that he himself and his family having experienced much attention from Dr Verling, had often recommended the Emperor to see him professionally, but that he had uniformly objected to it, because he [Verling] would not accede to the conditions presented by the Emperor. I then signified to Count Bertrand that I would wish the object of my visit to be conveyed to General Bonaparte, and that I would wait at Longwood to know the result. He said that he would communicate the message to the Emperor, and that Dr Verling and I might call on him again. In about an hour afterwards, Count Bertrand sent for Dr Verling and myself to his house. In this second interview he told me he had been with the Emperor and that he would see me, provided I was authorised to give my opinion in writing, to sign and leave it with him. I replied I would not promise to do that without first communicating with you, that I considered my visit strictly professional, and that as such I would act to the best of my judgment but on no other terms would I visit General Bonaparte. 'Oh!' then he replied, 'you are acting under the influence of the Governor.'

At the same moment the Count took from his side pocket a written paper from which he read several conditions, the purpose of which tended to absolve the person who should have the medical charge of General Bonaparte from your control, and every other military authority. He put the question to me, if I were authorised and willing to give my assent to those articles. I then consequently told the Count …

We are deprived of the denouement in Arnott's own words but he predictably refused the Grand Marshal's offer. It must be remembered that this was the summer of Stokoe's trial – the court-martial was only two weeks after this meeting – and it would have been an act of gross stupidity to accept the conditions.

Bertrand could not have been surprised by the outcome but he was frustrated, launching an uncharacteristic attack on Lowe. Why did the Governor send Arnott when he knew that nothing had changed and that there was no chance of his being acceptable to the Emperor? The Governor, he said, obviously believed Napoleon to be ill or he would not be offering a different doctor. So why did he insult him so much? His officers had orders to harass him and to spy on him so that he had to hide behind closed doors and windows. 'Are these the medicines and remedies that the Governor sends to the sick? What barbarity!'

Verling called on Montholon who was astonished at the Grand Marshal's offer. He believed Bertrand to have exceeded his authority from Napoleon; the Emperor had only permitted him to say that if the conditions were met, he would then choose a medical man. The Grand Marshal later approached Verling and confessed that he had not meant to offer Arnott the post, simply to establish the conditions which would have to be met by any British doctor. Perhaps the language proved problematic; both doctors interpreted the Frenchman's words as an offer of the post of the Emperor's physician. In truth, Bertrand's intent was academic as there was no chance of the newly arrived doctor being conferred this honour unless either the British authorities or the Emperor was prepared to make an unexpected concession.

Despite this stuttering introduction to Longwood, Arnott became friendly with the Bertrands and was a frequent visitor to their house. He assisted Verling and Livingstone in the medical management of the Countess and her children. The Grand Marshal also sought his professional advice; in his diary, he writes, 'If only the Emperor would consult him!'

With such close relations with the French, it was inevitable that should the Emperor again become seriously ill, Arnott's name would be called. Thus it was that, in March 1821 – fully eighteen months after Arnott's first visit to Longwood – Bertrand and Montholon, alarmed at the physical deterioration of their master, became determined that the doctor should be asked to assist Antommarchi.[3]

The pressure on the Emperor to see another British doctor had been building over the previous few months. Lowe again formally offered Arnott's services in December 1820, writing to Montholon that the medical officer would act as he would for an 'ordinary private patient'. This was not an altruistic gesture. The Governor was unsettled by reports from Bathurst that Napoleon was planning to escape and he was determined to place one of his subordinates in Longwood to improve surveillance of the prisoner. He informed Montholon that unless the Orderly Officer or a British medical officer was allowed access to the Emperor, he would have to resort to force to gain proof of his presence. The Count, motivated by a different sort of anxiety, had been trying to convince Napoleon to see Arnott since November. He told Lutyens that his master had dismissed his entreaties. 'I shall be better in a few days, there is no danger.'

Arnott was edging closer to the Emperor. He met with Antommarchi to discuss the symptoms of the illness. Although he had not seen the patient, the British surgeon concluded that the fever described was not dangerous. He was equally confident that the current illness had no connection with the previous liver trouble. Montholon was now so desperate that Napoleon should see Arnott that he begged him on his knees but, as Marchand relates, he met more resistance.

'What need is there to call another doctor? Will he understand my disease any better? If Corvisart or Larrey were here, I should have confidence and some hope; but these ignoramuses know nothing of my illness. A good ride on a horse – that is what I need! Get a book and read me something.'

Undeterred, Montholon and Bertrand continued to press the case for a second opinion and, at the end of March, Napoleon finally cracked. Marchand explains his decision as being due to the renewed pleading of his two companions and also to a realisation that his strength was draining away. This sudden change of heart was still a surprise to those close to him; Saint-Denis admits that it was 'contrary to all their expectations'. It was a not a gracious acceptance.

'Your British doctor,' the Emperor said to Bertrand, 'will go and report my condition to that executioner. It will give him far more pleasure to learn of my agony; but afterwards what else can he do even if I agree to see that doctor? Well! It is more for the satisfaction of the people around me than for my own, for I expect to gain nothing from his opinions!'

Now that they had obtained their objective, the French were quick to brief Arnott as to how he should behave. Bertrand's diary entry for 31st March:

> General Montholon spoke to Dr Arnott and asked him if he would give his word of honour to look upon himself as a civilian doctor dealing with an ordinary private person? If he would care for the Emperor as though he were a City doctor attending a London merchant? If he would issue no bulletins or spoken or written reports unless he were so authorised, and would first submit a copy for approval. If he would not speak of the patient other than to say 'he is well or ill' without specifying anything about the nature of the illness?

Arnott stated that he was willing to see the Emperor and could be sent for through the intermediary of Bertrand. He asked if he should sign any bulletin together with Antommarchi as this was usual practice in the case of a private patient. Finally, he sought assurance that if, in the Emperor's bedroom he were to use 'another form of address', that the Governor would not be informed.

The doctor was nervous of Lowe and did not want his every word to be communicated to Plantation House. Although the Governor had authorised the consultations with the Emperor and had not asked for any bulletins, he was unimpressed at the prospect of another British doctor entering Longwood. He had earlier observed to Verling that any change 'might give rise to intrigues'. Arnott had a meeting with Lowe prior to the consultation and although we are not party to the details of this, we have the surgeon's comment that the senior officer was both petulant and furious. This was not unusual for Lowe, but Gorrequer's contemporary diary entry is explicit as to the Governor's misgivings.

> Mach's tortuous proceedings, surrounding every proposition of Medico 20th [Arnott] as well as the fair ones from Veritas [Montholon], with all sorts of captious, peevish objections and difficulties, and agreeing to nothing; evidently wishing, if he could, to prevent him being called in, if he could forge any deceitful or plausible (to Big Wigs at Home) pretext. His repeatedly saying that he should not see him in presence of suite, except Ninny [Reade]

was present, or Ninny and Cercueil [Brigadier-General John Pine-Coffin]
laying great stress upon making Ninny a part.

Pine-Coffin had succeeded Bingham in command of the troops. Napoleon
took a morbid delight in his name. Arnott was not trusted by either his
patient or his military superior.[4]

It will be helpful to pause and consider the nature of Napoleon's disease.
An understanding of the illness is important in telling the story of Arnott,
a man who was to be haunted by a misdiagnosis. Prior to his demise on
St. Helena, Napoleon had enjoyed good health. His iron constitution sustained him through the extremes of the scorching heat of the Egyptian
expedition and the piercing cold of the retreat from Moscow. Various
authors have tried to attach a number of diagnoses to the Emperor but
these do not stand close scrutiny. Segur, in his classic monograph of the
Russian campaign, says that Napoleon only ever complained of rheumatism
and of dysuria – an irritation on passing urine which may have been caused
by bladder stones.

Following Napoleon's arrival on the island of his exile, it is possible
to divide the history of his health into three phases. The first of these,
comfortably the longest, extends from October 1815 to September 1820.
During his first two years at Longwood he was mostly well. However,
in September 1817 and January 1819 he complained of severe pain in
the upper abdomen, pain in the right shoulder blade, nausea and headache. O'Meara was in attendance during the first of these attacks and
Stokoe paid his five visits during the second. From this point on, he never
regained full health. His physicians noted vomiting, pallor, and constipa-
tion alternating with diarrhoea. He also suffered from sporadic episodes
of fever, chills, jaundice and darkening of the urine – symptoms which
suggest a possible liver problem.

Concerns regarding the Emperor's health increased in the summer of 1820
but the second phase of his symptoms can be best defined as being between
October 1820 and February 1821. During this period, Antommarchi was on
duty and Napoleon's health greatly deteriorated. Montholon wrote to his
wife, 'The illness of the Emperor has definitely worsened. His pulse is weak;
his gums, lips and nails are colourless.' Every effort was a Herculean task. He
complained of persistent abdominal pain, difficulty in swallowing, constipa-
tion, night sweats and fever. He was profoundly weak, had no appetite and was
losing weight. Madame Bertrand told Assistant Surgeon George Rutledge of

the 20th Foot that whilst the others were eating, Napoleon chewed small pieces of under-done meat which he spat out after extracting the juice.

The final phase was the two months preceding the Emperor's death, March to May 1821. Antommarchi remained on the scene and Arnott gave his assistance during the last 35 days. The dying man continued to suffer severe abdominal pain, vomiting and fever. The sweating was now so profuse that he had to change his clothes several times every night. His mental state was also in decline; he was intermittently confused and often mistook Arnott for Stokoe or O'Meara. It took a monumental effort and a transient remission in the worst symptoms for the Emperor to dictate his will to Montholon and Marchand. April was marked by a grim accentuation of all the symptoms and, on the 27th he had a 'coffee ground vomit' and passed black tarry stools. This, accompanied by an increase in his pulse, was consistent with bleeding from the stomach or the upper part of the gut. In the final week he became first delirious and then comatose. Napoleon remained in this condition until eleven minutes to six on the evening of 5th May 1821, when he died.[5]

More clues as to the cause of the disease and death can be gleaned from the post-mortem performed on 6th May by Antommarchi. Seven British doctors, including Arnott, supervised the autopsy. Napoleon's body was extremely pale. On internal examination, the crucial findings were in the stomach. This was filled with dark material resembling coffee grounds, a sure indication that there had been a sizeable bleed. This was very likely the immediate cause of death. On closer inspection of the wall of the stomach there was a very large ulcer with hard, irregular borders. Separate from this lesion was a second smaller ulcer with adhesions to the liver. There was also some altered blood in the colon, part of the large bowel. The other organs were mostly normal although there was disagreement between those present with regard to the size and state of the liver and there were a few enlarged hardened lymph glands around the stomach.

As we will never have the opportunity to take a biopsy from Napoleon's stomach for pathological analysis we have to rely on the combination of his clinical symptoms and the eyewitness observations at the post-mortem to postulate a diagnosis. It is almost certain that he had cancer of the stomach (gastric carcinoma). The nature of the ulcerated lesion in the stomach wall described by Antommarchi corresponds very well with the classical appearance of gastric cancer. A team of pathologists from Dallas have meticulously compared the tumour described in Napoleon's post-mortem report with modern digital images of stomach cancer and have concluded that it was a particular ulcerating subtype of the disease and that the enlarged lymph glands were proof of spread beyond the organ itself. Even with modern surgical treatment, the prognosis of this type of tumour (stage IIIA) is dismal with less than half of patients still alive one year after diagnosis.

Why did the Emperor contract this devastating disease? We now know that there are a number of factors which can predispose to the development of gastric cancer. It is possible that he suffered from a chronic infection of the stomach (*Helicobacter Pylori*) that caused both an earlier benign peptic ulcer and ultimately increased his risk of cancer. The separate smaller ulcer found at post-mortem was most likely benign – it was stuck to the liver and was probably the cause of the earlier attacks of abdominal pain. The duration of Napoleon's symptoms is overly long for stomach cancer alone and the presence of two sorts of disease in the stomach, both benign and malignant, would explain this. His risk of gastric cancer may also have been increased by a high salt intake. His diet was that of a veteran of the *Grande Armée* and was rich in salt-preserved foods with a dearth of fruit and fresh vegetables.

Certain types of gastric cancer have a familial predisposition; members of the family carry a genetic abnormality which significantly increases their chance of developing the disease. This may have been the case for the Bonapartes. Napoleon's father, Charles Bonaparte, died at only 39 years. At post-mortem, he was found to have a tumour the size of a large potato in the lower part of his stomach. Other members of the family did not have autopsies performed and the causes of their deaths are therefore uncertain.[6]

Napoleon had a longstanding infection of the stomach, which caused first a benign ulcer and then a fatal cancer. A massive bleed from the tumour hastened his death. This version of events is supported by most doctors who have studied the St. Helena literature but we must also briefly consider the poisoning hypothesis which has its fervent advocates and which has received much publicity. Supporters of this theory claim that Napoleon was deliberately poisoned with arsenic; Montholon is generally held to be the guilty party. The evidence for such a murder is entirely circumstantial and the objective medical information available makes poisoning a very unlikely cause of death. It must be admitted that high levels of arsenic have been found in samples of Napoleon's hair from St. Helena. This has been presented as scientific proof that arsenic was the cause of his demise.

In fact, the hair sample analyses – there have been several performed – are inconclusive. Arsenic and many other potentially dangerous compounds may have entered the hair in a number of innocent ways. Its presence, even in elevated amounts, is neither proof of poisoning nor conclusive evidence that arsenic was the lethal agent. The metal was in widespread use in the early nineteenth century, being a common constituent of drugs and of everyday effects. The wallpaper in the Emperor's study at Longwood contained significant amounts. Chronic environmental exposure is the likely cause of the laboratory results. This interpretation is strongly supported by a study on sequential hair samples performed in 2004 in Munich. The scientists analysed not only Napoleon's hairs from St. Helena but also hair samples taken seven years earlier during his incarceration on Elba. All the samples contained equally elevated levels of arsenic in addition to eighteen other metallic elements.

The post-mortem findings are also against poisoning as the cause of death. Characteristic autopsy features of fatal arsenic ingestion – skin and nail changes, haemorrhage into heart muscle, multiple tumours – are all absent. Devotees of the murder hypothesis also claim that Napoleon could not have died of cancer as he did not have the weight loss inevitable in the terminal stage of this disease. Sten Forshufvud, the Swedish doctor and Napoleonic buff who started the debate in 1961, writes,

> There is one thing which, first of all, makes the diagnosis of cancer very shaky. Napoleon did not show the characteristic condition of cachexy – that is extreme weight loss of flesh and wasting away – found, generally speaking, in persons who die of cancer.

French historians, René Maury and François de Candé-Montholon (a descendant of the alleged murderer), writing forty years later, perpetuate this view. They quote Walter Henry's post-mortem observations.

> On exposing the contents of the abdomen, the omentum was seen loaded with fat of which the quantity was very great … The kidneys were embedded in an immense quantity of fat … The heart was small but proportional to the size of the body, at least before it became bloated and oppressed with fat.

This objection to the proposed diagnosis of cancer is not unreasonable and it provoked a group of pathologists in Basle to make a study of Napoleon's weight over the last twenty years of his life. They first used an ingenious method reliant on the waist measurement of trousers worn by the Emperor at different times. Four pairs worn before the exile were measured at the Musée National du Château de Fontainebleau and five pairs worn on St. Helena were measured at Fontainebleau or at Malmaison. Three more trouser waist sizes were obtained from Napoleonic authorities and the *Fondation Napoléon* making a total of twelve measurements up to the time of his death.

Modern data confirm a close correlation between trouser waist size and the subject's body mass index. As Napoleon's height is known (167 cm) it was possible for the researchers to derive a model which allowed calculation of his weight at different dates. To double check his weight at his death, a second method based on autopsy abdominal subcutaneous fat measurement was also used; Antommarchi recorded this as one and a half inches. The trouser size model suggested a weight increase from 67 kilograms to 90 kilograms by 1820. This reflects the well known transformation of slender General Bonaparte into the corpulent Emperor Napoleon. The trousers worn at the time of his death were consistent with a weight loss of 11 kilograms (to 79 kilograms) in the last year of his life. The abdominal fat calculation gave a similar figure (76 kilograms) to the trouser method. Taking the results of both techniques together, it is fair to state that Napoleon lost between 11 and 14 kilograms during his final illness. This is a substantial amount and quite in keeping with what is seen in modern patients suffering from the disease. The post-mortem fat observed by Henry and others simply reflected the fact that the Emperor was obese before his last illness and that his body had retained significant fat deposits despite his alarming weight loss.[7] So the poison theory is all mouth and no trousers.

We can assume that when Archibald Arnott entered Napoleon's bedroom on 1st April 1821, he was about to consult with a patient in the last stages of a fatal malignant disease. It was 9pm and, according to Marchand, the scene was only dimly lit by a covered lamp in the adjacent room. The valet lifted the mosquito net and Arnott approached Napoleon. Antommarchi was also present but said nothing. Bertrand acted as an interpreter. The British doctor said a few words and then felt the patient's pulse and performed a summary examination of the abdomen. He commented that he wanted to discuss the ailment with Antommarchi and asked for permission to return the following morning. He immediately reported back to Lowe.

> The room was dark so that I could not see him but I felt him or someone else. I examined his pulse and state of skin. I perceived that there was considerable debility, but nothing that indicated immediate danger.

Arnott believed himself to be duty bound to keep the Governor fully informed. Equally, he was suspicious of the French, intimating that the room was darkened deliberately in order to conceal the patient's identity. This initial impression of deception may have coloured the surgeon's conclusions regarding Napoleon's illness.[8]

After this inauspicious start, Arnott visited the Emperor once or twice daily during the last month of his life. At first, both men were cautious. Arnott did not attend spontaneously but preferred a formal summons from Longwood. Bertrand guessed that this was not due to any lack of zeal on the doctor's part but that he was afraid of the Governor. The Emperor, accustomed to the intimacy of a small group, was nervous at the introduction of an outsider. According to the Grand Marshal, the slightest unfamiliar thing upset him. During his early visits, the doctor noted that his patient's pulse always quickened upon his arrival and that he grew calmer with time. This awkwardness soon abated, the meetings became more open and candid, and a good relationship formed between the two old soldiers.

Napoleon believed that he had met Arnott previously but although the doctor had once seen the great man in Paris during a sightseeing tour, he had not been presented to him. A cloud threatened rain and, as he was only lightly dressed, he thought it better to head for his lodgings. When Arnott related this anecdote, Napoleon commented, 'Ah, a far-seeing Scot'. The Emperor appears to have genuinely enjoyed the company of the surgeon and he paid him a number of compliments, referring to him in chats with Bertrand as a 'brave, sensible and observant man'. He instructed Antommarchi that he did not want any English medical man to touch him after death but that, if this was unavoidable, it was Arnott alone who was to be employed in the task. Napoleon was, however, reserving judgment as to his new doctor's medical prowess; on one occasion, he commented to Antommarchi, 'You are much inferior to Dr Arnott ... I don't know whether he is a good doctor but he has a good manner and I will receive him.'

By the time of Arnott's attendance, the Emperor had low expectations. 'I know the truth, and I am resigned' he calmly remarked. Despite this pessimism as to the final outcome, Napoleon retained a keen interest in the details of his disease. This only faded in the final days when he became first confused and then frankly delirious. In response to the patient's direct enquiries as to the state of his health, Arnott adopted the familiar strategy of bland reassurance. Napoleon was too astute to be fobbed off with platitudes.

He was convinced that his disease was fatal. On 17th April, he complained of lassitude and refused all food. Bertrand witnessed the consultation.

'It is true that Your Majesty is weaker,' Dr Arnott said, 'but I have seen many patients in an even weaker state than you make a recovery. You must therefore have hope.'

'Words, words and phrases fit for women and children,' Napoleon said wearily, 'but to men and especially to soldiers like us, you should speak the truth.'

'I have told you the truth,' Arnott rejoined. 'I have said what I think.'

'What is the strongest remedy you have? Mercury?' Napoleon asked.

'In certain cases, but it is useless in cases of weakness,' Dr Arnott replied.

'Mercury? Opium? Quinine?' the Emperor repeated.

'Yes, in certain illnesses, but in other cases to let blood is one of the strongest remedies.'

'You English, you let too much blood,' Napoleon remarked.

This exchange must have reminded the Emperor of his conversations with Warden on the *Northumberland*. His scepticism was entirely justified. A bleeding would have very likely caused harm, leaving him more debilitated. The Emperor concluded the consultation by declaring that, although he had none of the symptoms of immediate death, he was so weak that it would not take a cannon ball to kill him – a grain of sand would suffice.

Whilst he retained his mental faculties, Napoleon enjoyed engaging Arnott in wider conversations. Bertrand records a number of these in his journal. For instance, on 24 April, a relatively good day for the patient, the two had a discussion lasting an hour in the morning and again in the evening. Napoleon's boundless curiosity was still in evidence; he quizzed Arnott on all sorts of matters including the relative merits of British and French medicine, drinking habits in England, the bravery of British and French soldiers undergoing surgery, and the beauty of London compared to Paris. The Emperor was particularly interested in Arnott's pay and expenditure. The surgeon had gained a reputation on the island for being careful with his money. He laughed when Napoleon quipped, 'All Scotsmen are misers!'[9]

It was in the course of one of these friendly exchanges that Napoleon informed the doctor that he had decided to present a book on the campaigns of Marlborough to his regiment. The Emperor had always admired the British General and the very fine book had been presented to him in the previous October by Robert Spencer, an opposition politician who briefly visited the island. The three separate volumes were luxuriously bound and contained the Imperial title. After telling Arnott to put them in his regimental library, the Emperor added, 'If I have consented to see you, doctor, it is to satisfy the people around me, and because you are a man of honour, respected by the officers of your regiment.' Marchand says that Arnott was visibly moved by the present and Bertrand, who had translated his master's words into English, expressed the surgeon's gratitude in French.

On the following day, the Emperor asked Arnott what his fellow officers had said regarding the book. The doctor replied that they had not yet had a chance to read it. 'Does not some committee look after the library?' the Emperor enquired. Arnott responded that it was administered by a commissioner. Napoleon smelt a rat – it was obvious that appreciation of such a generous gift was not dependant on a thorough reading of the text. He later commented to the Grand Marshal that Arnott must have been rebuked by Reade for receiving the book. The Emperor was correct to suspect foul play although it was actually Lowe who had intervened. The volumes had originally been left in the room of the Orderly Officer, Engelbert Lutyens, who was informed of Napoleon's intent by Arnott. Both men were nervous of censure and Lutyens therefore immediately informed the Governor of the gift. Lowe instructed Major Jackson, who was in temporary charge of the 20th, to return the book to Montholon. It could not be given to a British regiment because it contained the Imperial title and it had been donated through improper channels.

Lutyens was so irritated by the confiscation that he behaved in a manner that was judged to be insubordinate and was removed from his post. Lowe, concerned that Arnott might be becoming another O'Meara, wrote to the doctor.

> The attempt to make you the channel of communication in such matters, they well know, is foreign to your professional duties, and it will probably, therefore, not have been made without some ulterior design in view.

This episode reveals Lowe at his worst. Forsyth is forced to concede that, in refusing to allow the gift, the Governor had 'acted with an overstrained sense of duty'. Young describes Lowe's action as 'ungracious' and acknowledges that he was adhering too rigidly to regulations. As on other occasions, the Governor had insight into his own unreasonableness but was ultimately unable to restrain himself. He raised the affair with Gorrequer.

He [Lowe] broke out that it was expected that he should be so delicate, because Neighbour [Napoleon] was said to be dying, it was what he himself had no idea of. [He said] that Neighbour knew very well what his opinion had always been of him, and it would never be on account of his being in a dying state that he would alter his line of proceeding. That he'd be damned, or some such expression, if he'd pursue any other. He cared very little about it.

Others did care, and not only the French. Bertrand says that the officers of the 20th Regiment were very angry. Captain Lutyens was ashamed. 'What a cowardly business,' he exclaimed. 'The wretch, to rebuff a dying man in such a fashion!'[10]

Napoleon's medical care was shared by Arnott and Antommarchi. It was only near the end of the Emperor's life, when he was delirious, that Lowe insisted that Thomas Shortt, Physician to the Forces, who had recently arrived on St. Helena, and Charles Mitchell, Surgeon of the flagship *Vigo*, be sent to Longwood for a consultation. Shortt and Mitchell discussed the case with Arnott but were reluctant to give an opinion without seeing the patient. This was refused. Nevertheless, the consensus of the three British doctors was that Napoleon should be given a strong dose of a purgative (calomel). Antommarchi was unimpressed by the plan as he judged the Emperor to be on the verge of death and he believed all such efforts to be pointless. He was worried that the strength of the medication might make things worse. The Corsican physician has been much criticised and lampooned but he deserves credit for understanding the terminal nature of the disease and opposing futile and distressing treatment.[11]

At this meeting, Arnott also conceded that the Emperor's days were numbered. However, for much of the previous month, he had argued that Napoleon's problems were more of a mental than physical nature. Astonishingly, he had made a diagnosis of 'hypochondriasis'. It is difficult to understand how such an experienced doctor could have made such a crass misdiagnosis but the contemporary records are explicit and, if taken literally, allow no other explanation. Arnott's written and verbal reports (the latter recorded by Gorrequer) to the Governor and Reade are contained in the Lowe Papers in the British Library. These, combined with the eyewitness accounts of those around him, enable us to build a detailed picture of the doctor's approach to Napoleon's illness.

From the start, he wanted to believe that his patient was not sick at all. On 5th April, four days after the first consultation, Bertrand comments in his journal that Arnott was 'in seventh heaven' because there was no trace of fever. Although the French were conscientiously reporting the symptoms to him, he was disinclined to listen. Even when his colleague, Antommarchi, reported that the patient had had a bad night, his reaction was sceptical. He wrote to Gorrequer, 'I did not find him labouring under any of the symptoms there detailed.' On the 6th, Reade wrote to the Governor.

> Dr Arnott informed me that he had never found him, during any of his visits, in the state of which he had been described by Antommarchi. From what I could learn generally, out of Dr Arnott's conversation, he appears to think that General Bonaparte is not affected with any serious complaint, probably more mental than any other. Count Bertrand had asked him his opinion of General Bonaparte: he told him that he saw no danger whatever. During his visit this morning he recommended General Bonaparte to rise and get shaved.

Arnott agreed that Napoleon looked unwell as he was pale and had grown a very long beard. Equally, he denied that the the patient was emaciated; he felt his pulse regularly and he had a 'stout' wrist, indeed as fleshy as the doctor's own. Reade wrote to Lowe that he was persuaded by Arnott's tone that 'Bonaparte will be out again very soon.' It was probably nothing more than a 'fit of bile'.

Arnott's predecessors, O'Meara and Stokoe, had made a diagnosis of liver disease but he was unconvinced of this. Napoleon went so far as to pull up his shirt and point to the region of the liver, asking the doctor to examine him. Bertrand explained to Arnott that the Emperor was sure that this was the site of the problem. The surgeon examined the abdomen and Napoleon complained of some tenderness. Arnott commented to Bertrand that he could find 'no hardness or swelling whatsoever'. The Grand Marshal translated his words into French and the patient acknowledged them with a disbelieving look before changing the subject.

On 17th April, Antommarchi noted that Napoleon was suffering from a cold sweat but Arnott was oblivious to this; he found the pulse to be unaltered and there to be no evidence of fever. The Corsican physician believed that 'the dust of a ball' would be enough to carry the patient off and Montholon told Lutyens that he could not survive more than a few weeks but Arnott continued to press his original diagnosis, a fact recorded by Gorrequer.

Dr Arnott remarked to the Governor that if General Bonaparte took no more sustenance than what Dr Antommarchi and his followers said he did, he must finally sink under it. Dr Arnott added that he became more and more confirmed in the opinion that the disease was hypochondriasis; no symptoms of immediate danger about him, but if some alteration for the better did not take place the ordinary results of the disease might be expected. His mind seemed to be particularly affected. Dr Arnott had remarked a singularity in his manner that morning. He was sitting in a chair and began whistling, when, suddenly stopping, he opened his mouth quite wide, projected it forward, and looked steadily at Dr Arnott in the face for a short time with a kind of vacant stare.

The Governor asked Dr Arnott whether it might be advisable to excite General Bonaparte in some way, to procure some change for him – to get him into the new house, for instance. Oh, said Dr Arnott immediately, anything occurring to break the present association of ideas would doubtless have a good effect. If, for example, a seventy-four [a ship of the line] was to arrive from England to take him away, I have no doubt he would soon recover. This would put him on his legs again directly.

Lowe pointedly asked whether the air on St. Helena had exacerbated this affliction. The surgeon reassured him that the disease would be just the same in a prison elsewhere.

On 22nd April, only a week before Napoleon became moribund, Arnott repeated the same message to Lowe.

General Bonaparte's malady was hypochondriasis – having many dyspeptic symptoms; – the cure probably tedious because he, Dr Arnott, could not give him that which would set him right. On asking Dr Arnott what that was, he immediately replied, liberty ...

The Emperor, Arnott continued, had improved over the previous week; he acknowledged this himself. He had complained of his liver, crying out '*le foie*' and complaining of the '*chaleur*' over it, but this, the doctor observed, was a symptom of hypochondriasis. Antommarchi stated that the patient was now very ill with fever and had difficulty in swallowing but Arnott thought him 'decidedly not worse'. Lowe was becoming a little uneasy. Were swallowing problems, abdominal pain and vomiting really symptoms of mental disease? Arnott reassured him that they were. The Governor ordered the doctor to consult him immediately if there was any deterioration so that he might obtain a second medical opinion. He wrote to Bathurst that Arnott had repeatedly told him that the prisoner was in no immediate danger.

Napoleon, at least whilst he remained alert, understood Arnott's thoughts. He discussed his disease with Montholon and Bertrand. He informed the latter that he knew that Arnott did not believe him to be dangerously ill, whereas Antommarchi did. Word that the Emperor's symptoms were being exaggerated was also passed to the British officers in the vicinity. Lutyens had regular contact with Arnott and was repeatedly informed that the patient was 'better'. Charles Harrison wrote home on 22nd April:

> I don't know what to think of the invalid, but I now begin to firmly believe it is all humbug. He still continues confined to his bed, but from what I can collect is considerably better. His new doctor [Arnott] attends him twice a day regularly, and he tells me he is the most extraordinary man he had ever had to deal with in his life, and the conviction on my mind is, that if he were to be told there was a 74 arrived to take him back to France he would find the use of both his mental and bodily faculties.[12]

No patient ever died of hypochondriasis, a morbid fear of non-existent disease. We may ask at what point Arnott was forced to relinquish his diagnosis. He was certainly less optimistic in his conversations with Antommarchi than he was in his reports to the Governor and his communications with the other Longwood residents. As early as 18th April, the two doctors discussed the seriousness of the situation. Arnott opposed Antommarchi's proposal that all treatment was now useless but when his Corsican colleague challenged him to justify his bullishness – 'You are always spreading hopes amongst us; on what are they based?' – Arnott had no satisfactory answer. Antommarchi writes cryptically in his memoirs that the British surgeon 'soon gave up a conviction which he had not held'. In their private discussions, Arnott had also admitted the possibility of hereditary gastric cancer.

When Napoleon's condition deteriorated between 25th and 27th April with increasing debility and signs of bleeding from the stomach and bowel, Arnott was forced to backtrack and publicly acknowledge that he was attending a patient with a life-threatening disease. On the 28th, the Governor wrote to Admiral Lambert telling him that Arnott had that morning informed him that Bonaparte had become considerably worse than he had ever seen him before and that the disorder 'bore a very serious aspect'. By 1st May Arnott was in constant attendance and reported to Lowe that the patient was delirious; 'I think he rather raves more than he did in the morning.' On the 2nd, he finally admitted that Napoleon was probably dying. 'Danger is to be apprehended in the course of the day ... allowing the probability is that he may last until tomorrow or the next day.' His reports still contained surprising notes of optimism – for instance, at 9pm on 4 May, less than 24 hours prior to death, he insisted that the patient was better than a day earlier and that he had taken a 'considerable quantity of nourishment'.

At the end, Arnott's actions were motivated by a desire to accommodate Lowe's directive that everything possible should be seen to be done. The Governor had written to Montholon, 'In short, M. le Comte, I am strongly desirous that English medical science should at all events have the chance of saving his life.' Lowe was influenced by the case of a sick sailor treated at Plantation House who had been declared beyond hope by O'Meara but who had been unexpectedly restored to health by the exertions of Baxter. Arnott must also have been embarrassed by his diagnosis of a mental disorder, now so dramatically disproved, and he was keen to restore his credibility with some decisive action. On 3rd May the Emperor was too weak to swallow and the surgeon suggested an enema. Bertrand writes in his journal,

> On the subject of the enema, Arnott said that professional men would be unable to understand his having left the Emperor for three days without a motion. It was therefore absolutely necessary to obtain one, either by means of medicine or by means of an enema. He did not think that this would save the Emperor, as he was certainly in the greatest danger, with almost everything against him, but that nevertheless as a professional man and for the sake of his own reputation, he had to induce a motion. It was absolutely necessary, and it was possible, without moving the Emperor and by leaving him on his back, to lift his legs and to put a sheet folded in four or in eight under him to receive ...

Antommarchi opposed this useless procedure and Napoleon was spared the indignity.[13]

Arnott's medical reports to Lowe are not the only account he made of Napoleon's illness and death. In 1822 he published a book, now very hard to find, entitled *An Account of the Last Illness and Decease and Post Mortem Appearance of Napoleon Bonaparte*. In the introduction, Arnott says that he was solicited to write the work by his friends in England. The slim volume contains a series of daily medical reports in which are documented both the chief symptoms and the means adopted for their relief. If the entries in the book are compared with Arnott's reports to Lowe, it is immediately evident that there are significant differences. In his contemporary bulletins, Arnott clung to a diagnosis of hypochondriasis until only a week or so before Napoleon's death; as late as 22nd April he claimed that an offer of freedom would restore his patient's health. Whilst he remains reluctant to offer a specific diagnosis in his later book, he describes, in the archaic medical language of the day, serious symptoms quite incompatible with a mental disorder. Furthermore, these alarming symptoms and signs were present from the outset.

A few selected quotes from his book make the point. As early as 2nd April, Arnott notes that Napoleon was 'remarkably pallid' and in a 'very exhausted state', and he added that the stomach was very 'irritable'; the patient was unable to take food or medicines. On the 4th he was feverish and 'much distressed' with 'tension of belly'.

Three days later there was persistent fever and vomiting and 'very profuse perspiration', and then, on the 10th; 'nausea and vomiting returned ... His strength appeared to be sinking rapidly'. By the 13th we learn that he was 'seized with a paroxysm of vomiting', and two days later 'his strength had shrunk considerably; he was covered with a cold damp perspiration ... the skin has a clammy feel.' For 17th April – still several days before Arnott's final bulletin to Lowe confirming hypochondriasis – Arnott records in his book,

> There was an aggravation of all the symptoms; the vomiting increased and his strength sunk, the pulse was small, frequent and irregular; the whole surface was cold. He was comatose, and, when roused, complained of a sense of suffocation.

He continues to describe the relentless deterioration with vomiting of blood on the 27th and the appearance of 'tarry stools' the following day. On occasion he notes that the patient rallied a little, even becoming 'cheerful', but these are only brief respites and the overall picture is that of a man struggling against a terminal disease. Arnott concluded the substantial part of his work with a description of the Emperor's death. He also appended an account of the post-mortem examination and a letter to Lowe but these add little to the main text.

The profound difference between Arnott's complacent contemporary account of the disease to Lowe and Reade and the retrospective description in his book can only be explained in one of two ways. One possibility is that the surgeon genuinely believed that his patient had hypochondriasis and the later work was a belated attempt to restore his medical reputation. The second is that the book version is his true assessment and that his contemporary reports were fabricated for political and personal reasons. In the first case, he can be charged with medical incompetence. In the second, he is open to a charge of cowardice, as he presumably played down Napoleon's illness to please the Governor and his deputy. Arnott was aware that O'Meara and Stokoe had been hunted down by the British authorities for daring to state that Napoleon was seriously ill.[14]

There is no evidence to suggest that Arnott was an incompetent doctor. He was the possessor of a medical degree from Edinburgh and used clinical methods which were state of the art in the early nineteenth century. For instance, he regularly recorded his patient's temperature. This is routine now, but the technique of 'clinical thermometry' was not much used in England until fifty years after Napoleon's death. Arnott had probably learnt to use a thermometer during his attachment to the prestigious Royal Infirmary at Edinburgh. There are clues in the Longwood memoirs that the experienced British doctor understood the severity of Napoleon's disease. Arnot not only discussed the nature of the symptoms with Antommarchi but he admitted to Bertrand, on 1st April, that he agreed with his medical colleague that the Emperor was 'dangerously ill'.

The best evidence that Arnott was acting duplicitously comes from the pen of Gorrequer. In his diary, the Military Secretary repeated the comments not only of the Governor but also of his wife.

And on the 4th [April] [Lady Lowe] having said also loud at pranzo to Ego [Gorrequer] that Medico 20th [Arnott] would take care to make out the case of our neighbour [Napoleon] as much better than it really was. Represent him in much better health that he really was because he knew it would please, and he was much too much of a Scotsman not to be regulated by what he knew was desired or expected.

This conversation took place only a few days after Arnott first met Napoleon. On 7th April, a week after the first consultation, Gorrequer writes the following.

Mach's [Lowe] talking to Medico 20th [Arnott] respecting our Neighbour's [Napoleon's] complaint, laying it down that it was a disease of the mind, and not of the body. Medico had for some time (probably to give Mach satisfaction) declared it to be hypochondriasis, having often been told by Mach it was the state of his mind. [And that it was] the reflection of his [Napoleon's] impolite conduct here, and his behaviour to him [Lowe], (and how differently he would play his game now, if he had to play it over again) that he was more suffering from. And he [Lowe] added with a furious satisfaction and the grin of a tyrant: 'If a person was to go in there (his apartments) and make a great clamour, it would be the most likely thing to revive him. Depend upon it.' This was the cure he prescribed for rousing him from the state of despondency and hypochondriasis Medico represented him in.

At least one British historian has represented Arnott as a victim; a man brainwashed by Lowe. The French are less generous. Gilbert Martineau describes the doctor acting out of 'political sagacity'. He concludes that he had a grave responsibility for the Emperor's death. He was as ignorant as Antommarchi but more malevolent. This is arguable, as we have seen that Arnott was not ignorant, and to blame him for the Emperor's demise is unfair. By the time of Arnott's consultations, no medical intervention could have saved Napoleon's life. This would be the case today. Some have suggested that the treatment adopted by Arnott – the administration of the toxic drug calomel – hastened the death. This may be the case but is impossible to prove.

Arnott was not Napoleon's executioner but neither was he an innocent bystander. His attempts to win favour from the Governor succeeded. Gorrequer tellingly compares the official treatment of Arnott with that of Stokoe. Arnott attended Bertrand's house without authority and he there informed the Grand Marshal of Napoleon's condition. He regularly referred to Napoleon as 'the patient' in his reports. All this was done with impunity.

The secretary was in no doubt that Arnott was in the Governor's pocket. He also believed the doctor to be actively exploiting this connection for his own ends. It was one of Arnott's duties to make medical inspections of the ships in the harbour.

Medico 20th [Arnott] not withstanding that he frequently got the bastiments [ships] boarded by his deputy [Rutledge, Assistant Surgeon of the 20th], pocketed the guinea; whilst he was at the same time receiving a pound daily for attending Neighbour [Napoleon] and 10 shillings for health medico. Notwithstanding his activity in the conspiracy, always a guest of Mach [Lowe], and enjoying every mark of favour; no remonstrance with him, evidently however to have him in reserve, by this attention and kindness, in case any future need or emergency in explaining matters respecting Neighbour's health satisfactorily.

As the only British medical man in a position to express a first-hand opinion regarding the Emperor's illness, Arnott was too important to be allowed to be a free agent. Lowe was determined to control him. Reade was exasperated with the surgeon. The Deputy Adjutant-General warned the Governor that Arnott was 'much too civil to Bonaparte's followers' and that this was 'in a manner at your expense'. It may be that he was jealous of the doctor's closeness to Lowe. Gorrequer was also irritated by Arnott's privileged contact with the Governor. On 1st April, the date of the first consultation, he writes

> Soon after this day Medico 20th began addressing all his reports to Mach, instead of Ego [Gorrequer] about Neighbour in order to conceal them from him. Most likely to turn it to some advantage on his side when necessary.

It is probable that this relationship between doctor and Governor was based on expediency rather than on any genuine warmth. Whilst Lowe is cautious in his comments regarding Arnott, the doctor, at least in the company of fellow medics, was less discrete. Gorrequer's diary, 15th August, 1821:

> Medico Longo [Thomas Shortt] also told Ego [Gorrequer] that Old O.P. archy medico [Arnott] had abused both Mach and Sultana [Lady Lowe] through thick and thin, when dining at his house the preceding week.[15]

Napoleon was ignorant of the misrepresentation of his illness and he rewarded Arnott for his attendance. Although conspiring with the Governor, the doctor had at least treated his patient with good manners and kindness during his thirty-five consultations. The ailing Emperor took a gold snuff box and laboriously engraved an 'N' upon it with the point of his scissors. This box, containing 600 Napoleons, was handed to Arnott by Montholon after the Emperor's death. Reade commented to the surgeon that he was surprised it was not 1,500 Napoleons; a bad case of sour grapes. When Lowe received a note from Arnott just before 6pm on the 5th containing the words 'He has this moment expired', he sent Shortt and Mitchell to confirm the death. Montholon asked that Arnott, the British officer most trusted by the French, should stay in the room until midnight to watch over the body before being relieved by one of his colleagues. At seven o'clock the next morning, Lowe and his staff entered the death-chamber to formally identify the remains.

Once the autopsy was completed, the body was sewn up. Some sources state that Rutledge was entrusted with the morbid task of guarding the dissected corpse but Arnott was in attendance for at least part of the time. Marchand says that Arnott had been requested not to leave the Emperor's body until it was interred and also to keep watch over two vases containing the heart and the stomach. Saint-Denis confirms that Arnott or his 'substitutes' were ever-present as the Governor was fearful that the remains might be interfered with or stolen. Arnott later described his nocturnal vigil to the Edinburgh Professor Sir James Young Simpson. He lay in bed with two pistols under his pillow ready to repel any French attempt to seize the post-mortem specimens which were in basins of water. Hearing a splash, he jumped to his feet to find that it was only the Longwood rats trying to get at the flesh. The surgeon then kept the silver dish containing the heart in his bed. The most famous rat anecdote from St. Helena concerns the two animals that jumped out of the Emperor's hat when he was putting it on but Arnott's story is the most unpleasant. At the funeral on 9th April, a beautiful winter day, the hearse could not easily reach the tomb in a valley below Hutt's Gate and the casket was carried by Montholon, Bertrand, Marchand and young Napoleon Bertrand. The British surgeon walked near the front of the procession with Antommarchi.

Arnott retired from the army in 1826 having completed thirty years service. He lived for the remainder of his life on his estate, Kirkconnel Hall, in Dumfriesshire. In addition to the gifts from Napoleon, he was in receipt of £500 from the British Government. He remained unmarried and died at the age of eighty three. His tombstone in Ecclefechan churchyard carries an inscription:

> At St. Helena he was the medical attendant of Napoleon Bonaparte whose esteem he won and whose last moments he soothed.

Arnott was reluctant to discuss the St. Helena episode in his later years. He presumably wanted his book of 1822 to be his last word on the subject. When this publication appeared, Lowe took umbrage and wrote to the Colonel of the 20th Regiment complaining of the doctor's conduct. Arnold Chaplin, in his account of Napoleon's illness, is puzzled by the Governor's objection but Lowe's irritation is understandable. He had taken considerable trouble to manipulate Arnott and he could not have expected the doctor to belatedly produce an honest account of Napoleon's last weeks. Now it would be possible for the public to read both Arnott's contemporary medical reports and his book and to understand that that the surgeon's actions on St. Helena were the result of the climate of fear created by the Governor.[16]

Notes

1. Gorrequer, Major G, *St. Helena during Napoleon's Exile*, pp. 221, 63, 131–3, 172; Chaplin, A, *A St. Helena Who's Who*, p. 29; Young, N, *Napoleon in Exile*, Vol. II, p. 272.

2. Wilson, JB, *Dr Archibald Arnott*; Chaplin, *A St. Helena Who's Who*, pp. 33, 51–2; Chaplin, A, *The Illness and Death of Napoleon Bonaparte*, pp. 100–102; Richardson, F, *Napoleon's Death: An Inquest*, pp. 152–3.

3. Markham, JD, *Napoleon and Dr Verling on St. Helena*, pp. 83–4, 140–2; Forsyth, W, *History of the Captivity of Napoleon*, Vol. II, p. 72; Young, Vol. II, p. 159; Bertrand, Général, *Cahiers de Sainte-Hélène*, pp. 383–5; Bertrand, General, *Napoleon at St. Helena*, p. 131.

4. Forsyth, Vol. II, pp. 130, 148–50; Lutyens, E, *Letters of Captain Engelbert Lutyens*, pp. 62, 67, 101–4; Bertrand, *Napoleon at St. Helena*, pp. 132–5; Marchand, *Mémoires de Marchand*, Vol. II, pp. 290–2; St. Denis, LE, *Napoleon from the Tuileries to St. Helena*, p. 261; Wilson; Markham, p. 98; Lowe Papers 20214 f. 159; The National Archives J 76/4/1 ff. 21–2; Gorrequer, p. 219.

5. Chaplin, *The Illness and Death of Napoleon Bonaparte*, pp. 6–47; Lemaire, J-F, *Autour de 'L'Empoisonnement' de Napoléon*, pp. 22–31; Lugli, A, *Napoleon Bonaparte's Gastric Cancer*.

6. Lugli; Chaplin, *The Illness and Death of Napoleon Bonaparte*, pp. 48–75.

7. Lin, X, *Elemental Contents in Napoleon's Hair*; Lugli; Forshufvud, S, *Who Killed Napoleon?*, p. 182; Maury, R, *L'Énigme Napoléon resolue*, p. 135; Lugli, A, *Napoleon's Autopsy: New Perspectives*.

8. Marchand, Vol. II, p. 292; Young, Vol. II, p. 212; Ganière, P, *Napoléon à Sainte Hélène: La Mort de L'Empereur L'Apothéose*, pp. 194–5; Frémeaux, P, *The Drama of St. Helena*, p. 277; Antommarchi, F, *Les Derniers Moments de Napoléon*, Vol. II, pp. 49–50.

9. Wilson; Bertrand, *Napoleon at St. Helena*, pp. 254, 152–80, 215, 199–206; Masson, F, *Autour de Sainte-Hélène*, Vol. III, p. 246; Kemble, *Napoleon Immortal*, pp. 266–9; Frémeaux, p. 283.

10. Young, Vol. II, pp. 215–6; Marchand, Vol. II, p. 299; Lutyens, p. 135; Bertrand, *Napoleon at St. Helena*, pp. 157–8; Frémeaux, p. 287; Forsyth, Vol. II, p. 153; Gorrequer, p. 222; Lowe Papers 20157 f. 18.

11. Young, Vol. II, p. 224; Antommarchi, Vol. II, pp. 107–8; Bertrand, *Napoleon at St. Helena*, pp. 254–5.

12. Chaplin, *The Illness and Death of Napoleon Bonaparte*, pp. 35–6; Bertrand, *Napoleon at St. Helena*, pp. 147, 170; Young, Vol. II, pp. 212–21; Lowe Papers 20133 f. 18, 20207 f. 341, 20157, ff. 2–28; Forsyth, Vol. II, pp. 151, 640; Lutyens, p. 119; Glover, G, *Wellington's Lieutenant Napoleon's Gaoler*, p. 290.

13. Lowe Papers 20157 ff. 17, 29–34, 20133 f. 107; Antommarchi, Vol. II, p. 76; Young, Vol. II, pp. 219–23; Chaplin, *The Illness and Death of Napoleon Bonaparte*, pp. 45–6; Forsyth, Vol. II, p. 155; Bertrand, *Napoleon at St. Helena*, pp. 252–3.

14. Chaplin, *The Illness and Death of Napoleon Bonaparte*, pp. 35–6; Arnott, A, *An account of the Last Illness and decease and PM appearance of Napoleon Bonaparte*, pp. iii–iv, 3–23; Richardson, pp. 155–7.

15. Richardson, p. 155; Kemble, pp. 264–5; Bertrand, *Napoleon at St. Helena*, p. 161; Gorrequer, pp. 220–1, 243–4; Korngold, R, *The Last Years of Napoleon*, p. 390; Martineau, G, *Napoleon's St. Helena*, pp. 213–4; Chaplin, *The Illness and Death of Napoleon Bonaparte*, pp. 37–8.

16. Marchand, Vol. II, pp. 336–54; Young, Vol. II, p. 225; St. Denis, p. 281; Richardson, pp. 176–7; Wilson; Chaplin, *The Illness and Death of Napoleon Bonaparte*, pp. 100–102; Chaplin, *A St. Helena Who's Who*, pp. 51–2.

9

DEATH MASK

With Napoleon dead, it may be thought that there was little chance of more medical men becoming ensnared in the web of conspiracy that surrounded him. This was not the case. Two more British doctors were to be trapped and the first of these was Thomas Shortt who arrived on St. Helena in December 1820. Shortt was the most outstanding of all the Army and Navy doctors on the island. He was born in 1788 near Dumfries and received his medical education in Edinburgh. In 1806, at the age of eighteen, he was appointed Assistant Surgeon to a battalion of the Foot Guards. He served in the Mediterranean and soon transferred to the Royal Artillery. In Egypt in 1807, his talents were recognised and he was placed in charge of a hospital for the sick of the artillery, the engineers and the Staff Corps. He also had responsibility for supervision of an eye hospital in Alexandria. In the following years he served with distinction in Sicily with the Chasseurs Britanniques and was appointed Surgeon to the 29th Light Dragoons in 1813. He declined the opportunity of a Staff Surgeon post but at the end of the war he was offered the post of Physician to the Forces which he accepted.

All this represented a brilliant and rapid military career. Shortt had been promoted to the prestigious post of Physician at only twenty seven years of age, an unusual achievement even in a time of conflict. With hostilities over, he was now on half-pay and he returned to his old medical school to obtain his doctorate. After starting a glittering career in private practice in Edinburgh, including the honorary post of 'Physician Extraordinary to the King of Scotland', Shortt was appointed as Baxter's successor as

Principal Medical Officer to St. Helena in 1820. This was a well judged selection in view of his proven medical and administrative expertise, and his fluency in Italian and French. Understandably, the talented physician was not enthused by this turn of events – he was very well established in Edinburgh and must have had an enviable lifestyle – but he complied with the order and he arrived in Jamestown five days before Christmas, accompanied by his wife Henrietta.[1]

The decision to appoint Shortt was taken by James McGrigor, the veteran chief of the Army medical service, who had proved so valuable to Wellington's cause in the Peninsular War. McGrigor was mindful of Baxter's problems and he had sent a man who, he hoped, would be able to act with more autonomy. Lowe, irritated that he had not been consulted prior to the appointment, was immediately sensitised to the presence of Shortt. When the new senior medical officer said things which were helpful to the Governor – he roundly condemned O'Meara and confirmed the healthiness of the local garrison – Lowe perversely complained to Bathurst in a letter of February 1821 that the doctor was trying too hard to please. He suspected that Shortt might be sending different reports to McGrigor. Despite his reservations as to his loyalties, the Governor felt obliged to formally offer the services of his most highly qualified doctor to the French. No reply was received.[2]

Shortt's integration into the St. Helena community was not helped by Lady Lowe, who took a dislike to him and his wife. His medical reputation had preceded him; Lady Lowe commented to Bertrand that it was a pity that Napoleon was not seeing the new doctor. 'He was much the most capable man to have reached the island since she herself had arrived on it, not excepting Mr Baxter.' Despite this respect for his professional abilities, a rift developed between the Lowe and Shortt families. It is possible that the doctor and his wife, fresh from their life in Edinburgh, found the society on St. Helena claustrophobic and were not seen to be adequately respectful. Only a few days after the Shortts' arrival, Gorrequer records Lady Lowe's anger that they had decided to visit Admiral Lambert for tea rather than her. The Military Secretary notes that there was a perfectly good reason for this and that no offence was intended. He adds phlegmatically, 'The more you tried to be civil and attentive the worse it was, and that was the return that you got for your civility.'

Lady Lowe shared her husband's paranoid tendencies; she was convinced that there was 'a party against her' on the island. In June 1821 she claimed at dinner that the Shortts had behaved with incivility and rudeness. Thomas Shortt was under no illusion as to the Lowes' sentiments. He told Gorrequer that he knew that the Governor's wife regarded him as an enemy. Henrietta Shortt, who also left a diary of her time on St. Helena, believed that the only real complaints that Lady Lowe had against her were her 'Scotch accent and her long waist'. She hints that Her Ladyship was not altogether popular and admits to having a 'terrible fracas' with her.[3]

In such a closed community, social infighting of this sort was inevitable and it need not in itself have damaged the working relationship between Shortt and Lowe. But there was more. Although Shortt never met Napoleon, we have seen that on one occasion, on 3rd May, he did have the opportunity to visit Longwood and to discuss the Emperor's illness with Arnott and Mitchell. The two doctors who had been excluded from the patient were reluctant to commit themselves to a definite diagnosis. However, Shortt, on the basis of the second-hand information which he had received, did favour liver disease; this was the reason he strongly supported the administration of a large dose of calomel, a medication that can only have exacerbated the symptoms of stomach cancer. The doctor incautiously made his opinion public and it is inconceivable that the Governor was unaware of his views. Lowe had not forgiven O'Meara and Stokoe for making the politically inconvenient diagnosis of liver disease and he had no reason to change his attitude now.[4]

Napoleon had informed his associates that he wished to have an autopsy performed. He understood that the findings would have political as well as medical connotations – particularly if liver disease was found to be the cause of death – and he instructed Bertrand that he preferred that Antommarchi should perform it either alone or with Arnott. He accepted that Shortt, as the senior British doctor, would probably also be present and he told the Grand Marshal that every precaution was to be taken to see that 'no nonsense' was inserted in the official report. The Emperor may have lost his battle with disease but he was determined not to be defeated by Lowe.

The post-mortem examination was arranged for 2pm on 6th May, the day following death. Marchand and Saint-Denis describe a table in the billiard room being prepared with a sheet. The room was only fifteen by eighteen feet and was poorly lit by two side windows. Into this cramped dark space were packed seventeen people; not at all what Napoleon had envisaged. Antommarchi, wearing an apron and holding a scalpel, was to perform the autopsy. Also in attendance were the following: Thomas Reade, Major

Charles Harrison, Captain William Crokat (three British officers); Thomas Shortt, Archibald Arnott, Francis Burton, Matthew Livingstone, Charles Mitchell, Walter Henry, George Rutledge (seven British doctors); Bertrand, Montholon, Marchand, Saint-Denis, Vignali and Pierron (six French). Shortt, as the senior medical man, was to oversee the procedure and to draw up the official report. He ordered Walter Henry to take notes. All present were aware that the findings and conclusions would be sent around the world and that this was more than a purely medical matter. The French remained convinced that the post-mortem would reveal that death was caused by hepatitis induced by the climate of St. Helena. Lowe's followers were equally determined that this should not be the case. Archibald Arnott, who had for so long touted a diagnosis of hypochondriasis, must have been particularly apprehensive. All were ignorant of the real cause of death.

The post-mortem took two hours; the essential findings have already been described. All present were soon convinced that a cancer of the stomach was the fatal disease. Even the French were accepting of this. Bertrand admitted that the stomach was the 'seat of all the trouble' with the tumour clearly visible. Montholon wrote much the same to his wife in Europe. Rutledge describes the surprise of the French and their pressing enquiries.

> Madame Bertrand went so far as to satisfy herself as to the precise part in which the disease existed that she actually introduced the point of her little finger through the cancerated hole, and said that cancer was what the Emperor had always said to be the matter with him, and of which he anticipated his death.

The Grand Marshal's wife was not present during the autopsy and she was presumably allowed to view the dissection afterwards. There was actually relief among Napoleon's followers that his death was due to an inexorable process which could not be attributed to the conditions of his captivity. The post-mortem findings exonerated all his Longwood companions from any possible blame.

There were five different post-mortem reports. Three of these might be termed 'contemporary' and two were conceived at a later date. Thomas Shortt wrote the official report and then amended it to produce a second definitive version – we will return to the reason for this. Antommarchi refused to sign this British document. When it was translated to him, he said that he agreed with it but it is alleged, by Francis Burton, that Bertrand forbade him to add his name because the deceased was not referred to as the 'Emperor Napoleon'. The Grand Marshal makes no mention of this in his memoirs and Antommarchi later claimed that he did not sign because it was not his report. The Corsican penned his own account of the dissection on 8th May and then elaborated on this in a more detailed version, which he appended to his memoir of 1825. The final report was created in 1823 by Walter Henry. He did this following a request from Lowe and he used his original notes to compile it. This entered print in 1839 in Henry's *Trifles from my Portfolio.*[5]

Once it became obvious that the stomach was the site of the fatal disease, the state of the liver was of secondary medical importance. Nevertheless, all present realised the political significance of any hepatic abnormality; even a secondary disorder of the organ might provide ammunition for those who were opposed to the British Government's treatment of the prisoner. Rutledge helped Antommarchi remove the abdominal organs from the corpse. As the liver was inspected there was an expectant hush. Would O'Meara, Stokoe and Antommarchi be vindicated in their diagnosis of hepatitis? Thomas Reade's report to Lowe was written only a few hours later. The Governor was too squeamish to attend in person. After giving Lowe details of the appearance of the stomach, Reade describes what happened next.

The liver was afterwards examined. The moment the operator [Antommarchi] took it out Dr Shortt instantly observed 'it was enlarged'. All the other medical gentlemen differed with him in this opinion, particularly Dr Burton, who combated Dr Shortt's opinion very earnestly. Dr Henry was equally divided with Dr Burton. Dr Arnott said there was nothing extraordinary in the appearance of the liver, it might be a large one, but certainly not larger than the liver of any man of the same age as General Bonaparte. Dr Mitchell said he saw nothing extraordinary, and Mr Rutledge said it certainly was not enlarged. Notwithstanding all these observations, Dr Shortt still persisted in saying 'it was enlarged'. This struck me so forcibly that I stepped forward and observed to the medical officers generally, that it appeared to me very important that they should all be prepared to give a decided and prompt opinion as to the real state of the liver, and I recommended a very careful re-examination of it. Dr Shortt made no more observations, but all the other gentlemen reiterated their first opinion to me. At this moment, the liver was in the hand of the operator, and upon my appearing desirous to see it closer, he immediately took his knife and cut it open from one end to the other, observing to me, 'It is good, perfectly sound, and nothing extraordinary in it.' He observed at the same time that he thought it was a large liver. This opinion, however, did not appear to have been made in the manner as Dr Shortt had expressed, viz. 'that the liver was enlarged'. There is a large difference between a 'large liver' and 'a liver being enlarged'. I made this observation to Dr Burton and Dr Arnott who coincided.

Reade's distinction contains some truth but he had misinterpreted Antommarchi's opinion. In his own report, written only forty eight hours later, the Corsican physician described the liver as being 'congested and larger than normal'. The majority medical opinion at the post-mortem was against liver enlargement but the most experienced anatomist and the most accomplished doctor in the room, Antommarchi and Shortt, both expressed the view that the organ was larger than normal. In his official report, Shortt described the cause of death – 'The internal surface of the stomach to nearly its whole extent was a mass of cancerous disease' – and added the following;

> The convex surface of the left lobe of the liver adhered to the diaphragm, and the liver was perhaps a little larger than natural. With the exception of the adhesions occasioned by the disease in the stomach no unhealthy appearance presented itself in the liver.

He presumably thought this to be a reasonable compromise. The insertion of the word 'perhaps' acknowledged that his own opinion was not universally accepted. This report was signed by Shortt, Arnott, Mitchell and Burton. The two most junior doctors, the Assistant Surgeons Rutledge and Henry, were excluded as the Governor had ordered that only those of the rank of Surgeon or above should be signatories. Livingstone was not included as he was not present during the final stages of the autopsy. Shortt did not approve of the presence of an employee of the East India Company and he had found an excuse to remove him before the end.[6]

Lowe remained vigilant and he immediately raised two objections to the post-mortem report. He complained that the signature of Livingstone had been omitted and he brought attention to the statement regarding the liver, as he understood this not to be the opinion of all the doctors present. He was determined that there should not be even a hint of liver disease. We have no record of the subsequent discussions which must have taken place between the Principal Medical Officer and the Governor. A second post-mortem report was produced; this made no reference to enlargement of the liver and contained the signature of Livingstone. Shortt kept a copy of the redundant first report with his papers and it can still be inspected in the British Library. The sentence, 'The liver was perhaps a little larger than natural' is crudely crossed out and there is a footnote in Shortt's handwriting, 'The words obliterated were <u>suppressed</u> by the order of Sir Hudson Lowe, Thomas Shortt, PMO.' There is no date to this addition.

Forsyth avoids any mention of the change to the autopsy report. Lowe thought the matter important enough to require some explanation and he wrote to Bathurst on 10th May.

> With reference to what I mentioned in the previous letter I addressed to Your Lordship respecting the state of the liver on dissection, I beg leave to enclose a letter which Sir Thomas Reade had addressed to me on the subject [Reade's report of the post-mortem quoted earlier]. I regret the point of view in which it exhibits the conduct of Dr Shortt whose attachment to every part of his public duty and private professional duty has been calculated to give very general satisfaction, and I trust, therefore it may not be necessary to advert to it again … I have to add that Mr Livingstone (whose proper line of conduct in some discussions with Dr Verling I had occasion to mention), who being present when the stomach and liver were examined, and being asked by me in Dr Shortt's presence if he had observed any largeness in the liver, directly said he had not. Some degree of contrivance it appeared to me had been previously used to prevent Mr Livingstone from being present during the dissection, though specifically named by me to attend and even to send him away before the dissection was over.
>
> P.S. Dr Arnott has appeared to me to have conducted himself as a perfectly honest and upright man in not encouraging, at the dissection of General Bonaparte, the desire evinced to ascribe his disease to the liver and showed his judgment also in having an opinion to the contrary. Dr Shortt thought the disease produced from the liver without having ever seen the patient alive, but he feels a little ashamed, I believe, of the opinion he has offered.[7]

Norwood Young does describe the amended post-mortem report. He defends the Governor against any accusation of wrongdoing by claiming that Shortt was not coerced into making the alteration. He had, Young claims, a change of mind. The author suggests that the doctor's initial opinion that the liver was enlarged was simply a 'hasty assertion which he afterwards regretted'. Young supports his theory that the physician was the victim only of his own mistake by quoting two letters written by Shortt on the day after the autopsy. The first, to his brother-in-law in Dumfries, was later published in the *North British Advertiser* in 1873.

St. Helena

7th May, 1821

My Dear Sir

You will, no doubt, be much surprised to hear of Bonaparte's death, who expired on the 5th May, after an illness of some standing. His disease was cancer in the stomach that must have lasted some years, and been in a state of ulceration some months. I was in consultation and attendance several days, but he would not see strangers. I was officially introduced, the moment he died. His face was in death the most beautiful I ever beheld, exhibiting softness and very good expression in the highest degree, and really seemed formed to conquer. The following day I superintended the dissection of his body – (at this time his countenance was much altered) – which was done at his own request, to ascertain the exact seat of the disease (which he imagined to be where it was afterwards discovered to be), with the view of benefiting his son, who might inherit it. During the whole of his illness he never complained and kept his character to the last. The disease being hereditary, his father having died of it, and his sister, the Princess Borghese, being supposed to have it, proves to the world that climate and mode of life had no hand in it and, contrary to the assertions of Messrs O'Meara and Stokoe, his liver was perfectly sound; and had he been on the throne of France instead of an inhabitant of St. Helena, he would equally have suffered, as no earthly power could cure the disease when formed.

A second letter of the same date, containing much the same information, was published by a member of the Shortt family in the *English Review* in 1831. If we take his comment that the liver was 'perfectly sound' literally, then the doctor had indeed had a dramatic change of opinion. This is improbable as there had been no reason for him to revise his original medical assessment in the twenty four hours after the autopsy. It is more likely that he was telling his brother-in-law only part of the truth. He would not have wanted to admit to a close relative that he had been bullied into changing a crucial medical report for political reasons. Neither would he have wished to place such an explosive revelation into the public domain; the post on St. Helena was censored and the contents of his letters were almost certainly scrutinised by Lowe's staff. That he was forced to change the official report against his will is confirmed by an entry in Gorrequer's diary for 7th May, the same day on which Shortt wrote his letters home.

> Mach [Lowe] worried Dr Shortt and Dr Arnott to make them alter the report of the dissection, and the whole of the doctors concerned, who after much noise and much rage on his part did alter it. By dint of persevering in worrying the above two named, he obtained letters from them, to annex to reports subsequently sent, saying that Napoleon would not have lived so long had it not been for the adhesion of the liver.

Lowe not only demanded the erasure of any reference to the liver as a possible source of disease; he wanted to portray the organ as a positive influence. Arnott, who had originally thought that the liver was large, had evidently sided with Shortt but both doctors had been forced to capitulate. Lowe was correct in his claim that Shortt was ashamed but this was not for the reason he inferred.[8]

The Governor had a personal reason to be grateful to his Principal Medical Officer. His son became seriously ill with croup and Shortt successfully treated him. Lowe showed the doctor no public ill will. He praised him in his General Order of 25th July 1821. Conversely, Shortt never forgave Lowe for forcing him to act unethically. When O'Meara's book appeared, the doctor joined in the attacks on the beleaguered ex-Governor. He was consulted by Sir Walter Scott who was working on his *Life of Napoleon*; much of Scott's prejudice against Lowe was derived from Shortt.

It is possible that Shortt departed from St. Helena sooner than he wished. The reasons for this are obscure. One would have thought that he would have been keen to return to his lucrative private practice but his inclination to stay on the island is suggested by a conversation of Reade's, cryptically documented by Gorrequer in late June. According to the Deputy Adjutant-General, Shortt 'only wanted to be asked to remain here ... but was disappointed'. He adds that the doctor 'would have given anything to stay'. Shortt sailed for home in September and resumed his previous work in Edinburgh. In 1827, he refused a further call up from the Army Board and, following an application to the Duke of Wellington, he was granted £1,000 in lieu of his half-pay. His successful career culminated in his appointment as Inspector of Prisons in 1842. He died from pneumonia the following year at the age of fifty-five and was buried at Newport on the Isle of Wight.[9]

After the autopsy, Saint-Denis and Marchand dressed the Emperor in the complete uniform of the mounted chasseurs of the Imperial Guard. They carried the body to his former bedroom, which had been draped in black and turned into a mortuary chapel. He was laid on the field bed on which he had died and, as has been related, was guarded by Arnott and Rutledge. It was now decided to make a cast of the Emperor's face; a death mask. Both valets say that Madame Bertrand was the chief proponent. She wanted to take an imprint of the Emperor's features, both for his own family and for posterity.

There was nothing surprising in this. It was the fashion of the time to take casts of the face or the whole head, both in life and after death. The technique was not straightforward. Even in the hands of an expert, death-moulding was unsatisfactory as nothing could prevent the sinking of the eyes, the compression of the nose, and the drawing in of the cheeks. The normal method was to shave the head, to block up the orifices (in life a thin quill was inserted into the nose for breathing) and then to place a thin sheet of muslin on the skin. One or two silk threads were laid on to allow the eventual removal of the mould. The plaster, prepared from gypsum, was then applied in layers over the whole head and allowed to set hard. The threads were pulled and the mould came apart, often in three pieces. These were re-soldered together with wet plaster and bound with string to form the final mould. The casting involved pouring in, at the throat, enough plaster to line the inside. The mould was rocked to ensure that this filled every cranny and more plaster was added until the cast attained a thickness of around one inch. The whole was allowed to set and dry for a few hours and a chisel was then used to chip away the mould leaving the cast of the head. Ideally, this was a perfect reproduction but, particularly if performed after death, there was often the need for a sculptor to repair cracks and beautify the final product.

At first, there was little public reference to Napoleon's death mask. A letter to *The Times* in September 1821 alluded to a conversation in which Antommarchi described fashioning a mask. This was penned anonymously and was very likely a forgery as it contained a number of obvious inaccuracies. Three years later, Antommarchi published his memoirs, *Les Derniers Moments de Napoléon*, in which he made reference to the existence of a mask and claimed that he was the maker. Although Antommarchi wrote that he moulded the face before the post-mortem – all other witnesses indicate that it was done afterwards – his assertion was not challenged. In the nineteenth century, it was commonly assumed that it was 'Antommarchi's mask'. However, the waters were already becoming muddied. There was more than one mask in circulation and the story of the creation and subsequent fate of the original was becoming part of St. Helena mythology. Which mask was the true version? There were almost as many different theories as for the cause of death of the Emperor. In the first decade of the twentieth century, the story of the mask took a dramatic turn – an eminent French historian stated that the true author of the mask was a British army doctor.[10]

Francis Burton was born in 1784 at Tuam in County Galway and he studied medicine at Dublin. He joined the British army in 1805 and served in the Peninsular War, first as Assistant Surgeon in the 36th Foot and then as Surgeon to the 4th Regiment. He also saw action in the Walcheren Campaign and at Waterloo. He was highly regarded both by his comrades and medical superiors. At the end of the war, the officers of his regiment presented him with a piece of plate as testimony to their gratitude. He resided in Edinburgh for some time before he was recalled to active service at the special request of James McGrigor. It was in the capacity of Surgeon to the 66th Regiment that he arrived on St. Helena on 31st March 1821.[11]

Burton had a reputation for integrity both during his university years in Dublin and through his later military career. This is important as we are greatly dependant on his papers and letters in unravelling the story of Napoleon's death mask. There are three main sources for the doctor's version of events. In 1835, seven years after Burton's death, the celebrated Dublin pathologist Professor James Graves gave two lectures on the subject of Napoleon. Graves was Burton's cousin and he had unique access to his correspondence. In the second of his lectures, the professor declared that Burton was the author of the death mask. This should have caused a stir and seriously undermined Antommarchi's pretensions but the talk was delivered to a handful of medical students on an ordinary professorial round and was published in the highly specialised *London Medical and Surgical Journal*. It only reached a very limited number of people and it is unlikely that word spread across the Channel. Graves's revelations were quickly forgotten and only received wider attention over seventy years after the original lecture. The second source is a letter written by Burton to *The Courier* in September 1821 and the third is correspondence between Lowe and Bathurst in which the Governor gives the surgeon full credit for the creation of the mask.

Burton states that he had previous experience of taking casts in plaster of Paris but he does not elaborate. He asked the Governor for permission to make a death mask 'both before and after the death of General Bonaparte'. He later adds that he was 'very anxious' to take a 'bust' of the Emperor. Lowe gave the doctor permission to proceed. Marchand remembers that the Governor offered Antommarchi the services of a doctor who was adept at plaster casts to help him take that of Napoleon but the Corsican replied that he needed only plaster and not assistance. Burton is not mentioned by name but this incident agrees with his own account.[12]

What happened next is best told in Burton's own words. The doctor sometimes uses the term 'bust' rather than 'cast'.

> I accordingly [having received Lowe's approval], the morning after General Bonaparte's death [6th May], proceeded to Longwood. On my arrival there, Dr Antommarchi informed me that he intended taking a cast: I asked his permission to be present, and also to take one myself to which he agreed. Dr Antommarchi, however, on trial of the material sent to him, said it could not succeed; upon which I returned to Jamestown and found that there was no plaster to be had in the shops but learned that the crude material (sulphate of lime) was to be found scattered about in different parts of the island. The Admiral [Robert Lambert] was then applied to, who allowed his boats to proceed in search of it, Mr Payne [John Paine], ornamental house-painter, employed at Longwood, having offered his services in preparing the plaster.
>
> As soon as it was ready, I had it conveyed to Dr Antommarchi under the feeling that the friends of the deceased ought to have the first trial; he, however, on seeing the plaster, said it could not succeed, and positively refused even to attempt it. This occurred in the presence of Madame Bertrand, several British officers, Mr Payne, Mr Rubridge [Joseph Rubridge, the portrait painter] and many of the household. On seeing Dr Antommarchi positively refuse the take the cast, Madame Bertrand not only gave me permission, but urged me even to attempt it. With little difficulty I succeeded in forming the mould, but at so late an hour that a second could not be taken. Dr Antommarchi, after the only difficulty had been surmounted, thought it proper to assist. Next morning [7th May], the bust was taken from the mould, but finding the plaster very bad, I was most reluctantly obliged to sacrifice the mould to preserve the bust perfect.

The last comment suggests that Burton had no experience of making death masks. It was routine practice to destroy the mould. His previous handling of plaster was probably limited to surgical procedures in live patients. He continues,

> Here then lay a difficulty; for although the person [Antommarchi] employed by the friends of the deceased could not execute the business, I thought it a necessary compliment that the friends should have one of the best busts that I could execute; and under this impression I have ever acted. I represented to them, through Dr Antommarchi, the great danger of trying to take a second mould from the bust [i.e. a secondary or piece-mould from the original cast in order to multiply casts] owing to the badness of the plaster; but to obviate the difficulty, proposed that it should not be attempted until our arrival in England, which was agreed to, and Dr Antommarchi proposed that it should be done at the Sablonière Hotel, London, to which he intended going.

From Burton's account, it seems that the room was full of people when he fashioned the mould for the mask. In addition to himself and Antommarchi, there was Madame Bertrand and a number of members of the household, including Marchand and Saint-Denis, and perhaps as many as ten British spectators. Very few have left accounts of who did what and the eyewitness evidence that we do have is contradictory. Marchand says that Antommarchi made the mask with Burton's help but this is dubious. The valet wrote his memoirs long after the appearance of Antommarchi's book and he would not have wanted to publicly accuse his companion in exile of lying. Saint-Denis gives equal credit to the British and Corsican doctors. The two British sources available, Ensign John Ward of the 60th Regiment and Ensign Duncan Darroch of the 20th, insist that Burton was the chief operator. Darroch's account has an air of authenticity; he remembers that he was unable to remain long in the room because of the 'horrible stench'.

To understand subsequent events, it is important to appreciate that Burton made his cast in two parts taken from two separate moulds. There was a larger front part containing the features of the face and the ears and a smaller back part with the outline of the back of the head. Again, this suggests that the doctor was an amateur at making death masks. A more experienced practitioner would have joined the two moulds together to produce a single cast of the whole head.[13]

Despite his inexperience, the surgeon had succeeded in creating a recognisable mask. He had shown more determination and had overcome more difficulties than he later admitted; to fashion the object from crude material taken directly from the soil was a considerable achievement. Well satisfied with his efforts, Burton left the two halves of the cast to dry and retired to his quarters for some refreshment. Here he recounted his efforts to his brother officers who were keen to see the mask. On being informed that it was at Longwood, one of the more senior officers, whom Burton does not identify, immediately exclaimed, 'You have been deceived, you will never see the mould again.' Here, Burton uses the word 'mould' when he actually means the cast.

The doctor naively protested that it was impossible that the mask could be spirited away as he had made it in front of so many witnesses. He was, however, unsettled enough by the remark to return to Longwood – it is unclear whether this was later the same day or early the following morning. Here he found the suspicions of his worldlier companion to have been fully justified. The front, or face part, of the cast had been taken. The back part was left behind; the theft was committed by someone who did not fully understand the significance of the two halves.

Burton retained the back portion and went in search of Madame Bertrand. The Countess admitted, in the presence of her husband, Antommarchi and a British officer, Major Anthony Emmett, that she was in possession of the face mask. She assured the doctor on her honour that he would be provided with a copy of the cast as soon as suitable plaster was available. In all likelihood, this would be following their return to Europe. Burton was unimpressed. 'Having been thus cajoled and ungraciously treated, I was anxious to have Madame Bertrand's promise in writing.' There now followed a vigorous correspondence between the surgeon and his two adversaries, Count and Countess Bertrand.[14]

On 22nd May, Burton sent a firm but polite letter to the Countess. In it, he reminded her that the mask could not have been made without his exertions and that Antommarchi had played only a secondary role. He pointed out that he was still in possession of the crucial back part of the mask without which it was incomplete. The surgeon requested that the object be returned to him and promised that, upon his return to London, he would make a faithful copy for the French. Having received no reply by the following day, Burton dispatched a second short note from Jamestown asking for a definitive response to his claim. This was also ignored and, realising that the precious relic was slipping through his fingers, he decided to write a more assertive letter to Count Bertrand.

23rd May 1821

Sir,

Having twice done myself the honour of addressing myself by letter to Countess Bertrand, on the subject of the bust of Napoleon being detained by some person at Longwood, and as she has not thought proper to answer either of my letters, of which conduct I feel duly sensible, I beg leave to address you on the subject, as the person legally concerned for your wife and to refer to my letter of the 22nd to the Countess, in which I claim the bust as my private property having exclusively procured the material and formed it myself with your consent. At the same time I beg to repeat my positive engagement to give you one of the best casts that can be taken from it on my arrival in London, and even if you need the original itself as soon as I take a cast from it for myself; than which I think nothing can be more liberal on my part. If however it is not agreed to, in justice to myself I am compelled distinctly to state that if the bust is not handed over to me today I shall immediately have recourse to every legal measure this Island affords of detaining it here under seal until our respective claims are determined and that if this Island does not afford the means, the same ship which carries you to England shall also carry my claims to the Authorities there, as well as to the Customs House officers, with a statement of the whole transaction, not only to that country but to France, where I have no doubt the merits of the case will be fully investigated and the notices duly appreciated.

 With feelings of great regret for being compelled to express myself this strongly.

I have the honour to be, Sir,

Your most obedient and humble servant

Francis Burton

The Grand Marshal could hardly have expected that he would be threatened with legal action by a British army doctor in his final hours on St. Helena. He decided that a reply was in order but instead of writing directly to Burton, he composed a letter in collaboration with Montholon. It is actually the latter's name at the bottom but it is the Grand Marshal speaking. In a carefully worded response, Bertrand first states that it was he and Montholon who requested that Antommarchi should make a mask. The role of Burton is both acknowledged and belittled.

> Never, Sir, did you set forth to me any claim to this mask being your property. Nor did you obtain my consent in this matter. I had not the honour to know you, either personally or by name, although I now assume you to have been one of the doctors who were present at the post-mortem examination of the Emperor's body. You assisted Monsieur Antommarchi and I witnessed with gratitude the trouble you took.

It was convenient for Bertrand to pretend that Burton was no more than Antommarchi's assistant. The Grand Marshal then refutes the surgeon's claim to the mask on the basis that it was commissioned by the French and that the doctor was merely the artist or sculptor. Bertrand argues that an artist commissioned to paint a portrait was not the owner of the work; it instead belonged to the client who initiated the contract. The letter finishes as follows.

> I cannot therefore, Sir, admit that you have any kind of right to the ownership of the original cast, nor even that of one of the copies. But I shall always be ready to testify to the readiness with which you assisted Monsieur Antommarchi in the operation which had been entrusted to him, and I have no doubts that the Emperor's family will show its gratitude by presenting you with one of the finest examples of the Emperor's death mask.

There are a number of corrections to the wording, suggesting that Bertrand and Montholon gave careful thought to their response. No doubt they hoped that the complimentary references to Burton's participation and the promise of a fine copy would placate the surgeon and end the matter.[15]

On 27th May 1821, the whole of the Longwood contingent together with some officers of the 66th embarked for England on the store-ship *Camel*. The party reached Portsmouth at midnight on 31st July. Here, the Bertrands and Montholons were treated with great civility. They were visited by senior naval and military men and were able to renew acquaintance with the officers of the *Northumberland*. After a few days, they travelled on to London. The *British Press*, the only newspaper to record the fact, noted that General and Madame Bertrand and family, General Montholon and family, and Professor Antommarchi had booked into Brunel's Hotel on

Leicester Square. The papers were generally polite although the *British Monitor* chose to refer to Bertrand as 'noodle' and Montholon as 'doodle'. Among the Grand Marshal's papers, which were only fully disclosed in 1946, is a note referring to the mask. It is undated but must have been written at the time of his arrival in London. Bertrand states that he has placed a copy of the original cast into the hands of a 'Monsieur X' for safe-keeping. This was so that if the original ever became damaged, more faithful copies might be made. It was his intent to send the actual mask to Madame Mère in Rome.[16]

Burton left St. Helena on 13th June on the *Abundance*. Lowe had given him a package with instructions to deliver it to Earl Bathurst. This contained the private papers and diary of Las Cases although the surgeon was unaware of this. He also carried with him the back part of Napoleon's death mask. An entry in Gorrequer's diary for May 1821 – the exact date is not specified – provides more information on the making of the mask and Lowe's role in its procurement. According to the Military Secretary, a number of small plaster of Paris figures were broken up to provide material for its construction. These were almost certainly the source of the plaster that Burton poured into the two moulds. Gorrequer says that the cost of these ornaments was £22-10-00; a substantial amount of money at the time. He adds that the Governor encouraged Burton to claim ownership of the mask and that Lowe suggested to the doctor that he should tell Madame Bertrand that the British authorities might intervene in the matter. Lowe wished to enjoy one final small victory over the French.

In a letter to Bathurst written on 13th June, the Governor recommends Burton and makes reference to the mask.

Dr Burton has not been very well used by the Count and Countess Bertrand. They wished to have a cast of General Bonaparte's head in plaster of Paris. Professor Antommarchi undertook to have it done, but could not succeed. Dr Burton, by a happy combination of skill and patience, succeeded, though with very indifferent material, in obtaining an almost perfect cast. The Bertrands have kept the face; Dr Burton has preserved the back of the skull, or craniological support. There was a contest on [sic] correspondence between them on the occasion, and I have only to approve of Dr Burton's delicacy in seeing it was a subject upon which he could not with propriety refer to me for a decision.

With the Governor not prepared to back his case publicly, Burton was left to fight for the mask on his own. The surgeon reached London on 9th August bearing his dispatch from Lowe and soon had an interview with Goulburn and Bathurst at the Colonial Office. This was probably a routine debriefing; Lowe had promised Bathurst that the surgeon would be able to give 'the fullest information on every matter'. The mask may well have been discussed but there is no evidence that the Government officials gave Burton any practical help to retrieve it.[17]

Burton now wrote to Count Bertrand asking for his copy but was rebuffed with a letter informing him that an application would have to be made directly to Napoleon's family. The surgeon decided that legal action was the only recourse left to him and, after consultation with a lawyer, he applied to Bow Street magistrate's court for a search-warrant.

This was granted and two officers of the Crown went to the Bertrands' hotel in Leicester Square. When they arrived and had made known the nature of their errand, they were remonstrated with both by Bertrand and Sir Robert Wilson. The latter was a notorious British army officer who had seen a great deal of action in the wars and was a willing magnet for publicity. One biographer calls him as a 'dedicated controversialist' and another describes him as being a 'sensationalist'. Wellington famously declared that he was 'a very slippery fellow'. Wilson was attracted to the partisans and followers of the fallen Emperor and it is typical that he was in the company of Count Bertrand at this moment. The officers were impressed by the protestations of such celebrated men and they waived their right of search.

According to a contemporary journalist writing in *The Courier*, Bertrand made Burton an offer of compensation but the doctor indignantly refused. The subsequent hearing at Bow Street was a bitter disappointment to Burton. The Grand Marshal argued that the mask was the property of the family of the deceased, to whom he was an executor, and that he was not authorised to surrender it. Although the authorship of the mask was not questioned – Antommarchi made no claim to it during the legal proceedings – the magistrate decided that it was a matter beyond his jurisdiction. If Burton chose to press his case for ownership, he would have to seek another tribunal. Wilson begged to observe that he believed that the Bertrands and their party had been treated abominably and he applauded the court's officers for not insisting on a formal search. Only a week later, the renegade soldier was castigated for fomenting trouble at Queen Caroline's funeral.

Burton thought the case to have been misrepresented in the news-papers and he wrote to *The Courier* to give his version of events. Of the actual court proceedings and the outcome, he makes the following brief comments:

> Mr Birne [the magistrate], on hearing both sides, declined acting any further in the business, on the principle that it involved a question of Executorship. Now, it is possible to look upon the bust as the property of the friends of the deceased and not that of the person who procured the material and executed the work, unemployed by them, and without meeting the slightest hindrance on their part – I leave the world to decide.[18]

The world had weightier matters to consider and the affair of the mask was quickly forgotten. It seems that the surgeon made no further efforts to gain possession of his creation. He probably believed that this would be futile, particularly once the mask had been taken to France by the Bertrands. Sir Richard Burton, the orientalist and explorer, was a nephew of the doctor. Lady Burton, in her biography of her husband, says that Dr Burton had a letter from Antommarchi in which the latter acknowledged that the British surgeon was the author of the mask. We cannot know if this was true but, if it was, Burton decided against its publication. After all, even conclusive proof of authorship would not win him back the prize. He returned to obscurity as Surgeon in the 12th Lancers and died suddenly in London in October 1828 from a haemorrhage into the lungs.

When Burton was alive, Antommarchi had been reticent regarding his role in the making of the mask. Now, he seized his chance. The fate of the original face mask is shrouded in mystery but it is probable that Antommarchi took a secondary or piece-mould from it when he was the guest of the Bertrands in Paris in the summer of 1822. This allowed him to take a secondary cast from which he could produce any number of plaster and bronze masks. The news of Burton's death filtered through to Antommarchi around 1830. According to the editor of a later edition of Antommarchi's memoirs, the Corsican physician 'suddenly remembered that he had moulded the head of the dying hero'. Blowing the dust off his masterpiece, Antommarchi now spent several years publicising it. In July 1833, 'at the request of the most eminent men of the Empire', he issued a prospectus in which he described himself and his role on St. Helena as follows.

[Antommarchi is] a generous citizen who did not hesitate to leave his country and his family and so abandon all the advantages of a magnificent position acquired by his efforts to go and reside in a mortal climate, whence he disputed with death the existence of the Great Man.

He then described his moulding of the mask and invited subscribers. This was primarily a financial venture but, despite touting far and wide, he failed to sell the expected number of reproduction masks and he soon became disillusioned.

There are currently many Napoleon death masks in museums and private collections around the world. Some are classified as copies but a number are said to be originals. The 'official' death mask, on display in the army museum of *Les Invalides* in Paris, was approved by Antommarchi and Napoleon's mother and has been known of since the 1830s. There is widespread scepticism regarding its authenticity. Many Napoleonic scholars believe the mask to be a fake; one theory is that it shows the features of the Emperor's *maitre d'hôtel*, Cipriani. French Government departments are at loggerheads over the issue. The Culture Ministry contends the claim of the curators of *Les Invalides* and states that the true mask is held but not displayed at another museum in the outskirts of the capital. To complicate matters further, there are claims for several other masks. One is attributed to Archibald Arnott. Another version which was displayed at the Royal United Services Institute in London between 1947 and 1973 has more determined advocates. It was sold at Christie's auction house in 2004 and has not been seen since. Unlike the Paris masks – in which Napoleon appears unnaturally young – the London mask is that of a bloated old man. The French authorities detest it and entirely reject its provenance. These are all face masks. The fate of Burton's back part of the mask is unknown. The doctor died intestate and the trail is cold. It could easily have fallen into the hands of his eminent cousin, Professor Graves, but there is no trace of the relic in the medical museums of Dublin.[19]

The story of the mask, like that of Napoleon's exile on St. Helena, is unfinished. Burton received belated recognition for his role in the mask's creation. At the start of the nineteenth century, historians began to question the honesty of Antommarchi. It was Frédéric Masson, an exhaustive researcher of all things Napoleonic, who unearthed Graves's lecture and, in his *Autour de Sainte Hélène* of 1909, gave the young army surgeon the lion's share of the credit. In his own lifetime, Burton was deprived of any reward or wider recognition for his cameo role on St. Helena. Compared with some of his medical colleagues, he escaped lightly. Nevertheless, he can be included in the line of Anglo-Irish Army and Navy doctors – Warden, O'Meara, Stokoe, Verling, Arnott, Shortt and Burton – who were attracted to Napoleon but were ultimately harmed and disappointed. For them all, the Emperor was nothing less than a curse.

Notes

1. Chaplin, A, *Thomas Shortt*, pp. 7–26; Drew, R, *Commissioned Officers in the Medical Services of the British Army*, Vol. I, p. 192.
2. Chaplin, pp. 7–26; Richardson, F, *Napoleon's Death: An Inquest*, pp. 172–3; Forsyth, W, *History of the Captivity of Napoleon*, Vol. II, pp. 133, 155–7.
3. Bertrand, General, *Napoleon at St. Helena*, p. 221; Gorrequer, Major G, *St. Helena during Napoleon's Exile*, pp. 204, 244–5, 250–4; Chaplin, A, *A St. Helena Who's Who*, p. 97.
4. Young, N, *Napoleon in Exile*, Vol. II, pp. 227–8; Bertrand, pp. 227–8; Ganière, P, *Napoléon à Sainte-Hélène: La Mort de L'Empereur L'Apothéose*, p. 259.
5. Young, Vol. II, pp. 227–35; Bertrand, pp. 181, 261; Richardson, pp. 165–6; St. Denis, LE, *Napoleon from the Tuileries to St. Helena*, p. 279; Marchand, *Mémoires de Marchand*, Vol. II, p. 337; Forsyth, Vol. II, pp. 162–7; Chaplin, A, *The Illness and Death of Napoleon Bonaparte*, pp. 48–9; Henry, W, *Surgeon Henry's Trifles*, p. 181; Montholon, Comte de, *Lettres du Comte et de la Comtesse Montholon*, pp. 80–1; Chaplin, *Thomas Shortt*, p. 81; Lowe Papers 20214 f. 202; Antommarchi, F, *Les Derniers Moments de Napoléon*, Vol. II, p.126.
6. Chaplin, *Thomas Shortt*, pp. 7–26; Ganière, p. 259; Young, Vol. II, pp. 229–32; Montholon, CJT de, *Récits de la Captivité*, Vol. II, p. 559; Bertrand, p. 262; Henry, p. 181.
7. British Library Eg. 3718 ff. 164–5; Lowe Papers 20214 ff. 195–6; Young, Vol. II, pp. 232–5; Chaplin, *Thomas Shortt*, pp. 23–4; Chaplin, *The Illness and Death of Napoleon Bonaparte*, p. 53; Kemble, J, *Napoleon Immortal*, pp. 276–7; Ganière, pp. 261–2.
8. Richardson, p. 173; Young, Vol. II, pp. 233–4; Gorrequer, p. 234.
9. Chaplin, *Thomas Shortt*, pp. 7–26; Young, Vol. II, p. 235; Lemaire, J-F, *Autour de 'L'Empoisonnement' de Napoléon*, p. 21; Gorrequer, p. 247; Drew, Vol. I, p.196.
10. St. Denis, p. 283; Marchand, Vol. II, p. 339; Watson, GL de St M, *The Story of Napoleon's Death-Mask*, pp. 44, 113–19; 10–21; Antommarchi, Vol. II, p. 115.
11. Drew, Vol. I, p. 180; Chaplin, *A St. Helena Who's Who*, pp. 64–5; Watson, pp. 40–3.
12. Watson, pp. 38–54, 124–32, 150–2; Young, Vol. II, p. 244; Marchand, Vol. II, p. 337.
13. Watson, pp. 125–8, 154, 44–8, 133–5; Marchand, Vol. II, p. 341; St. Denis, pp. 283–4; Lutyens, E, *Letters of Captain Engelbert Lutyens*, p. 192; Veauce, E de, *L'Affaire du Masque de Napoléon*, pp. 50–4; Paoli, F, *Le Dr Antommarchi ou Le Secret du Masque de Napoléon*, pp. 172–6.
14. Watson, pp. 45–7, 128–9.
15. Bertrand, pp. 277–81; Watson, pp. 206–7; Veauce, pp. 206–7.
16. Forsyth, Vol. II, p. 183; Young, Vol. II, p. 257; Watson, pp. 14–15; Bertrand, p. 280.

17. Watson, pp. 150–7; Gorrequer, p. 242; Veauce, pp. 168–9.
18. Watson, pp. 120–3, 130–2, 157–8; Marchand, Vol. II, p.390; Veauce, pp. 203–5.
19. Watson, pp. 21–8, 35–6, 158, 193–7; Roy-Henry, B, *Napoléon L'Enigme de L'Exhumé de 1840*, pp. 69–101; Veauce, pp. 211–5; Richardson, pp. 244–5; Young, Vol. II, p. 247; Lichfield, J, *The many faces of Napoleon*.

APPENDIX I

CHRONOLOGY OF MAIN EVENTS

1815

15 July	Napoleon boards the *Bellerophon*
7 August	O'Meara appointed as Napoleon's doctor
8 August	Napoleon departs for St. Helena on the *Northumberland*
15 October	The *Northumberland* arrives at St. Helena with Napoleon and entourage and O'Meara
12 December	Napoleon moves to Longwood House

1816

8 March	Warden dines with Napoleon at Longwood
14 April	Hudson Lowe and Staff, including Reade and Baxter, arrive at St. Helena
17 April	First meeting of Napoleon and Lowe
17 June	Malcolm replaces Cockburn
19 June	Cockburn and Warden depart St. Helena on the *Northumberland*
30 December	Departure of Las Cases from St. Helena

Late 1816 First publication of Warden's Letters

1817

29 June	Stokoe (and Plampin) arrives on St. Helena

1818

14 March	Departure of Gourgaud from St. Helena
2 August	Departure of O'Meara from St. Helena
25 August	Arrival of Verling at Longwood

1819

17th–21 January	Stokoe's consultations with Napoleon
March	Arnott's arrival on St. Helena

2 July	Departure of Madame Montholon
30 August	Stokoe's court-martial
12 September	Stokoe's final departure from St. Helena
20 September	Antommarchi arrives on St. Helena and Verling departs Longwood

Late 1819

| | Departure of Baxter from St. Helena |

1820

| 23 April | Departure of Verling from St. Helena |
| 20 December | Shortt's arrival on St. Helena |

1821

31 March	Burton's arrival on St. Helena
1 April	Arnott's first consultation with Napoleon
5 May	Death of Napoleon
6 May	Post-mortem examination
6–7 May	Moulding and casting of death mask by Burton
9 May	Napoleon's funeral
27 May	Remaining exiles – including Bertrand, Montholon and Antommarchi – depart St. Helena
25 July	Departure of Hudson Lowe from St. Helena

1822 Publication of O'Meara's *Voice* and Arnott's account of Napoleon's illness

1823 Court case: Lowe versus O'Meara

1825 Publication of Antommarchi's memoir

APPENDIX II

NOMINAL LIST OF PERSONS COMPOSING THE ESTABLISHMENT AT LONGWOOD, 25 MARCH, 1816

Officers:
General Bonaparte
Count Bertrand
Count de Montholon
Count de Las Cases
Baron Gourgaud
Monsieur Emanuel de Las Cases
Captain Piontkowski   7

Ladies:
Countess Bertrand
Countess de Montholon   2

Children:
3 of Count Bertrand
1 of Count de Montholon   4

Foreign domestics of General Bonaparte:
Marchand, 1st Valet de Chambre
Saint-Denis, 2nd Valet
Noverraz, 3rd Valet
Cipriani, Maître d'hôtel
Lepage, Cook
Pierron, Butler and Confectioner
Santini, Valet
Rousseau, Valet

Gentilini, Valet
Archambault Snr, Coachman / Groom
Archambault Jnr, Coachman / Groom   11

Count Bertrand's foreign domestics:
Bernard Snr, Valet
Bernard, Valet   2

Foreign female servants:
Collette Bernard, Waiting-maid
Josephine, Waiting-maid   2

General Bonaparte and suite   28

British Officers	2
English sailors/soldiers	11
Men of the Island	7
Women of the Island	1
British Officer's servants	3

British contingent   24

TOTAL   52

APPENDIX III

BRITISH MILITARY AND NAVAL OFFICERS ON ST. HELENA 1815–1821

<u>Military</u>

Governor: Lt.-General Sir Hudson Lowe
Deputy Adjutant-General: Lt.-Colonel Sir Thomas Reade
Military Secretary: Colonel Edward Wynyard
Aide-de-Camp: Major Gideon Gorrequer
Inspector of Coasts and Volunteers: Lt.-Colonel Thomas Lyster
General Officer Commanding the Troops: Brigadier-General Sir George Ridout Bingham
   (replaced in August 1820 by Brigadier-General John Pine-Coffin)
Brigadier-Major in Charge of Engineers: Major Anthony Emmett
In Command of Artillery: Major James Power
In Command of Dragoons: Cornet J.W.Hoath
In Command of the Staff Corps: Lieutenant Basil Jackson
Orderly Officers at Longwood (at various periods):
Captain T.W. Poppleton
Captain Henry Pierce Blakeney
Lt.-Colonel Thomas Lyster
Captain George Nicholls
Captain Engelbert Lutyens
Captain William Crokat

Naval

Admirals in Command of the St. Helena Station:
Rear Admiral Sir George Cockburn (October 1815–June 1816)
Rear-Admiral Sir Pulteney Malcolm (June 1816–July 1817)
Rear-Admiral Robert Plampin (July 1817–July 1820)
Rear-Admiral Robert Lambert (July 1820–September 1821)

BIBLIOGRAPHY

Manuscript Sources

British Library:
Lowe Papers Add. 20,125; 20,126; 20,128; 20,133; 20,145; 20,146; 20,154; 20,157; 20,207; 20,214.
Eg. 3714–20 (Grangerised copy of Forsyth's *History of the Captivity of Napoleon*).

The National Archives (London):
J 76/8/1 (Gorrequer's diary)
J 76/4/1 (Medical attendance on Bonaparte)

Printed Sources

Antommarchi, F, *Les Derniers Moments de Napoléon*, 2 Vols., Paris, 1898.
Arnott, A, *An Account of the last illness and decease and PM appearance of Napoleon Bonaparte*, London, 1822.
Aubry, O, St. Helena, London, 1937.
Balmain, Count, *Napoleon in Captivity: The Reports of Count Balmain Russian Commissioner* (ed. J Park), New York, 1927.
Bertrand, Général, *Cahiers de Sainte-Hélène*, Paris, 1959.
Bertrand, General, *Napoleon at St. Helena* (ed. PF De Langle), London, 1953.
Cabanès, Docteur, *Au Chevet de L'Empereur*, Paris, n.d.
Chandler, DG, *Dictionary of the Napoleonic Wars*, London, 1979.
Chaplin, A, *A St. Helena Who's Who*, London, 1919.
Chaplin, A, *The Illness and Death of Napoleon Bonaparte*, London, 1913.
Chaplin, A, *Thomas Shortt*, London, 1914.
Chevallier, B, et al, *Sainte-Hélèna Île de Mémoire*, Paris, 2005.

Cockburn, Sir George, *Napoleon's Last Voyage*, London, 1888.

D'Hauterive, E, *Sainte-Hélène au Temps de Napoléon et Aujourd'Hui*, Paris, 1933.

Drew, R, *Commissioned Officers in the Medical Services of the British Army 1660–1960*, Vol.I, (A Peterkin, W Johnston), London, 1968.

Forshufved, S, *Who Killed Napoleon?*, London, 1962.

Forsyth, W, *History of the Captivity of Napoleon at St. Helena*, 2 Vols, New York, 1853.

Frémeaux, P, *Napoléon Prisonnier: Mémoires d'un Médecin de L'Empereur à Sainte-Hélène*, Paris, 1901.

Frémeaux, P, *The Drama of Saint Helena*, London, 1910.

Ganière, P, *Napoléon à Sainte-Hélène: La Mort de L'Empereur L'Apothéose*, Paris, 1962.

Glover, G, *Wellington's Lieutenant Napoleon's Gaoler*, Barnsley, 2005.

Giles, F, *Napoleon Bonaparte: England's Prisoner*, London, 2001.

Gonnard, P, *The Exile of St. Helena*, London, 1909.

Gorrequer, Major G, *St. Helena during Napoleon's Exile* (ed. J Kemble), London, 1969.

Gourgaud, Général Baron, *Journal de Sainte-Hélène 1815–1818* (ed. O Aubry), 2 Vols, Paris, 1947.

Gregory, D, *Napoleon's Jailer: Lt. Gen. Sir Hudson Lowe A Life*, Madison, 1996.

Henry, W, *Surgeon Henry's Trifles* (ed. P Hayward), London, 1970.

Henry, W, *Trifles from my Portfolio*, 2 Vols, Quebec, 1839.

Howard, M, *Napoleon's Doctors: The Medical Services of the Grande Armée*, Stroud, 2006.

Howard, M, *Wellington's Doctors: The British Army Medical Services in the Napoleonic Wars*, Staplehurst, 2002.

Jackson, Lieut-Col B, *Notes and Reminiscences of a Staff Officer* (ed. R C Seaton), London, 1903.

Journeaux de Sainte-Hélène, Paris, 1998.

Kemble, J, *Napoleon Immortal*, London, 1959.

Korngold, R, *The Last Years of Napoleon*, London, 1960.

Las Cases, Le Comte de, *Le Mémorial de Sainte-Hélène*, 8 Vols, Paris, nd.

Lemaire J-F, et al, *Autour de 'L'Empoisonnement' de Napoléon*, Paris, 2001.

Lichfield, J, *The many faces of Napoleon*, The Independent on Sunday, 23rd August 2007.

Lin, X, et al, *Elemental contents in Napoleon's hair cut before and after his death: did Napoleon die of arsenic poisoning?*, Analytical and Bioanalytic Chemistry (2004), Vol. 379, pp. 218–20.

Lugli, A, et al, *Napoleon's Autopsy: New Perspectives*, Human Pathology (2005), Vol. 36, pp. 320–4.

Lugli, A, et al, *Napoleon Bonaparte's gastric cancer: a clinicopathological approach to staging, pathogenesis, and etiology*, Nature Clinical Practice Gastroenterology & Hepatology (2007), Vol. 4, pp. 52–7.

Lutyens, E, *Letters of Captain Engelbert Lutyens* (ed. Sir Lees Kennedy), London, 1915.

Macé, J, *Dictionnaire Historique de Sainte-Hélène*, Paris, 2004.

Maitland, Captain FL, *The Narrative of the surrender of Bonaparte and of his Residence on board HMS Bellerophon*, London, 1904.

Malcolm, Lady, *A Diary of St. Helena* (ed. Sir A Wilson), London, 1929.

Marchand, L-J, *In Napoleon's Shadow* (ed. Proctor Jones), San Francisco, 1998.

Marchand, *Mémoires de Marchand* (ed. J Bourguignon), 2 Vols, Paris, 1952.

Markham, JD, *Napoleon and Dr Verling on St. Helena*, Barnsley, 2005.

Martineau, G, *Napoleon's St. Helena*, London, 1968.

Masson, F, *Autour de Sainte-Hélène*, 3 Vols, Paris, 1909–12.

Masson, F, *Napoleon at St. Helena*, Oxford, 1949.

Maury, R and Candé-Montholon, F de, *L'énigme Napoléon résolue*, Paris, 2000.

Montholon, CJT de, *Récits de la Captivité de L'Empereur Napoléon à Sainte-Hélène*, 2 Vols, Paris, 1847.

Montholon, Comte de, *Lettres du Comte et de la Comtesse de Montholon (1819–1821)* (ed. P Gonnard), Paris, 1906.

Napoleon I, Emperor, *La Correspondance de Napoléon I*, 32 Vols, Paris, 1858–70.

O'Meara, B, *Napoleon in Exile; or a Voice from St. Helena*, 2 Vols, London, 1827.

O'Meara, B, *An Exposition of some of the transactions that have taken place at St. Helena since the appointment of Sir Hudson Lowe as Governor of that island*, London, 1819.

Paoli, F, *Le Dr Antommarchi ou Le Secret du Masque de Napoléon*, Paris, 1996.

Richardson, F, *Napoleon's Death: An Inquest*, London, 1974.

Roseberry, Lord, *Napoleon The Last Phase*, London, 1900.

Roy-Henry, B, *Napoléon L'Énigme de L'Exhumé de 1840*, Paris, 2000.

St. Denis (Ali), LE, *Napoleon from the Tuileries to St. Helena*, New York, 1922.

Seaton, RC, *Napoleon's Captivity in Relation to Sir Hudson Lowe*, London, 1903.

Seward, D, *Napoleon's Family*, London, 1986.

Shorter, C, *Napoleon and his Fellow Travellers*, London, 1908.

Shorter, C, *Napoleon in his Own Defence*, London, 1910.

Smith, BS, *A Guide to the Manuscript Sources for the History of St. Helena*, Todmorden, 1995.

Sokoloff, B, *Napoleon A Medical Approach*, London, 1938.

Stanhope, Earl, *Notes of Conversations with the Duke of Wellington 1831–1851*, London, 1998.

Stokoe, J, *With Napoleon at St. Helena being the memoirs of Dr John Stokoe Naval Surgeon Translated from the French of Paul Frémeaux by Edith S Stokoe*, London, nd.

Tulard, J, *Dictionnaire Napoléon*, 2 Vols, Paris, 1999.

Veauce, E de, *L'Affaire du Masque de Napoléon*, Paris, 1957.

Warden, W, *Letters written on board His Majesty's Ship the Northumberland and Saint Helena*, London, 1816.

Watson, GL de St M, *A Polish Exile with Napoleon*, Boston, 1912.

Watson, GL de St M, *The Story of Napoleon's Death-Mask*, London, 1914.

Weider, B, and Forshufved, S, *Assassination at St. Helena Revisited*, New York, 1995.

Wilson, JB, *Dr Archibald Arnott: Surgeon to the 20th Foot and Physician to Napoleon*, British Medical Journal (1975), Vol. 3, pp. 293–5.

Young, N, *Napoleon in Exile: St. Helena (1815–1821)*, 2 Vols, Philadelphia, 1915.

INDEX

Medal struck in 1815, 'Napoleon on St Helena'. It depicts Napoleon seated on a rock with his head down, despondent. History on her knees urges him to take up the pen, while Fame flies overhead with a trumpet.

Lead medal entitled 'The Death of Napoleon' – 'He died on a rock'. It depicts the island with ships and a symbolic setting sun. An eagle with a palm branch flies overhead. These images are from *Napoleon's Medals: Victory to the Arts* by Richard A. Todd, published by The History Press.

ALSO AVAILABLE FROM THE HISTORY PRESS

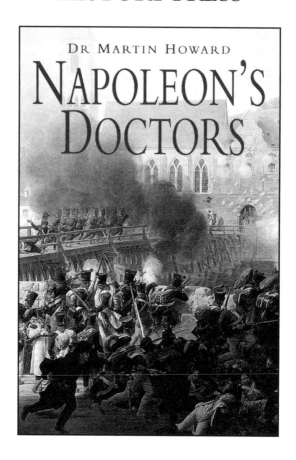

DR MARTIN HOWARD

NAPOLEON'S DOCTORS

Napoleon's attitudes to his sick and wounded men, and to his own medical service, were complicated and unpredictable. He supported his favourite doctors but often appeared indifferent to the wider *Service de Santé*. The ordinary French army doctors struggled to gain real status and to survive campaigns including Egypt, the Peninsular War, the merciless attrition of Russia and the final defeat at Waterloo. Despite constant infighting with their own administrators they contrived to provide some sort of medical care on all the battlefields of the Revolution and Empire and in the army's loathed hospitals – the 'Tombs of the *Grande Armée*'. In *Napoleon's Doctors,* Martin Howard draws on eyewitness accounts of soldiers and doctors, many translated for the first time from the original French, to give the first comprehensive account in English of life in the medical services of the *Grande Armée*.

ISBN 978-1-86227-324-5

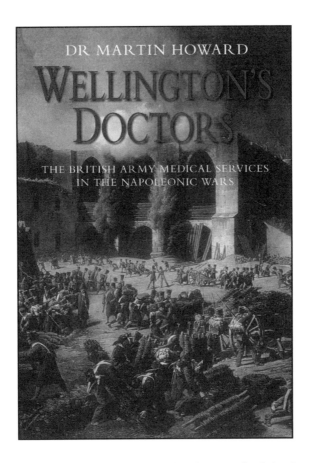

The doctors of Britain's Napoleonic army played a crucial role in the war against France. Wellington was the first British general to praise his doctors in dispatches. Despite their importance, Wellington's doctors receive little attention in most accounts of the wars. In this groundbreaking study, many rare contemporary Napoleonic memoirs and letters have been consulted to give a unique and vivid picture of the army doctors and those in their care.

'*Wellington's Doctors* is a fine piece of scholarship, combining authority, readability and the human element.' *The British Army Review*
'Dr Howard has left no stone unturned … This is the definitive source on the medical arrangements in the British Army of the Napoleonic Wars.' *First Empire*

ISBN 978-1-86227-493-8